ACTA UNIVERSITATIS STOCKHOLMIENSIS

Stockholm Studies in Sociology

New Series 47

D1809417

To Bev
with many thanks
from Elias

Stockholms
universitet

Class, Place and Identity in a Satellite Town

Elias le Grand

© Elias le Grand and Acta Universitatis Stockholmiensis,
Stockholm 2010

ISSN 0491-0885
ISBN 978-91-86071-50-9

Printed in Sweden by US-AB Tryck & Media, Stockholm 2010
Distributor: eddy.se ab, Visby, Sweden
Cover image by Claudia Young

To my parents.

Contents

Acknowledgements

First of all, I am really grateful to all the young people in Satellite Town who took part in this study. Many thanks also to Gary at Northside and Sarah at Greenwood. Apologies are due to Nicky and Sarah for what happened that fateful evening more than two years ago. Hopefully, I learnt something from it.

Patrik Aspers has been an enthusiastic and inspiring supervisor throughout the project. His continuous support, encouragement and belief in my work have been invaluable. I owe him a lot. I am also grateful to my associate supervisor Lars Udehn, who contributed with many thoughtful comments and suggestions.

The study would not have developed as it did, or maybe not been realized at all, without the great generosity of Bev Skeggs, who let me spend 14 months at the Sociology Department at Goldsmiths, University of London. Bev also suggested that I do the study in Satellite Town. At Goldsmiths, I also want to thank Kimberly Keith, Bridget Ward, Anamik Saha, Helena Holgersson and Madli Maruste. During the initial stages of fieldwork, Alex Hensby at Roehampton University generously shared some useful tips and advice on how to proceed.

I want to thank friends and colleagues at the Department of Sociology, Stockholm University, who lit up its dull corridors with their presence. Warm thanks in particular to Lambros Roumbanis and Daniel Castillo, without whom these past years certainly wouldn't have been as enjoyable. I also want to thank Lambros for his many valuable ideas and suggestions on this project, and for his support during its final weeks. Other colleagues have read and provided valuable comments on the text. I am grateful to Stina Blix, Caroline Dahlberg, Barbara Hobson, Magnus Haglunds, Martin Hällsten, Jens Rydgren and Betty Thompson. Thanks also to Göran Ahrne, Isabelle Andersson, Maria Bagger-Sjöbäck, Karin Bergmark, Nihad Bunar, Moa Bursell, Gergei Farkas, Thomas Florén, Saemundur Grettisson, Karin Halldén, Maria Lind, Thomas Nordgren, Mikaela Sundberg, Richard Swedberg and Maria Törnqvist.

I am very grateful to Mats Trondman at Linnaeus University, who was the discussant at my 'final seminar', where the bulk of my thesis was presented. His many valuable comments and suggestions on the manuscript certainly helped to improve it.

The Network for the Studies of Cultural Distinctions and Social Differentiation (SCUD) provided a stimulating intellectual and social environment, and I am really grateful to Johs Hjellbrekke for letting me participate in the network. A draft of what is essentially Chapter 4 in this book was presented at the last SCUD workshop at the Open University in April 2010. I am grateful to workshop participants, particularly Mike Savage who was the discussant, as well as Annick Prieur and Kristoffer Chelsom Vogt, for their constructive comments and suggestions. I also want to thank Vegard Jarness and Nobumi Kobayashi-Hillary.

Warm thanks to Lena Gunnarsson from whom I have learnt a lot. Lena also read and provided valuable criticism on the text. And my gratitude goes to Pär Engholm for his sharp comments and intellectual passion, and for our enduring friendship. Apologies are due for losing track of time all those times in London. Thanks also to Maria Bäckman for advice on ethnographic fieldwork, to Raoul Galli for constructive input, and to Karen Rockow for professional and thorough proof-reading.

I have dedicated this book to my fantastic parents, Toshiko and Carl. I am immensely grateful for all the love and support they have given me throughout the years. Love and thanks also to my brother Taro and his wife Ulrika.

Finally, I want to send my heartfelt thanks and love to Claudia.

1. Introduction: Class, Place, Identity

This multi-method ethnography—written from the perspective of a Swedish, Anglophilic, middle-class academic—is primarily based on fieldwork conducted in an area situated on the periphery of one of south London's outer boroughs, a borough with a large, centrally located town as its 'capital'. Lying in the margins of the borough, the area is, to quote one of the locals, 'the satellite town of a satellite town'. I will call it Satellite Town for short. Satellite Town is predominantly working-class, white—although with a significant Black African and Caribbean population—and with a history of social marginalization including a large proportion of council house estates and high rates of intergenerational unemployment and teenage pregnancy. I lived in the area for five months, and worked as a volunteer youth worker at the two youth clubs located in the area, on and off for about a year. I also conducted extensive studies of web sites, news media and popular culture.

The book focuses on the white, working-class youths of Satellite Town. Its central purpose is to examine the processes of identity formation among these young people, particularly in relation to class and place. Identity is a multi-facetted concept and we will deal with it in more depth shortly, but for now, suffice to say that it is about the dynamic and dialectic processes between identity constructed from the 'inside' and the 'outside'. Identity as constructed from the 'inside' involves inquiring how the respondents construct their *self-identities*. How do they perform their selves through dress, gesture, posture, ways of speaking and so forth? And how are these performances acted out in different social contexts? What people, practices and objects do they identify with or disassociate from, and on what grounds? And further, what is their 'sense of' and relationship to place? That is to say, what sense of belonging do they express to different places—where do they feel at home or, conversely, out of place? How is their sense of safety related to different places? What is their mobility in space, and what constraints and opportunities in this regard do they experience?

Identity constructed from the 'outside' involves how the respondents are *categorized by others*. How are they represented and positioned in public codes and narratives? How do other people talk about them? What consequences do these categorizations have for their self-identities? Are they aware of these categorizations, and if so, how is this awareness experienced and expressed?

But while the study is about the formation of identity among these young people, we need to recognize that ethnographic knowledge is not generated from a disembodied, objective view from nowhere, but always in relation to a situated, positioned and embodied researcher who brings her particular experiences and preconceptions to the analysis. The fact that this study is about the white, young people of Satellite Town cannot be separated from the fact that it is made and written by a middle-class Swede situated in a white, British, working-class space. In parts of this study, I have striven to carefully use my own experiences in relation to the field and its actors as a source of limited, although potentially important, sociological insight. Thus, as I argue in Chapter 2, including the ethnographic self in one's account enables not only greater transparency, accountability and reflexivity, but is also epistemologically productive.

The 'Chav' Phenomenon

The wider context and the *raison d'être* for undertaking this study—which is explored more in-depth in Chapter 3—is the recent emergence of a moral panic in the British public realm[1] about white, working-class youths labelled 'chavs'. The term is commonly used to denote white British youths dressed in tracksuits, sneakers, baseball caps, designer brands and jewellery. The moral panic emerged in the early years of the 21st century, where 'chav' became a widely discussed and contested issue in news media as well as on blogs and web sites (Hayward & Yar, 2006; Tyler, 2008). In 2004 'chav' was chosen the buzzword of the year in a book published by Oxford University Press (Dent, 2004) and included in the *Collins English Dictionary* and the *Oxford English Dictionary*.

The figure of the chav has become a highly stigmatized stereotype, a 'folk devil' against which strong moral-aesthetic boundaries are constructed, often through mockery. Chavs are associated with marginalized spaces and places. They are said to live in council estates and to gather in gangs occupying public spaces such as street corners, shopping centres and McDonald's restaurants. They smoke, binge drink and live on a diet of cheap and unhealthy food, especially fast food. In general, the appearance and lifestyles of chavs is overwhelmingly associated with excessive, vulgar and crude taste.

Moreover, chavs are portrayed as loud-mouthed and aggressive. Male chavs are often associated with violence and petty crime, such as football

---

[1] While Habermas (1989) talks about the public sphere in the singular, contemporary scholars generally agree that it is more plausible to talk about the existence of a plurality of often competing public spheres in contemporary Western (and indeed non-Western) societies (Jacobs, 1996). With this in mind, I use the term 'public realm' to denote the realm within which these public spheres exist.

hooliganism, vandalism, assaults and muggings. Chavs are also described as promiscuous and sexually irresponsible, and this is especially the case for female chavs who are depicted as 'sluts' with no control over their sexuality. They are also associated with teenage pregnancy and motherhood. Chavs are often portrayed as lazy, unemployed welfare cheats lacking any willingness to work, who are happily using the welfare system paid for by hardworking respectable people. In sum, they are people who lack moral education.

Chavs have been the subject of widespread mockery in public discourse. Highly stereotypical images of chavs have been widely spread on web sites such as *Chavscum*, *Chavtowns*, and *YouTube*. 'Chav jokes' are spread via emails, and one can take 'chav tests' on *Facebook* and other web sites to establish 'how chav' one is. Humorous representations of chavs are also found in popular culture, such as *The Catherine Tate Show* in the UK, in the internationally popular British TV-series *Little Britain*, and in the comic strip *The Neds* featured in the *BeanoMAX* children's comic. Moreover, the chav phenomenon has been used to create and market commodities and services such as books, stickers, games, mouse pads, baby clothing, night club events, holidays and gyms. In this way, chavs have become the subject of entertainment. Lastly, in the wake of the moral panic, new and existing forms of policing have targeted people with the appearance of chavs Shopping malls, pubs, night clubs and other public establishments have started banning people wearing hoodies, baseball caps or brands associated with chavs (Hayward & Yar, 2006). This is clearly a way of excluding an unwanted, potentially troublesome and low status segment of the population.

My contention is that the term chav has emerged as a new label of class contempt, a new means of demonizing non-respectable white working-class people, which has widespread legitimacy. In this way, I argue that understanding the chav phenomenon is of crucial importance for understanding class formation and the cultural dimensions of class and identity in present-day Britain.

Recently, several studies about the public representations of chavs have been published (M. Adams & Raisborough, 2008; Brewis & Jack, 2010; Edensor, 2009; Hayward & Yar, 2006; Johnson, 2008; Raisborough & Adams, 2008; Tyler, 2008; Tyler & Bennett, 2010), as well as some interview-based qualitative studies discussing the chav phenomenon (Hollingworth & Williams, 2009; McCulloch et al., 2006). But apart from Anoop Nayak's (2003, 2006) study of a group of 'charvers'[2] in Newcastle, very little in terms of ethnographic research has been published about chavs (though see also Rimmer, 2010). This book draws on these studies, and with its focus on the dialectics of identity formation as constructed from the 'outside' and 'inside', it provides not only an analysis of the public discourse of chavs, but also ethnographic knowledge about the lives of people who are positioned

---

[2] 'Charver' is a local term for chav used in the Newcastle area. See Chapter 3.

and categorised as chavs in these discourses, and their thoughts about chavs and other phenomena. Thus by exploring the dialectical ways in which identities in Satellite Town are constructed, I study the complex, contradictory ways in which the lives of the respondents in Satellite Town intersect with larger public discourses. This, of course, reflects C. Wright Mills' (1959) contention that the aim of sociological research is to relate public issues to individuals' concerns and biographies.

As I show in Chapter 3, people who are labelled chavs form a largely voiceless group in the widespread public debate about the chav phenomenon. This study is therefore important as it seeks to 'give voice' to people who are positioned in the codes and narratives constructed around the term, although it needs to be critically recognized that this is mediated by the ethnographer. And more broadly, I believe this study will contribute in two main ways. Firstly, by increasing our knowledge of the particular category or group chavs it will contribute to research on youth (sub)cultures. Secondly, it also contributes to more general debates about social class.

Theoretical Framework

I will now present the theoretical framework that I have developed during the course of the research. I will discuss the core concern of the study, identity, and how it is bound up with two other concepts, those of positioning and spatiality. I will argue that the two latter are essential for making sense of the dynamics of identity formation, not the least in this study.

Identity

As Paul Ricoeur notes, two basic components of identity are sameness and selfhood (Ricoeur, 1991). Identity as selfhood means that it is an answer to the question *who* one is. This is a fundamental, inescapable, existential matter of being human in a social world. Yet identity also denotes some sense of sameness or similarity—of continuity—of this self in time-space. But here things become more complex as identity also implies *non*-identity, that there is someone or something which identities are defined *against*. Thus similarity is intrinsically bound with *difference*, just as self is intrinsically bound with *other*. That is why identities always have an excluding aspect: to define who one *is*, is also to state who one is *not*. As Stuart Hall (1996, p. 5) writes: 'Throughout their careers, identities can function as points of attachment and only because of their capacity to exclude, to leave out, to render "outside", abjected'.

The inherently social and relational nature of identity means that a person cannot decide her identities solely by herself, since it always involves the recognition or mis-recognition (Fraser, 2000) made by other people. Identities are constructed in spatio-temporal processes through a 'dialectics of identification' (Jenkins, 2008 [1996]; cf. Lawler, 2008) between self and other. Drawing on Jenkins, I will conceptualize this dialectics as an interplay between 'internal' processes of the formation of *self-identity* and 'external' processes of *social categorization*. Of course, these processes are often intermingled in complex ways and one could argue that to distinguish between the 'external' and the 'internal' is a crude, indeed positivist way of conceptualizing identity formation. However, as I will argue, these processes are not necessarily intermingled but may work according to different logics, thus the need to analytically distinguishing between the two.

Processes of identity formation that are 'external' to the person involve processes of social categorization, where she is classified, defined and evaluated by others—be they people, organizations or more impersonal cultural codes and narratives. Categorizations can be extremely powerful in shaping a person's identity. Take the notion of stigma, which involves labelling processes where certain attributes are tied to negatively loaded (stereotypical) characteristics 'marked' or 'inscribed' onto a person who displays these attributes, and who ends up with a 'spoiled' identity (Erving Goffman, 1963; cf. Link & Phelan, 2001). Thus, this form of 'marking' can profoundly shape who she 'is' in society, regardless of her own thoughts on the matter.

As regards the internal processes of identity construction, those of self-identity, I distinguish between two aspects or dimensions. *Self-understanding* has to do with tacit knowledge and is aptly captured by Goffman's (1951) notion of a person's sense of place. Bourdieu (1985, 1989) also draws on this concept when he talks about the practical sense (*la sense pratique*) with which actors make their way through the world. Self-understandings denote a person's tacit, intuitive and routine sense of being located in social and physical space. It is both a cognitive and affective process. For instance, a person might feel more at home and comfortable in certain social settings than others. In this way, self-understandings relate to a person's sense of belonging, and with her ontological security (Giddens, 1984, 1991)—her fundamental sense of feeling safe in the world.

Self-identification signifies that a person identifies with something, such as an attribute or characteristic—e.g. being British, a bodybuilder, hardworking, gay, black, woman, handicapped. This entails 'to characterize oneself, to locate oneself vis-à-vis known others, to situate oneself in a narrative, to place oneself in a category' (Brubaker & Cooper, 2000, p. 14). Self-identifications are often highly contextual and may therefore have a weak, fluid and shifting character. And while self-understandings are mostly tacit, self-identifications are more consciously formed and articulated, and thus more about discursive knowledge.[3] Lastly, just as the construction of one's

---

[3] See Giddens (1979, 1984) for a discussion of the distinction between tacit and discursive knowledge.

5

identities involves 'external' processes of social categorization, a central aspect of constructing one's self-identity also involves categorizing others. This may involve drawing symbolic boundaries against those others; to identify with someone or something is relationally bound to disassociating oneself with someone or something else.

This takes us to the distinction between personal and collective identity; on the one hand, identity can refer to a singular, particular and unique person in the world, on the other hand, it can denote her belonging to a plurality, i.e. a category. The formation of strong, affective forms of collective identity, Brubaker and Cooper (2000, p. 20) note, involves three criteria: categories, social networks and what Weber calls *Zusammengehörigheitsgefühl*, 'a feeling of belonging together'. The latter is particularly associated with strong exclusionary forms of social categorizations, i.e. symbolic boundaries against those allegedly not part of this community.

How can we understand the relationship between 'external' processes of social categorization and the 'internal' processes of the construction of self-identity? In social interaction (face to face or mediated) people construct their self-identities through performances (Erving Goffman, 1959), which include a person's gestures, dress, posture and manner of speaking. An important aspect of performances of self is that of impression management where people try, often routinely, to control the impressions they give off to others and thus influence how they will be perceived and thus categorized by others.

But as Goffman (1959) observes, however people try and however skilful they are in impression management, they can neither fully control nor have complete knowledge of what impressions they give off in social interaction. A person marked with a stigma usually gets her self-identity fundamentally altered, e.g. in the form of feelings of shame and inferiority, and this often leads to a wish to become or at least pass as 'normal'. But people can also actively resist categorizations imposed on them from others, and thus construct their self-identities in opposition to these others, e.g. to form their own counter culture. It needs to be stated, however, that for all the power of external processes to affect or shape self-identity through labelling, these can also pass relatively unnoticed by the people that are categorized, and thus have very little influence on their self-identities. When asked, they may rather disassociate from the categorizations in questions (either not knowing or trying to get away from the fact that the categorizations apply to them). This means that there is a potential autonomy between categorization processes and self-identity construction—one's self-understandings and self-identifications might be quite different from how one is categorized by others.

Positioning

Identity formation, I argue, cannot be understood apart from how actors are positioned vis-à-vis one another (indeed, as we will see, 'external' processes of social categorization are one of the ways in which actors are positioned). Positioning here refers to the relational and unequal distribution of different sets of resources—economic, social and cultural—among individuals and groupings of such individuals as well as embedded in institutions and organizations in social and physical space. Moreover, positioning is about the processes where these resources acquire *value*. These ideas, I believe, are 'fundamentally sociological' and not the least do Bourdieu's (1984 [1979], 1985, 1986a) metaphors of capital form an important influence. I prefer to speak more widely about resources, however, as there are some problematic limitations to his ideas. The use and valuing of resources, i.e. forms of capital, should be understood within his 'symbolic economy' framework, which is about the 'struggles' between actors (primarily social classes and class fractions) in social fields, and the 'stakes' of the 'games' played by them in such fields. Actors acquire, use and exchange social, economic and cultural capital as a part of their strategies to gain power and status, and to become the dominant actor in social fields.

For Bourdieu, the fundamental driving force of actors is not, as would appear from this description, interests (see e.g. Honneth, 1986), but ultimately a striving for recognition, that is, dignity (Wacquant, 2006). Still, there is a utilitarian bent to how Bourdieu understands the valuing of resources in so far as they function as capital for actors to reach their ends. And much of Bourdieu's *oeuvre* focuses on different groups' quests for power and status. What is lacking from these analyses is a deeper engagement with the value rationality (Weber, 1979) of human behaviour. I want to stress that some resources may be valuable and meaningful in *themselves* for the person and cannot be reduced to power struggles in social fields. As Andrew Sayer puts it: 'The struggles [in social fields] are not merely for power and status but are about how to live' (2005, p. 3). This is especially important for understanding identity formation, an issue Bourdieu virtually ignores. Thus, unlike Bourdieu, I prefer to talk more widely about resources rather than capital so as to include their use in both ends- and value-oriented action.

The economic dimension to positioning people is relatively straightforward: economic resources include money and material assets. Social positions refer to the social relationships within which a person is embedded, and how they constrain and enable her actions. The concept of social capital (Bourdieu, 1986a; Coleman, 1990; Putnam, 2000) has been widely used to denote how people can gain access to resources by virtue of being embedded in social networks. It is important here to consider the relative institutionalization and closure of social relationships. Highly institutionalized and closed social networks are often tied to the formation of social boundaries (Lamont

& Molnár, 2002)[4] affecting, among other things, the social and spatial mobility among those embedded in these networks.

The cultural dimension in social life is here taken to be constituted by symbolic meaning structures (Geertz, 1973). Rather than conceived as values mysteriously hidden in people's consciousness, these take the form of public codes and narratives. 'Culture is public because meaning is' (Geertz, 1973, p. 12). Culture works by positioning people in codes and narratives but it also constitutes the resources with which people try to make sense of and act in the world. Cultural properties constitute the very material for identity formation. 'External' forms of social categorization serve to position people in codes and narratives. In the same way, people appropriate symbolic meanings in mnemonic, affective and embodied ways, and these meanings constitute the cultural resources they draw on as they make their way through the world. It is by way of cultural resources that people draw on and perform public codes and narratives to construct self-identifications, self-understandings and categorizations of others. A central aspect is through embodied social action, what Marcel Mauss (1973, 1979) calls body techniques, that is, the culturally learned ways in which we use our bodies when we engage in different practices with specific functions and purposes, e.g. swim, sit, stand, walk, run, sleep, dance, eat, drink, have sexual intercourse, greet each other, and so forth. Though usually routinely performed, body techniques are skilled accomplishments, sometimes difficult to learn or change. And *qua* culturally generated, they differ between the genders, generations, classes, ethnic groups, etc. Moreover, to return to Goffman, body techniques are performed in particular contexts of social interaction, through modes of self-presentation. Here is also where the normative aspect of body techniques comes to the forefront, as when someone fails to live up to the particular rules of etiquette by her 'incorrect' way of holding and using her knife and fork at the dinner table.

Spatiality

Identity formation and positioning are always spatialized, that is, processes situated in space and place. Space is geographical location conceived in a general, abstract and relational sense, such as the representations of localities on a map or through census data. While space 'is about having an address', place 'is about living in that address' (Agnew, 2005, p. 82). Places are spaces that are inhabited, lived and experienced through all the senses, and thus imbued with history and meaning, giving them particular characteris-

---

[4] Lamont and Molnár define social boundaries as 'objectified forms of social differences manifested in unequal access to and unequal distribution of resources (material and nonmaterial) and social opportunities. They are also revealed in stable behavioural patterns of association, as measured in connubiality and commensality' (Lamont & Molnár, 2002, pp. 168-169). In this sense, social boundaries are manifested in social networks and the allocation of resources.

tics, indeed identities (Tuan, 1974). In this sense, place is 'practiced space' (Merrifield, 1993, p. 524). Place and space should not be conceived as separate from one another but dialectically interrelated, for the one is conceived in relation to the other (cf. Lefebvre, 1991; Merrifield, 1993).

Both space and place are crucial for understanding identity formation and positioning. The construction of spaces through different representational devices can serve as powerful forms of social categorization, which position localities and people in cultural codes and narratives. Indeed, the concept of space stems from the of emergence of modernity (Giddens, 1990) and is connected to the rational control and regulation of people and locality through planning (cf. de Certeau, 1984) or the capitalist market (cf. Harvey, 1989; Lefebvre, 1991). Thus, spaces are generally constructed by powerful actors with ample access to economic, cultural and social resources.

Places both shape and are shaped by the deployment of economic, social and cultural resources, and are a fundamental context for identity formation. The identities of places are constructed through processes of categorization from the 'outside' as well as bound with the identifications and self-understandings of those on the 'inside'. Moreover, identifications with place are not only constructed dialectically between 'insiders' and 'outsiders', but also in relation to other places.

I will now tie together the three strands of positioning, spatiality and identity formation within the context of this study. Inquiring into the identity formation among the young people of Satellite Town involves the interplay between the 'internal' processes of identity work—the self-understandings and self-identifications—on the part of the respondents, and the 'external' processes of social categorization via public discourses, in social interaction, and by myself as inscribed in the form of this book. But the dialectics of these processes are bound with the actors' unequal social, cultural and economic positioning vis-á-vis one another. Lastly, identity formation and positionings are also bound to the spatial locality that is Satellite Town and its relation to other spaces and places.

Youth Studies, Identity, Class and Place

Having drawn out the central features of the theoretical framework put to use in this book, I will now, briefly, situate this study in previous scholarly work on youth cultures, as well as in wider trends in social and cultural theory, particularly in relation to class, place and identity.[5] The main purpose of doing this is to argue for the importance of class and place in understanding

---

[5] This will not be a lengthy review. The interested reader has already numerous detailed overviews at her service (e.g. Blackman, 2005; Huq, 2006; Williams, 2007).

identity formation. In this section, I will also devote particular attention to the concept of class, which I conceive as a form of positioning.

Conceptualizing Youth Subcultures: From Chicago to Birmingham

Early sociological work on youth cultures can be traced to the University of Chicago in the 1920s, where we also find early usages of the concept of subculture (see Blackman, 2005, p. 2), which has become one of the dominant analytical frames for interpreting young peoples' lives. 'Chicago School' scholars produced a range of ethnographies exploring the lives of marginalized groupings living in the city, including gangs (Thrasher, 1927), 'hobos' (N. Anderson, 1923) and taxi-dancers (Cressey, 1932). One should also mention William Foote Whyte's classical ethnography, *Street Corner Society* (1993 [1943]), on the delinquent behaviour among a group of 'corner boys' in an Italian slum neighbourhood. Characteristic of these urban ethnographies is that social problems and youth delinquency are tied to socio-economic marginality and place. Using a 'social ecological' perspective, this means that the 'deviant' lifestyles adopted by youth groups are interpreted with reference to the context of the city of Chicago, and thus neither conceived as a specific 'youth problem' nor as connected to wider social structures beyond the boundaries of the city.

This came to change in the post world-war period with the advent and subsequent dominance of the Parsonian structural functionalist perspective. *Contra* scholars of the Chicago School, deviant youth subcultures were here conceived as a specifically generational phenomenon emerging as a response to problems of integration into the wider social structure. A seminal study is Albert K. Cohen's *Delinquent Boys: The Culture of the Gang* (1955). In it, he argues that deviant youth subcultures typically emerge among working-class boys as a reaction and solution to their problems of status attainment— that is, of behaving according to the dominant norms in American society which are those of middle-class respectability. By creating their own oppositional norms, they create their own status hierarchy, and thus bypass this problem.

The notion of deviance was also developed in a symbolic interactionist direction by Howard Becker in *Outsiders: Studies in the Sociology of Deviance* (1997 [1963]), a study of marijuana use. His contention is that deviant behaviour is not intrinsic to a particular act, but rather the result of powerful actors *labelling* such behaviour deviant. According to this 'transactional' approach, deviance is constructed relationally so that focus must be just as much on the 'moral entrepreneurs' who label certain people deviant as on the deviants themselves. Moreover, Becker argues that labelling processes lead to 'deviance amplification' where the social reaction to the behaviour of people labelled deviant leads them to intensify such behaviour, which, in turn, leads to stronger social reactions from powerful actors, and so forth.

Up until the 1960s, American work dominated the field of youth studies, but later British work became increasingly influential. From the late 1960s to the early 1970s, the National Deviancy Conference spawned some important work, particularly Stanley Cohen's *Folk Devils and Moral Panics* (2002 [1972]). Drawing on Becker's transactional approach, he studies the 'moral panic' about mods and rockers—young people predominantly from a working-class background—between 1964 and 1966 in Britain, and the processes whereby the latter were labelled 'folk devils'.

In the 1970s, a group of scholars at the Birmingham Centre for Contemporary Cultural Studies (CCCS) produced what is arguably the most influential body of scholarship for today's students on youth cultures. As with earlier work, most CCCS studies focused on white working-class males, and just like the functionalist work, the formation of subcultures was interpreted as generational and class-based reactions and solutions to structural circumstances. Most studies were on the 'spectacular' sub-cultures that emerged in Britain in the post world-war period, such as teddy boys, mods, rockers, skinheads, rastafarians and punks. Moreover, *contra* earlier work, the analytical tools were mainly derived from French structuralism, especially semiotic analysis, and the Marxist notion of class opposition and struggle. As I will explain shortly, this also meant a shift in emphasis from deviance to style and resistance.

Phil Cohen's (1972) essay, 'Subcultural Conflict and Working Class Community', was an early formulation of these ideas. With a clear focus on place, he traced how urban planning, depopulation and subsequent repopulation of immigrants led to the fragmentation of the white working-class community in the East End of London. In this context, he interpreted youth cultures as a generational solution to this deterioration of community. Through participating in the 'new' consumer society, youths formed subcultures through which they created their own communities, and crucially, on a symbolical or semiotic level, 'magically' recreated the community once existing among their parents' generation. But this means that subcultures are only a symbolic solution to a structural problem, which largely remains unchanged. Thus, Cohen was sceptical of subcultures' capacity for resistance.

Cohen's text strongly influenced a central piece of CCCS work, the anthology *Resistance through Rituals*, edited by Stuart Hall and Tony Jefferson (Hall & Jefferson, 2006 [1976]). In the long introductory chapter (J. Clarke et al., 2006 [1976]), the authors but rather than focus on place and community, they were more interested in the wider social structural context in Britain. And as the title of the volume implies, they also bring the issue of resistance to the forefront. Drawing on Althusser (on ideological subject formation) and Gramsci (on hegemony), the authors talk about subcultures 'winning space' from the dominant class. They do this, firstly, on a terrestrial level through place-making, i.e. through sociality in public spaces where they create a sense of collective identity. Secondly, they 'win' space on a symbolic or semiotic level by creating subcultural styles through which they appropriate and thereby redefine the meanings of commodities, from reflecting those of the dominant class to those of the subculturalists themselves.

Dick Hebdige's influential *Subculture: The Meaning of Style* (Hebdige, 1979), takes the semiotic approach further by reading subcultural styles like texts. He draws on Lévi-Strauss' notion of *bricolage* to conceptualize the creative ways in which youths combine commodities when creating subcultural styles and how the latter serve to redefine and 'subvert' the dominant meanings imbued in these commodities. Thus, citing Umberto Eco, he interpreted subcultural styles as forms of 'semiotic guerrilla warfare' (Hebdige, 1979, p. 105), although this might not be registered on a phenomenological level by the youths themselves. Though Hebdige and the authors in *Resistance through Rituals* give more space for resistance than Cohen, their analyses are ultimately as pessimistic as the latter in that they see subcultural resistance as contributing very little, if anything, to social structural change.

Most CCCS works have been based on secondary sources and visual representations, and seldom dealt with the 'lived culture' of the youths they studied. One exception is Paul Willis' (1977) seminal ethnography of the oppositional culture developed among 'the lads', a group of white working-class youths in a school in the West Midlands. The lads' counterculture develops in opposition to the institutional environment of the school and 'the ear 'oles', 'conformist' kids. Willis also points to the affinities between the lads' counterculture developed in and outside school, and the culture on the factory shop floor. And ironically, their oppositional culture serves to guide them into working-class jobs, rather than a path to further education and possible class mobility. Thus, resistance ultimately leads to reproducing the class structure.

Moreover, most CCCS studies focused on young white males. Hebdige's (1979) analysis of Jamaican rude boy and rastafarian subcultures and Stuart Hall and his colleagues' (Hall et al., 1978) work on the moral panic about young, black working-class males associated with muggings, are some of the few studies discussing issues of race. And Angela McRobbie (McRobbie, 1978; McRobbie & Garber, 1976) is one of few CCCS scholars who focused on the role of girls in youth cultures. She argued that the absence of girls from earlier studies was due to the fact that they focused on the presence of subcultures in public spaces, e.g. the street corner, which are mainly populated by boys, whereas girls mostly gather in the private space of the home, especially the bedroom. Rather than engaging in resistance and nonconformity, McRobbie argues that girls' participation in youth cultural activities mostly involves the consumption of mass culture, such as teeny-bop stars and other mainstream pop music, and magazines such as *Jackie* and *Just Seventeen*. She concludes that this consumption of mass culture influences girls to conform to traditional gender roles, rather than engage in resistance against the latter. This serves to fix them in the private sphere of the home rather than empower them and engage them in the public sphere.

Socio-Cultural Change and the Emergence of Post-Subcultural Studies

From the 1980s and onwards, the CCCS tradition as well as the concept of subculture have received widespread critique (cf. Bennett, 2000; Bennett & Kahn-Harris, 2004a; G. Clarke, 1982; Huq, 2006; Muggleton, 2000; Muggleton & Weinzierl, 2003; Redhead, 1990; Thornton, 1995). One problem is the narrow focus on young, white, heterosexual, working-class males and their 'spectacular' subcultural styles, downplaying issues of race, ethnicity, gender and sexuality and largely ignoring more mundane youth cultural forms (Bennett & Kahn-Harris, 2004b). Another problem is the heroic, romanticized narratives of youths engaging in resistance against the hegemonic bourgeoisie system. Some have even argued that this has served to legitimize sexist and racist behaviour (Huq, 2006). Moreover, much CCCS work has been pre-occupied with the semiotic deconstruction of subcultural styles at the expense of the meanings constructed among the youths themselves. Youths have been interpreted as heroically subverting the hegemony of Bourgeoisie culture, but most often without themselves being aware of it. This has led to a questioning of the validity of such analyses. As Cohen in his scathing and oft-quoted critique, puts it: 'this is, to be sure, an imaginative way of reading the [subcultural] style; but how can we be sure that it is not also imaginary?' (S. Cohen, 2002 [1972]).

The above arguments have also been bound up with critiquing the very concept of subculture itself, especially as used within the CCCS tradition. The concept has been criticised for being essentialist, i.e. for making a crude distinction between dominant culture and subcultures conceptualized as 'cultures within cultures', and conceiving youths to form integrated, bounded and coherent groups. This homogenizes the different and shifting ways in which youths create and appropriate 'subcultural' styles. Many commentators see this monolithic notion of subculture as bound up with the conception of them as rooted in class. This has led many researchers to abandon the concept of subculture and critique the CCCS argument that youth cultural forms are class-based.

Sara Thornton, in her celebrated study of *Club Cultures* (Thornton, 1995)—taste based youth cultures formed around shared activities in dance clubs and raves (see also Redhead, 1997)—says she finds the CCCS notion of subculture 'empirically unworkable' but uses 'the term "subcultures" to identify those taste cultures which are labelled by media as subcultures and the word "subcultural" as a synonym for those practices that clubbers call "underground"' (Thornton, 1995, p. 8). Drawing on Bourdieu, she argues that it is the appropriation of what she calls subcultural capital, which gives status and access to resources in these club cultural contexts. Subcultural capital is stratified first and foremost by age, and also by gender, but 'it does not correlate in any one-to-one way' with class (Thornton, 1995, p. 12).

Since the 1990s, scholars with a postmodern bent have branded what they call 'post-subcultural studies' (Bennett & Kahn-Harris, 2004a; Muggleton, 2000; Muggleton & Weinzierl, 2003; Redhead, 1990), which completely reject the concept of subculture and the notion that youth cultural forms are structured by class. They do so not only on theoretical grounds but also in light of contemporary socio-cultural change. What has happened is 'that subcultural divisions have broken down as the relationship between style, musical taste and identity has become progressively weaker and articulated more fluidly' (Bennett & Kahn-Harris, 2004b, p. 11). In this sense, they argue that youth cultures have become increasingly fragmented in the last decades. New times are characterized by 'flux', 'fluidity', as well as 'new, hybrid cultural constellations' (Weinzierl & Muggleton, 2003: 3), which are not structured by class but largely based on the creative choices made 'in the supermarket of style' (Polhemus, 1996). *Contra* CCCS, youth cultural styles have not only formed through resistance, a form of class struggle, but are often interpreted as an engagement in capitalist markets. This also means that 'youth lifestyles have become de-territorialized' (Miles, 2000, p. 159; quoted in Nayak, 2003, p. 28), and though post-subculturalists are interested in the spatiality of youth cultural formations, these are not conceived to be structured and constrained by place.

Post-subculturalist scholars have replaced the concept of subculture with other concepts allegedly better able to capture the fragmented, fluid, hybrid conditions characterizing the contemporary moment. One is the concept of scenes (Shank, 1994; Straw, 1991, 2002; Ueno, 2003), which denotes the spaces inhabited by young people. These can be bound to place, such as the face-to-face contexts of the night club and the street corner, but can also be trans-local and denote conceptual spaces, such as those of shared musical tastes. Andy Bennett and others have drawn inspiration from Michel Maff-esoli's (1996) notion of neo-tribes, which are 'a series of temporal gather-ings characterized by fluid boundaries and floating memberships' (Bennett, 1999: 600), rather than stable, homogenous and bounded groups rooted in social structure. Bennett (1999; 2004) and others (Miles, 2000) have also used the concept of lifestyle to conceptualize youth cultural forms. Lifestyles denote the freely chosen activities related to consumption through which youths express who they 'are'. It thus 'reflects a *self-constructed* notion of identity' (Bennett, 1999, p. 607, italics mine).

Class, Place and the Cultural Turn

Post-subcultural studies reflect a general trend in the social sciences, the cultural turn, which has seen an increasing interest in the cultural dimension of social life, and relatedly, a declining interest in and mounting critique of the class concept. First, there is the argument that classes have 'died'. It is based on the lack of evidence for the existence of any coherent form of class consciousness, i.e. evidence that people consciously form their social identities around class. Thus, there is a clear lack of proof for the existence of collective, explicit class identities (e.g. Bottero, 2004; Grusky & Weeden, 2001; Savage et al., 2001; Scott, 2002).[6] Instead, research has indicated that in so far as people identify with classes, they do it in a hesitant, ambivalent way, and are more prone to emphasize their ordinariness—that they are just like everyone else (Bäckman, 2009; Devine, 1992; Savage et al., 2001). Here, the comparative quantitative research undertaken by Evans and her colleagues (M. D. R. Evans et al., 1992; Kelley & Evans, 1995) points to the effect of 'reference group forces', i.e. that people's perception of their class location tends to be shaped by the local milieu and the immediate social networks in which they are embedded, and that this leads to a 'biased' perception of class and inequality, in so far as they are 'overestimating the number of persons similar to themselves and their intimates' (Kelley & Evans, 1995, p. 158). The point here is that reference group forces lead people to perceive themselves as in the middle strata in a hierarchy, even if they have high or low socio-economic status. In other words, they tend to have a '"middling" self-image' (Bottero, 2004: 998).

In this context, Bauman (1982), Beck (1992; Beck & Beck-Gernsheim, 2001), and Giddens (1991) have argued that individualization processes have broken down traditional class structures, disembedding people from the former. This has led to increased reflexivity among people to choose and to construct their identities. Thus, as within post-subcultural studies, reflexively chosen, individualized lifestyles have taken the place of traditional class identities. As a consequence, many scholars have argued that class has become a 'zombie category' (Beck & Beck-Gernsheim, 2001)—an obsolete, modernist concept that is inadequate for understanding contemporary Western societies.

Moreover, in light of the cultural turn, the dualist, base-superstructure type of causal model underpinning traditional conceptions of class formation has increasingly come under critique (Savage, 2000). In both Marxist and Weberian traditions, classes are seen as 'empty' positions in the sphere of production forming an economic structure, which is 'filled' by people (cf. Sørensen, 2005). Social classes—i.e. classes as social groupings, collectivities, etc.—are formed through interaction among and between people similarly positioned in this class structure. Pahl (1989) has termed this the S-C-A-model where structural class position gives rise to class consciousness,

---

[6] One of the few recent studies to make the claim for the salience of a coherent class consciousness is the one by Marshall and his colleagues (Marshall, 1988). It has been criticized, however, for among other things the index consisting of six questions that is said to measure class consciousness for (a) the link between the questions and class position being unclear, and (b) inconsistency among the questions (M. D. R. Evans et al., 1992).

which in turn serves as the basis for collective action. This reflects a dualism between culture and economy (Devine & Savage, 2005) where class cultures are rooted in economic class position. The problem with this model of social class formation is that the economic dimension explains the cultural dimension in a simplistic way. The social imagery, values and norms of a class risk being reduced to the class position in which people are situated (Bottero, 2005; Devine & Savage, 2005; Savage, 2000).

We can see such tendencies in CCCS work (as well as in earlier structural functionalist work) where the emergence of youth subcultures is interpreted as a reaction to problems grounded in the class structure. Even Willis' (1977) sophisticated ethnography of 'the lads', while recognizing the relative autonomy of the cultural dimension, is built on a notion of class culture conceptualized around a base-superstructure model, that is, within a materialist analysis where economic class position is a fundamental pre-condition for the counter culture created by 'the lads'.

The post-subculturalists' emphasis on mobility through space and fleeting sociality in place is also tied to wider changes as regards conceptualizing the role of locality in late modernity. There has been a tendency to conceptualize people's '"sense of place" with memory, stasis and nostalgia' (Massey, 1994, p. 119), where place is conceived as a bounded, stable community, which thus becomes a romanticized notion bound up with the past (Agnew, 2005). In this sense, place has been associated with rootedness, 'home', and permanence, as opposed to the flows of space. 'If we think of space as that which allows movement, then place is pause; each pause in movement makes it possible for location to be transformed into place' (Tuan, 1977, p. 66). As Doreen Massey (1994) notes, this is a reified, essentialist, inward-looking, even reactionary notion of place, overstating the coherence of localities, which are conceived as if they only have a singular identity, rather than being shaped by multiple, contextually shifting forms of identification. But particularly, the concept of globalization has changed our ways of thinking about the role of place. One central aspect of globalization is that it is about 'increasing long-distance interconnectedness' (Hannerz, 1996, p. 17), i.e. 'the intensification of worldwide social relations which link distant localities in such a way that local happenings are shaped by events occurring many miles away and vice versa' (Giddens, 1990, p. 64). Globalization leads to time-space compression—an acceleration in our ways of overcoming spatial distances which serves to interconnect distant localities, as well as our experience of this process (Harvey, 1989). Jan Aart Scholte (2000) argues that these developments fundamentally undermined 'methodological territorialism', that is,

> the practice of understanding the social world and conducting studies about it through the lens of territorial geography. Territorialist method means formulating concepts and questions, constructing hypotheses, gathering and inter-

preting empirical evidence, and drawing conclusions all in a territorial spatial framework. These habits are so engrained in prevailing methodology that most social researchers reproduce them unconsciously (Scholte, 2000, p. 56).

Rather, globalization is a fundamentally *deterritorializing* process, a weakening of the rootedness in place, and instead a transcendence of the latter. This has seen a crisis in the community studies tradition (Savage et al, 2004; though see Crow, 2002) with its case study method focusing on the community making and reproducing practices through face-to-face interaction within places. Instead, focus has turned to transnational, deterritorialized forms of collective identification, such as 'post-place communities' (Bradshaw, 2008)—transnational, deterritorialized forms of belonging and attachment, based on categories like race, ethnicity, sexuality and gender (cf. Scholte 2000). This aspect is of course also apparent in the influential literature on diasporas (cf. Appadurai, 1996; Gilroy, 1993; Hall, 1990). This indicates that there is a general trend toward focusing on processes of symbolic boundary construction in a way which largely transcends locality, where the notion of place-based solidarities constructed and reproduced through face-to-face interaction is associated with an obsolete, territorialist notion of places as bounded entities (Amit, 2002).

Some early globalization theorists, like Jameson (1991), have argued that this means that we live in 'placeless' times; in a postmodern culture characterized by the surface play of signs. Many analysts, however, have seen this as vastly overstating the deterritorializing effects of global flows (though see Hardt & Negri, 2000) and stressed the crucial importance of the local. For instance, Roland Robertson (1995) conceives of the dialectical relationship between the global and the local as 'glocalization', where global flows, rather than simply homogenize localities and erode the notion of place, take on particular, local forms. Moreover, Manuel Castells (1997) has argued that, in the wake of global flows, local identities and cultures should be interpreted as defensive reactions to these flows. His narrative is one where progressive global flows move through space, whereas local cultures and identities are left behind, rooted in place and bound up with the past. In this sense, the local becomes a 'residue' of global processes (Savage et al., 2004).

Reinstating Class and Place

Given the critique of class and place, not the least for identity formation among young people, why conduct an ethnographic case study about the identities of working-class youths in a small town? Recently, the alleged decline of class and the placelessness of contemporary times in shaping the lifestyles and identities of people, not the least those of youths, have been recognized as exaggerated. A range of studies have shown how youth lifestyles, mobilities and transitions are bound up with locality and class (cf.

Back, 1996; Blackman, 2005; Böse, 2003; Jensen, 2006; McCulloch et al., 2006; Nayak, 2003, 2006; Shildrick, 2006; Shildrick et al., 2009; Tolonen, 2005; Watt, 1998). This is especially pertinent in the work of Robert MacDonald and his colleagues (Johnston et al., 2000; MacDonald, 1996; MacDonald & Marsh, 2005; MacDonald & Shildrick, 2007; Webster et al., 2004) on youth transitions in the poor neighbourhoods in Teesside in the North-East of England.

The continued salience of class and place has led many to the conclusion that the mobile sociology Urry (2000) advocates is premised on the appropriation of resources which are unequally distributed. Thus, while we may have a largely unconstrained and mobile cosmopolitan elite, some are more tied to place than others (Skeggs, 2004). Similarly, although many youth cultural forms do have elements of fluidity, flux and hybridity, these are not the kind of all-encompassing features as some post-subculturalists argue, but many youth cultural forms also display more integrated, collective forms of identifications and distinctions more akin to subcultures than scenes or tribes (Muggleton, 2005; Sweetman, 2004). Paul Hodkinson's (2002) study of goths is a recent example.

In the wake of these developments, new productive ways of thinking about class and place have been developed. Returning to our discussion about place, we can note Castells' conceptualization of place-based identities and cultures as 'residues' of global processes to reflect a flawed concept of place as bounded, reactionary, and bound up with a nostalgic past. Instead, and following Doreen Massey (1994), we can conceive of place in a 'progressive', 'outward-looking' sense. As she states:

> what gives a place its specificity is not some long internalized history but the fact that it is constructed out of a particular constellation of social relations, meeting and weaving together at a particular locus. If one moves in from the satellite to the globe, holding all those networks of social relations and movements and communications in one's head, then each 'place' can be seen as a particular, unique point of their intersection. It is, indeed, a *meeting* place. Instead then, of thinking of places as areas with boundaries around, they can be imagined as articulated moments in networks of social relations and understandings, but where a large proportion of those relations, experiences and understandings are constructed on a far larger scale than what we happen to define for that moment as the place itself, whether that be a street, or region or even a continent. And this in turn allows a sense of place which is extroverted, which includes a consciousness of its links with the wider world, which integrates in a positive way the global and the local (Massey, 1994, pp. 154-155).

Thus, places are not containers constructed, reproduced and changed within the locality itself but always in relation to its outside, to social relations beyond it. Places are 'open and porous networks of social relations' (Massey, 1994, p. 121). This also means that places are not constructed around a coherent identity, but just like people, have multiple identities. As people are differently positioned in terms of social, economic and cultural resources, and, of course differently spatially positioned, places are experienced in different ways, and therefore identified with and categorized in different, indeed contested, ways.

Places, then, are not necessarily *Gemeinschaft*-like communities built on tight bonds of kinship, and should not be conflated with the latter. Rather, places are constructed through symbolic boundary formation (B. Anderson, 1991 [1983]; Appadurai, 1996; Barth, 1969; A. P. Cohen, 1985), that is, through people's social categorizations, self-identifications and self-understandings of localities. Surely, as Castells and others have noted, identities, that is, a stronger sense of 'us' and sharper boundaries against 'them' can become more prevalent in times of insecurity and flux, but these need to be recognized within a framework that recognizes the dynamic notion of place. Moreover, to focus on place also serves as a correction to the tendency to overstate the deterritorialized nature of symbolic boundaries. The increasing focus on how community is imagined (B. Anderson, 1991 [1983]) has led 'towards the collapsing of community into the concept of boundaries' (Neal & Walters, 2008, p. 282). The problem, as Vered Amit (2002) notes, is that the focus on categorical forms of collective identification, has led to underplaying the role of social relations in constructing and sustaining notions of community. Turning again to Amit (2002: 10), 'the imagination of community is always fundamentally oriented towards the mobilization of social relations'. This means that 'proclamations of community' are 'first and foremost claims of, and for, social engagement, whether as recognition of an existing set of social relations or as call for the formation of new sets of social relations'.

Reconceptualizations of class have their basis in acknowledging that the root of its conceptual and empirical problems lies in the relation between class and culture. One of the classic class scholars, John Goldthorpe (1996) has responded by narrowing down his class concept so as to minimize the role of cultural factors. Instead, he focuses on the 'effects' of 'class'[7] on people's life chances. But 'bracketing off' the cultural dimension in social life from class analysis doesn't solve our problems. Goldthorpe narrows down class to exclude what has been one of the core dimensions of class analysis: to talk about *social* classes implies that we are talking about some sort of collectivities, some sort of groupings of individuals.

To reconceptualise class analysis, the first thing to overcome is the dualist, base-superstructure type of causal model where class culture or consciousness is the 'result' of economic positioning. What needs to be acknowledged is the relative autonomy of culture in constituting social classes.

---

[7] I write class in quotes since Goldthorpe works with a nominalist, deductive class schema, which at best, might work as a proxy for 'real' classes.

A fundamental insight for class theory in the wake of the cultural turn is that social classes are constituted by cultural elements that are *irreducible* to economic class position. According to this view, the cultural sphere is just as much located in the 'base' as the economy or the sphere of production, rendering the metaphors of base and superstructure obsolete. Here, Bourdieu's (1984 [1979], 1985, 1986b) class framework is seminal as he presents a more complex, multi-dimensional view of social classes as relational groupings constituted by collectives of individuals with an unequal access to, not only economic capital, but also cultural and social capital. This entails a broader notion of social class compared with the traditional Marxist and Weberian ones:

> The conceptual space within which Bourdieu defines class is not that of production, but that of social relationships in general. Class relations are not defined by relations to the means of production, but by differing conditions of existence, differing systems of dispositions produced by differential conditioning, and differing endowments of power or capital (Brubaker, 1985; quoted in Bottero, 2005, p. 60).

As the formation of social classes cannot only be understood as objective positions in the sphere of production, which can be grasped by the researcher without taking into account the life worlds of the people studied, this entails a processual and dynamic view of class, as also constructed, that is, made by people through symbolic means and social practices in their everyday lives. Class is *lived* and identity construction is a process that is fundamentally bound up with class. Steph Lawler (2005b, p. 797) puts this aptly:

> The dynamic character of class is related to classed identities, so that class is understood, not as a set of 'empty' signifiers (employment, housing, etc.) waiting to be filled by interchangeable social actors, but as also something we *are*.

In this book, I will treat class as intrinsically tied to positioning. Social class formation, inhering from unequal 'conditions of existence', is connected to how people are economically, socially, culturally and spatially positioned vis-à-vis one another. This means that actors accrue different sets of resources, which are differently valued depending on the context. And it is in these processes that people create their self-identities and categorize others. Returning to our earlier discussion about identity formation, it is clear that traditional research on class identity very much builds on a class consciousness model founded on strong, explicit, affective, collective identifications with class. Indeed, Bauman, Beck and Giddens all construct their arguments around a narrative where a modern, industrialized age built on social class communities has broken down by individualization processes. Yet, it is questionable if such strong, collective class identities have ever been particularly prevalent (Savage, 2000). The problem with this model is that it tends to ignore other types of weaker, more subtle ways in which class and identity are related. I want to pinpoint the more tacit and mediated ways that class identities are constructed in the form of classed social categorizations, self-identifications and self-understandings.

A person's ontological security or 'sense of place' is tied to certain spaces and contexts that are culturally coded in classed ways. A working-class person might feel uncomfortable in a certain social setting, e.g. expensive restaurant, and claim that 'I don't belong in this kind of place', that it's not for 'people like us'. Similarly, she might categorize and draw symbolic boundaries against middle-class people, not explicitly, but by saying that the restaurant is for 'posh people' or 'snobs' (which consequently are *not* 'people like us'). The sense of one's place, *qua* classed self-understandings, is therefore linked to an awareness and feeling of social distance and a largely intuitive understanding of where one belongs in a status hierarchy. Again, Bourdieu's (1984) work has been influential in focusing and drawing out these aspects. As he notes, while class may rarely be a concept around which laypeople consciously construct their identities, it is bound to their subjective meanings and practices, including their self-worth, status, beliefs, tastes and values.

Focusing on the mediated and subtle ways in which identities become classed, a recent group of primarily British researchers (Devine & Savage, 2005; Lawler, 2005b; Reay, 1998, 2005; Savage, 2000; Sayer, 2005; Skeggs, 1997, 2004) has drawn on Bourdieu's work (albeit in such different ways that it is difficult to talk of a new 'school'). Indeed, in recent years, articles drawing on a culturalist notion of class have come to feature widely in British sociology journals. This suggests that, at least in a British context, class is back on the map and, dare I say it, in a revitalized form.

The proponents of this new thread of research argue that processes of individualization and reflexivity have not lead to the death of class identities, but, on the contrary, are processes very much bound up with class. One central point here is that the construction of identity is bound up with the cultural resources people can acquire. This also allows us to interpret the lack of collective class identities as themselves class processes.

The ambivalence or claims of ordinariness Savage, Bagnall and Longhurst (2001) found among their interviewees is therefore not necessarily evidence of an absence of class identities but may point to a resistance of being categorized and 'fixed' into a certain category. Similarly, the fact that the working-class women interviewed by Skeggs (1997) resisted being categorized as working-class is not evidence of the death of class, but rather shows how working-class femininity had become a stigmatizing and sexualized signifier to these women. The point here, therefore, is that their disidentification with class in itself is evidence of the power of class.

Moreover, while reflexivity in an individualized age is described by Beck (1992) and Giddens (1991) as a more or less universal process, Skeggs

(2004) argues that it only reflects their own middle-class experiences. In this sense, reflexivity is a highly classed phenomenon since it is mainly middle-class people who have access to the cultural resources and thus the agency to construct reflexive selves. For instance, reality television programs such as *Ibiza Uncovered, The Villa* and *Sex on the Beach* do not display the kind of choosing, reflexive selves as conceptualized by Beck and Giddens, but on the contrary, very excessive and unreflected behaviour (see Wood & Skeggs, 2004).

These and a number of other studies show how class formation on the subjective level is bound up with how feelings of inferiority and superiority and the drawing of symbolic boundaries operate in an individualized fashion. Their point is that processes of individualization are compatible with recognizing class as formative in identity construction and the cultural realm more generally. Rather than seeing class identities as collective, they focus on how personal identities are shaped by class processes. There is, in other words, a move from collective class identities to *classed* personal identities.

In this chapter I have drawn out the theoretical concerns of the study including the conceptual framework that has been developed throughout its course. I have argued for the importance of class and place for understanding identity formation, not the least among youths, in the contemporary moment.

Chapter Outline

The subsequent chapter is about ethnographic research. In it, I discuss epistemological questions pertaining to ethnographic fieldwork, such as those of objectivity and reflexivity. I also provide an account of the research conducted in Satellite Town, the empirical material generated and how it was analysed. In Chapter 3 I explore the representations of chavs in the British public realm. The purpose is to inquire into the social categorization processes, the 'external' aspects of identity construction, in relation to my respondents. In this way, the chapter serves as the context for chapters 4-6.

In Chapter 4 we enter Satellite Town. In it I explore the dialectical interplay between 'external' and 'internal' processes of identification with Satellite Town conceived as a place and space. Proceeding from the 'outside and in', I begin by exploring how Satellite Town and its residents are categorized through statistics, place images on web sites and through ethnographic descriptions. I then study the construction of identity from the 'inside' by turning to the residents of Satellite Town, and I explore their 'sense of place', that is, their identifications or disidentifications with the area, as well as symbolic boundaries against other areas.

Chapter 5 studies the respondents' discursive articulation of identity in relation to style and appearance, what I call visual markers of taste. I focus particularly on visual markers associated with chavs, and how the respondents are positioned by, and position themselves, in relation to these markers. Chapter 6 turns to the respondents' embodied, and largely tacit, performances of identity in face-to-face interaction within the spaces of Satellite Town. I particularly focus on the performances characteristic among boys and how they are bound up with constructing masculine identity. Here I also include my own masculine performances as sources of data. Finally, in the concluding chapter I bring together the different strands discussed throughout the book and draw out its general implications for research on youth (sub)cultures and social class.

2. Knowing the Field

This chapter is about the process of doing ethnographic research, in general, and in Satellite Town in particular. It provides a narrative of how I located and entered Satellite Town and an overview of the research I conducted there, but crucially it also discusses the assumptions that have underpinned and guided my research, ranging from the sampling strategy and data analysis to epistemological issues and dilemmas in fieldwork practice.

I will start with the epistemological assumptions as they fundamentally affect one's field practice and analysis. With the breakdown of the classic objectivist approach to conducting fieldwork, in the last decades ethnographic research, especially anthropology, has undergone much soul-searching, and some would even say a crisis (cf. Clifford & Marcus, 1986; Denzin, 1997; Geertz, 1983). Let me reiterate the classic objectivist view of scientific research to make clear my own position. This view builds on a realist ontology and a positivist epistemology (cf. Fay, 1996). The ontology states that the social world exists independently of our knowledge of it and that this reality has its own internal structure. The epistemology states that this reality and its structure are knowable by the researcher who adopts a disinterested, detached attitude to neutralize her preconceptions or biases so that they don't distort her analysis. The end product (inscribed in the form of an article, monograph, report, etc.) is taken to be an objective account reflecting or mirroring the reality that exists outside the researcher. In this sense, objectivism builds on a correspondence theory of knowledge.

What Norman Denzin (1997, 2002) calls the crisis in representation refers to a realization of the inherently flawed nature of this type of objectivism. Indeed, it has been clear for some time (not the least in feminist theory) that there can be no such thing as an impartial, value-neutral and objective point of view from which one can conduct research. Rather, all research is made from certain standpoints, with certain pre-conceptions, values and interests, which fundamentally shape the process and product of research (Haraway, 1988). Impartiality is an impossibility. The researcher cannot simply transcend her standpoint through the use of the 'scientific method', and, so to speak, 'erase' herself and the perspective from which she studies the social world. As I have argued, the researcher is always positioned—socially, economically, culturally and spatially—vis-à-vis those researched, and this inevitably affects both the process and product of research.

For Denzin (1997, 2002), the crisis in representation in ethnographic research is tied to a crisis of legitimation: as there is no value-free, neutral standpoint from which to view the world and no way of gaining impartial, objective knowledge about it, there is, then, no way to legitimize the truth of one's research findings. Furthermore, Denzin argues that while 'post-positivist' ethnographers seek to legitimize their research by claiming that it is 'valid', that is just a rhetorical device, 'a mask of authority', to legitimize 'a particular regime of truth within a particular text (and community of scholars) to work its way on the reader' (Denzin, 1997, p. 7).

If objectivity in the traditional sense is obsolete, what is one to do? Are we on the road to relativism? I think not. Denzin seems to *reduce* all validity claims made by the ethnographic researcher to exercises of power over the reader of the ethnographic text. This is a quite extreme postmodern position and it is disappointing to see it expressed by one of the 'leading scholars' in ethnographic research and in a book that claims to embody what is at the forefront in this field (indeed, the book's subtitle is *Ethnographic Practices for the 21st Century*).

Let me present the less pessimistic and reductionist ideas on representation and legitimation that underpin this study. First, the fact that all knowledge claims are made from certain standpoints means that they are situated, or in the terminology used here: positioned. This means that we need to adopt a perspectivist orientation to knowledge production in ethnographic research. I will use the metaphor of vision (cf. Haraway, 1988) to illustrate the difference between an objectivist and a perspectivist understanding of knowledge production, which is aptly captured by Judith Okely (2001) in her distinction between seeing and looking. The latter refers to the classic objectivist observer's detached, neutral, disembodied 'view from nowhere'. Seeing, on the other hand, is situated, embodied and recognises all our senses (cf. Back, 2007). Following from this, ethnographic knowledge is not only situated but also local (Geertz, 1983) and partial (Clifford & Marcus, 1986). This means that we need to acknowledge the differences in resources, positionings, and thus, of power between researcher and researched.

Moreover, the partial, local and situated nature of all knowledge production means that we need to problematize the relationship between the researcher and the world 'out there'. The fallibilist notion of knowledge (Fay, 1996) I adopt in this study means that while I don't contest the realism advocated by classical objectivists that the world exists out there, the problem is epistemological. What I mean is that we cannot gain certain knowledge about whether we are correct or false about our statements about the world out there. We conduct research, construct concepts and theories of the social world, but there is no pre-given structure of this world which can be known for certain and to which our research findings can correspond. Brian Fay (1996) likens the social researcher to a map maker trying to make sense of what she experiences, constructing theories and concepts as she goes along.

Yet, contra relativism, fallibilism doesn't mean that anything goes, that any theory is just as good as any other. Just because we don't have 'reality as it *really* is' as a yardstick, we can still retain an idea of objectivity. But Fay's (1996) point is that we need to see objectivity as intrinsic to the process rather than the product of research. In this sense, to work objectively is to work in a transparent fashion open to critical scrutiny, which is also self-critical in that it problematizes the research and the researcher's own role in it. As Donna Haraway notes, this clearly bestows responsibility on the researcher (Haraway, 1988). Moreover, this also explains the inclusion of the present chapter in the book, rather than tucking it away in an appendix. Objectivity is also a precondition for legitimacy and why the latter cannot be reduced to the researcher exerting power over the reader of the ethnographic text. Finally, a central characteristic of working objectively is critical reflexivity on the part of the researcher. Reflexivity is a tricky term, so it will need some in-depth discussion, to which we now turn.

Reflexivity in Ethnographic Research

What does it mean to be 'reflexive' in one's fieldwork practice? In a way, the traditional objectivist researcher is reflexive in the sense that she takes a 'step back', so to speak, and becomes a detached, value-free observer. I am not arguing against the potential epistemological productivity of taking a step back and being detached. That is not what, *per se*, makes this position flawed (although I will also argue for the epistemological value of emotional engagement). The problems are, as we have seen, that it is founded on the naive notions that through the use of the scientific method, one can erase the researcher as a subject, whose analysis then becomes free from biases and prejudices. Instead, let me discuss Bourdieu's seminal notion of reflexivity. For Bourdieu, the fieldwork practitioner should engage, not in participant observation, but what he calls participant *objectivation*. As he puts it:

> Participant objectivation undertakes to explore not the 'lived experience' of the knowing subject but the social conditions of possibility—and therefore the effects and limits—of that experience and, more precisely, of the act of objectivation itself. It aims at objectivising the subjective relation to the object which, far from leading to a relativistic and more-or-less anti-scientific subjectivism, is one of the conditions of genuine scientific objectivity (Bourdieu, 2003, p. 282).

For Bourdieu, the central feature of reflexivity in fieldwork practice is to objectify the subjective analysis made by the researcher. To objectify entails critically studying the 'social conditions of possibility' of the researcher to make the kind of subjective analysis she makes. A reflexive analysis of these social conditions include, firstly, the standard practice of scrutinizing how the researcher is positioned in society—'her social origins, her position and trajectory in social space, her social and religious memberships and beliefs, gender, age, nationality, etc.' (2003, p. 283). But Bourdieu also stresses the importance of the researcher's position in social fields. As an academic, she is positioned in the field of power (constituted by the class fractions within the dominant class), and in the sub-field of cultural production, in my case, that of sociologists. The researcher's social background and position in social fields fundamentally affects the interests and motivations that underpin her research. Crucially, it is bound up with the internalization of a particular academic habitus that embodies certain classifying principles for interpreting and evaluating the world, which constitute the intuitively and preconsciously grasped 'cognitive structures' that work as dispositions to reason and structure one's academic practice in a certain way. Bourdieu talks about an academic 'unconscious' and the ethnographer's 'scholastic bias' (2003, p. 288).

Participant objectivation 'is one of the conditions of genuine scientific objectivity' (2003, p. 282), and a way for the researcher to avoid exerting symbolic violence on her It entails that the researcher critically scrutinize her own location in social space, the academic field, and her academic habitus. In this sense, Bourdieu is highly critical of scholars (such as Clifford & Marcus, 1986) associating reflexivity with introspection and an engagement with the researcher's subjective experiences. In so far as the researcher writes about her own experiences and uses them to inform her research, they must be 'objectivated' in the sense just described.

Although Bourdieu's view recognizes the positioning, values and interests of the researcher, it is still couched in the kind of old-school objectivist notion of neutralizing distorting factors that hinder an objective, unbiased analysis of the social world. It is a view that marries objectivism with classical critical social science in so far as participant objectivation is a methodological strategy which potentially enables the researcher to, so to speak, delve beneath the surface of the social world and uncover hidden power relations and forms of oppression.

My contention is that it is productive to think of participant objectivation as a crucial feature of working objectively in the sense explained earlier, which entails that we try to be as transparent and critically reflexive about our preconceptions and biases as possible and how these have informed our research. In the context of the present study and its framework, the positionings of me as researcher vis-à-vis the respondents in Satellite Town should be subject to continued critical scrutiny of how it might have limited and enabled certain views to be expressed and so forth.

However, Bourdieu's reliance on traditional objectivism means that he fails to fully consider the potential benefits of engaging with the ethnographer as a thinking, feeling subject. To write about the ethnographic self includes analyzing the researcher's identity work and the roles in which she is positioned in the field (Coffey, 1999). This gives the analysis increased transparency and therefore increased legitimacy as the fieldworker is present and visible in the analysis.

Moreover, writing the ethnographic self can also be epistemologically productive (Coffey, 1999). It entails situating the analysis of the ethnographer's field experiences—including her thoughts, emotions, affects and performances—in the social world she studies, in order to increase our knowledge of it. As Staci Newmahr puts it:

> When ethnographic introspective questions like "Why did *I* respond this way?" How did I come to feel *this* way here?" are informed by the social and cultural context of the field, the life stories of the informants and the rituals of the community, these answers have the potential to greatly enrich ethnographic understanding' (Newmahr, 2008, p. 640)

This is very different from the kind of introspection that turns into narcissistic navel-gazing or 'diary disease' (Geertz, 1988, p. 89; quoted in Bourdieu, 2003, p. 282). For the reasons stated, I have, when deemed appropriate (see especially Chapter 6), tried to include myself as a situated, embodied, reflexive, affective and emotional being in the field. Lastly, I also want to make a point about the presence of the ethnographer in relation to the reflexivity of the respondents in the field. Here, the respondents' interpretations of the ethnographer can serve to shed light on the social world under study (see e.g. Venkatesh, 2002).

A Stranger in Satellite Town

What follows is a narrative of how I went about with my fieldwork—from the rationale behind choosing the research site to how I entered the field. In December 2006, I started with a pilot study of public representations of chavs on the Internet (among other things, I studied blogs, discussion forums and different news media). In mid-October 2007, I finally got the opportunity to move to London, which was possible thanks to an affiliation with the Sociology Department at Goldsmiths (University of London) and a small grant to enhance my salary so I could survive economically in the expensive city of London for what I planned to be six months. But as the six months approached, I realized that I had more work to do. Moreover, it wasn't so difficult to manage on my salary alone, and I enjoyed living in London, so I decided to stay. I finally left in mid-December 2008, 14 months after I first arrived.

How did I choose my research site? Since I was interested in doing an ethnography focusing on the chav phenomenon, the idea was to do a case study in an area with a large population of white working-class people adopting the visual markers associated with chavs and thus positioning them in the codes and narratives constructed around the term.

But before I tell you about how I finally ended up in Satellite Town, I will say something about one of the problems I had to confront before even trying to enter the field in the first place, namely my appearance and manners. Born and bred in Stockholm by a Swedish father and Japanese mother, I come from an academic social background, rich in cultural resources but more limited in terms of economic resources. My decision to do research on British, working-class youth cultures can in large part be explained by a longstanding interest in British popular culture—e.g. clothing styles, films, music, subcultures and football. And more generally, I have invested ample cultural resources in my lifestyle, which is based on knowledge and consumption of brands and clothing, contemporary music, films, food and drink. These form an important aspect of my identity work, of what one could call the performance of an 'aesthetic self'.

With this in mind, I was concerned that the way I spoke, dressed and gestured might not go down very well with some of the respondents. What if I appeared like some kind of 'posh' snob? I was also concerned about my own sense of ontological security; that looking very different from other people would make me too self-conscious about my 'otherness' and thus I would feel too much out of place. For these reasons I decided to make some changes to my appearance. But I did not try to 'pass' and perform as a 'native', like Gillian Evans (2006), a self-identified middle-class person, during her fieldwork in Bermondsey, a largely white working-class area in South East London. Evans consciously tried to hide her 'posh' middle-class accent and manners, and adopt those of the respondents, like talking in the local parlour and telling 'crude' jokes like a 'common' Bermondsey woman. For me, this was never an option. For one, wearing, say, a tracksuit just wouldn't be 'me'. I wouldn't have the cultural resources to be able to wear it as one was 'supposed to' in the milieu I was going to immerse myself in. It would be self-deception. And most importantly, it would be disrespectful to all those people who wear such clothing as part of their style.[8]

What I did was to choose dressed down clothes that I liked and felt comfortable in that replaced some of my usual clothes—jeans rather than slacks, boots and plimsoles rather than derbies, college sweaters rather than shirts, hooded jacket rather than coat, discreet shoulder bag rather than designer rucksack. I also shaved my hair to adopt the kind of short cropped coiffure common among British, working-class men, especially younger ones. Lastly, I made sure to always wear my contact lenses and never to be seen in my designer spectacles from Prada (the 'Harry Potter glasses', as one acquaint-

---

[8] As a sociologist doing her PhD at Goldsmiths at the time I was a visiting scholar, told me: 'Young people have really good bullshit radar. They can tell fake from a distance'.

ance put it) while in the field. The changes in appearance are displayed in Figure 2.1.

But despite this, I often felt out of place in Satellite Town and similar places. I felt that I looked too dressed up, and walked, talked and gestured in a posh, effeminate way. And in retrospect I probably overstated the importance of changing my appearance. When I returned to one of the youth clubs, a year after finishing fieldwork, in my new haircut, no-one seemed to take any notice. But perhaps dressing down was most important for my own sense of ontological security. As Elliot Liebow (1967, p. 166) perceptively notes: 'it seems as if the degree to which one becomes a participant is as much a matter of perceiving oneself as a participant as it is of being accepted as a participant by others'.

Figure 2.1. 'Before, during and after fieldwork'.
Photographs by Mikael Spång, Alessio Lana and Vegard Jarness.

Having changed my appearance I was ready to start exploring possible research sites. Knowing very little of the social, cultural and ethnic make-up of the different areas in and around London, I tried to learn by asking people I knew or met, and by surfing the net. On the basis of what I learned and the tips I received, I simply went to different areas around London and observed the people and the surroundings. But the outcome of my travels was disappointing. Although it is difficult to tell from one or a few visits to an area what kind of social, cultural and economic make-up it has, the places did not seem to fit my criteria for case selection: that is to say, they did not seem to be densely populated in terms of white young people appropriating the visual markers associated with chavs.

The breakthrough came when I spoke with Beverley Skeggs, who suggested that I go to an area located in the fringes of one of South London's outer boroughs. That was Satellite Town. To get there from central London, I took the 25-plus minute train ride until I reached the station where the main town or 'capital' of the borough is located. For a town, it is rather large and densely populated—perhaps it resembles more a small city—it has many concrete high rises, presumably built in the 1960s and 1970s, that give the area a grim feeling—and apart from all the administrative bodies of the council, it also hosts a middle-sized in-doors shopping centre and a few pedestrian malls. The train station is a lively spot with people walking to and fro. From there, I took a bus. As I sat on the bus, my pulse rose. Half an hour later, the bus stopped and I realized that it had reached the end station, that is, Satellite Town.

First, I was a bit surprised and, I'm embarrassed to admit, a bit disappointed that I did not see much from the surroundings that could imply marginality. I saw mostly two-storey brick houses hosting a few flats each and they looked quite homely and pretty to me. From where I stood, I could only see one high rise, which I found cold and grim-looking, and thus, according to my preconceptions, denoting 'marginality'. I thought the place would be full of such high rises. That this wasn't the case betrays my probably naive preconception based on the stereotypes of supposedly deprived spaces in Britain. I started walking and soon reached the small town centre. It was basically a street with a parking lot on one side and a long, narrow three-storey house in red brick at the other side aligned with a long string of shops. The parking lot and the well-trafficked small road next to it, goes parallel with the town centre street, made the place less pleasant.

As I was hungry, I started to look for a place to eat. I found a few eateries mostly serving different forms of what is normally categorized as fast food, e.g. fried chicken, kebabs, Chinese take away dishes and burgers. No representative from a Starbucks-esque coffee shop chain in sight. I chose the place that seemed to have the most comfortable chairs; little did I know that in the months to come I was going to spend many hours there. The place was empty except for the two black-haired, young-looking men working there. I went in and ordered an omelette with chips and tea—the 'today's special'—and then chose a seat by the window so I could look at the people passing by outside. Just ten minutes of looking at the people passing by where I sat led me to believe that this is just the kind of area suitable for the kind of research project I was undertaking. And this impression grew as time passed, and not the least after I finished the food and went for a stroll in the area surrounding the town centre.

In short, I saw many people who appropriated stylistic markers associated with chavs in public discourse. At least there seemed to be enough people I could talk to. Many white girls in their teens and twenties had their hair in ponytail, some wore tracksuits or jeans, and a few of them were pushing prams. Many of the white boys in their teens wore tracksuits, trainers and baseball caps, and sometimes 'hoodies' (hooded tops). A few were also cycling. After about two hours of fieldwork it was getting dark so I decided to head back home (not much point in doing fieldwork if you can't see your surroundings, I thought). On my way home felt a mixture of relief, excitement and thrill as I now knew I'd found my research site.

But now another obstacle emerged. I figured that to make contact with young people in the area, it would be difficult to just 'hang out in the street' and hope to strike up a conversation. The easiest thing, at least initially, would be to go through some kind of institution, like a school or even a church. I chose to try youth clubs. As spaces, they were more informally organized than schools, and were also focused around leisure activities, indeed enjoyment (cf. Wulff, 1988). I was not interested in the youth club *per se*, but rather as an entry point for meeting young people, and, hopefully gaining their trust. In Satellite Town, there are two youth clubs, one located in the Old Estate, and one in the more marginalized part of the area called the New Estate (see Chapter 4). I will call them Greenwood and Northside, respectively. I decided that the easiest way to make contact with the two youth clubs was simply to knock on the door and speak with those responsible for running the place. And that's what I did. Needless to say, when I arrived at the two youth clubs, it was with great anxiety. My heart was pounding. This was in the beginning of December, 2007. Matters, however, went remarkably easy. At both youth clubs, I presented myself as a Swedish PhD student doing a project about the fashion and lifestyles among British young people (which was true but obviously not the full story—I didn't say anything about my interest in the chav phenomenon and the white British working-class) and that I would like to work as a voluntary youth worker there. At Northside, the cheerful caretaker, a man in his late twenties wearing glasses and a baseball cap, said 'The more the merrier', and smiled. At Greenwood the middle-aged woman with straight light brown hair looked at me calmly when I spoke to her, and responded, 'We always need a pair of extra hands'. As I learnt later, they were used to people doing voluntary work as part of their education (e.g. in social work), and to get one more employee for free, I suppose, seemed like a good deal. I told them that I was going to write about people in the youth clubs and Satellite Town though all names would be anonymised. No one seemed to mind. The caretaker at Northside joked: 'How much do you want for writing nice things about me?' and laughed. I immediately started working as a voluntary youth worker at both youth clubs. I worked on the Senior's Nights, which was for young people aged 13-19. More or less weekly, I worked one evening at Greenwood and two evenings at Northside until May 2008, when an incident with a young person at Greenwood together with some bureaucratic issues (discussed in-depth in Chapter 6), forced me to quit working at both youth clubs. After the incident, I regularly visited Northside until I moved back to Stockholm in December of the same year, though no longer in the capacity of youth worker but rather as a friend 'dropping by to say hello'.

A Multi-Method Ethnography

I will now discuss the methods used and the empirical material generated. The fieldwork conducted in the youth clubs and in Satellite Town consisted of participant observation, informal interviews, and also a number of short, recorded interviews where photo elicitation was used. In addition, I analyzed numerous web sites, video clips, television series, newspaper articles and official documents about chavs and Satellite Town (see the Appendix).

Participant observation including informal interviews provided the most important source of empirical material. During the first few months of fieldwork, I mostly worked at the youth clubs and made an occasional trip to the town centre and surroundings. But I soon realized that this was not enough. There was so much I wanted to know about Satellite Town and its residents whose lives I was trying to make sense of. I realized that the best way was actually to live in the area. Eventually, I found a room in a flat for rent and lived there for five months (February–July, 2008). This was extremely valuable as it enabled me to get a richer sense of Satellite Town as a place and of the lives of its residents. I spent much time in the town centre. Among other things, I used to go a few times every week to the local diner where I spent several hours working with my laptop and chatting to the employees and some of the customers; I sometimes went to the library, to other eateries such as the local kebab shop, and to the market; I went a few times to the local pubs to watch football. I also made a few visits to night clubs in the main town of the borough, where I met a few people I knew from the town centre and from one of the youth clubs ('I'm underage, but don't tell anyone', one respondent said). Lastly, I wrote fieldnotes from casual conversations with people I met—friends, acquaintances and strangers—outside of Satellite Town about things that seemed relevant to my research.

The fieldnotes amount to about 95.000 words in total. Due to the high levels of stress and anxiety I often experienced during the fieldwork—particularly when I worked in the youth clubs—the fieldnotes are not as quantitatively lengthy as they potentially could have been. After long days of participant observation, I often felt too exhausted mentally to write elaborate descriptions of everything I had experienced, but rather tried to write accounts that were more 'to the point', and written down in order to trigger my memories and affects of the situations described. As others have pointed out (Coffey, 1999; Ellis, 2004), long-term fieldwork can lead to profound changes in the researcher's self, and this work is no exception. It was an intense experience and it left strong memories—deep mnemonic and emotional marks. Throughout the research project, I also wrote a memo—of about 35.000 words—which was used as a log book, chronologically recording the research process, but crucially also working as a reflexive tool: I wrote down ideas, reflections, as well as 'notes to self'.

During the fieldwork at Northside, I also conducted a number of recorded interviews. When I asked Gary, the caretaker at Northside, if I could interview some of the young people he said that he didn't mind as long as I conducted the interviews at the youth club and in the vicinity of other people. He explained to me that a youth worker in Britain is never allowed to be left alone with a young person. Doing as he said, the interviews took place 'in the open', usually in a corner of one of the rooms, and always with people nearby. I informed the interviewees that they would be anonymous, that they could walk out of the interview at any time, and that the interview would be recorded, but only because otherwise I would forget what we had been talking about. The fact that the interviews were done in the open, made them more a part of the rest of the fieldwork interaction setting, and potentially more informal and relaxed than they would have been if we had sat in a quiet room behind closed doors—music was playing, sometimes people played table tennis or watched TV at the other corner of the room, and one could often hear playing and shouting from adjacent rooms. Sometimes, when I interviewed one person, someone else came along and joined in or sat and listened in the background. A few respondents were interviewed twice. I tried to make the interviews as conversational as possible, and used my interview guide quite loosely. I also used photo elicitation in the interviews, that is, I showed the respondents pictures of places and people, and asked them what came into their minds when they saw these pictures. It proved a highly productive means of 'activating narrative production' (Holstein & Gubrium, 1995, p. 39). As I show in Chapters 4 and 5, it allowed me to introduce topics without directly asking the respondents—instead, I showed them a picture.

The caretaker had warned me that it would be difficult to interview the respondents for any longer period of time, as there would be too many distractions for them to maintain attention. And he was right. Two of the interviews had to be broken off or interrupted after 5 and 10 minutes respectively: one boy had to go as a game of football was about to start, and one girl had a game of pool coming up. Another interview was interrupted and continued later on. The interviews were thus generally quite short, and made with the young people with whom I had gained some trust. In all, I conducted 14 interviews, involving 16 young people, usually between 20-30 minutes and up to 40 minutes in length. All of the respondents where white except for one girl who defined herself as mixed race and two boys, one who was Black African and the other of Chinese origin. Moreover, all respondents' parents held what is normally conceived as working-class jobs, such as barmaid, carpenter, caterer and porter, except for one girl whose mother worked as a psychiatric nurse (her father was a painter and decorator).

The pseudonyms given the respondents were chosen to reflect their class connotations. Most respondents had working-class sounding names and were thus given names such as Gary, Abbey and Darren. A few had more middle-class connotations, and therefore got names such as Katie.

Analysis

How did I analyse the data? I started with a pilot study analyzing web sites, video clips, television series and newspaper articles about the chav phenomenon. I continued this throughout the research process. At a later stage, I also analyzed web sites and local newspaper articles about Satellite Town (see the Appendix). During fieldwork, I wrote down reflections, notes of peculiar interest, and possible themes in my memo and sometimes also in the fieldnotes. The next step took place when I was back in my office in Stockholm. With the necessary spatial and cultural distance from the field (cf. Ottenberg, 1990), I analysed the data—fieldnotes, interview transcripts, web sites, newspaper articles, videos, and images—by searching for themes, connections and narratives.

An important though limited feature of this process was coding the data with the assistance of the software programme Atlas.ti. Such programmes have been critiqued for introducing a positivistic aspect to the analysis of qualitative data. The argument is that it constitutes a formalized, depersonalized way of thinking about and analyzing one's ethnographic work, distancing it from the 'real' experiences of being in the field, such as its affective, emotional and embodied aspects (Coffey, 1999, pp. 152-154; Kelle, 1995). As Okely and Van Maanen put it:

> fieldnotes are records of evidence, direct quotations and even quantitative data, but they may also act as mnemonic triggers of a total experience. Making sense of fieldwork is also a bodily process. The writer recognizes themes and sorts out what seemed incomprehensible puzzles because she can feel it in her bones and flesh (Okely, 2007, p. 77).

> The heavy glop of material we refer to as fieldnotes is necessarily incomplete and insufficient. It represents the recorded memory of a study perhaps, but it is only a tiny fraction of the fieldworker's own memory of the research period (Van Maanen, 1988, p. 118).

These authors indicate that the 'data' generated from fieldwork cannot be reduced to one's fieldnotes which, in turn, are treated as a mere archive or filing cabinet through which one extracts information through coding. Rather, fieldwork as a 'total experience' transcends the written fieldnotes as it also exists in the researcher as cerebral and embodied memories (Okely, 2008), as 'headnotes' (Ottenberg, 1990), which also constitute forms of data used in the analysis.

But while I agree that software programmes sometimes 'can encourage an oversimplified and mechanistic application of analysis' (Coffey, 1999, p. 153), that does not necessarily have to be the case. On the contrary, it can also be constitutive of a reflexive process which triggers the creativity and imagination of the analyst (Aspers, 2007). While working with the software programme I made ample use of its memo function, i.e. I wrote down comments, ideas, analyses and reflections about text segments. Morcover, the coding process forced me to get close to the text, to each and every sentence. Lastly, the programme enabled me to analyse large amounts of different empirical material—text, images, video clips—within one framework. This helped me to order and grasp large amounts of data and this was instrumental in giving me an overview of the wide range of material used in the study, and to see connections between different segments of data. This fact also made it easier to explore the data, to jump between different segments, and thus made it easier to 'think with' the empirical material.

3. Creating a Folk Devil: The Moral Panic over 'Chavs'

> You're doing a PhD on chavs? Then maybe you can ask them why they dress so ridiculously.
>
> (Flatmate, November 2007)

> Hi u! Hope your [sic] not freezing. We're in some mega chav bar in the bush, not sure who is fat or pregnant, or both. X x jen.[9]
>
> (Text message, August 2008)

As I stated in the Introduction, the chav phenomenon is the *leitmotif*, the central context, within which this study has been undertaken. In this chapter, I explore the representations of chavs in the British public realm. My central focus here is on the 'external' aspect of identity formation, that is, on the categorization processes through which 'chav' is constructed. In many ways, this chapter lays the groundwork for chapters 4-6 were I explore how the codes and narratives constructed around chavs position the residents, and particularly the young people, of Satellite Town in cultural structures and how this is related to their identity formation. Thus, the full significance of what is discussed in this chapter will become clear in the chapters to come.

The chapter builds on an analysis of British news media, web sites, films and television series (see the Appendix). I will describe what I argue is a moral panic that has emerged over chavs, where the latter have become a folk devil, a stigmatized form of categorization where people with certain attributes are labelled 'chavs' and 'marked' or 'inscribed' with particular characteristics creating an extremely negative stereotype. This stigmatized identity is constructed relationally through moral and aesthetic boundaries where chavs are categorized and positioned as belonging to a 'rough' or 'non-respectable' fraction of the white British working-class that is strongly sexualized, gendered, spatialized and associated with a lack of economic, social and cultural resources. In this way, chavs are relationally constructed as a morally and aesthetically denigrated 'other' against whom middle-class and 'respectable' working-class people distinguish and define themselves.

---

[9] 'jen' is a pseudonym.

39

I begin by tracing the emergence of the moral panic around chavs and the etymology of the term. I then discuss the central aspects of chavs constructed as a folk devil. This is followed by a discussion of the contested character of the moral panic and how the public debates about chavs have been couched in an explicit vocabulary of social class and, to some extent, also race. Then follow two sections on more implicit forms of class boundary formation, focusing on aesthetic and moral boundaries, respectively, and one section looking at the spatial aspect of those boundaries. Finally, I analyze the consequences of the moral panic on chavs: how new and existing forms of policing have targeted chavs, how their alleged consumption of high-end brand Burberry has negatively affected the brand, and how they have been used as entertainment to market and sell commodities.

The Emergence of a Moral Panic

Moral panics are usually characterized by the sudden emergence of moral concern among a broad section of people in a particular social context (local, national, or transnational) over the behaviour of a person, group or category of people that are seen to threaten deeply-held values in 'society'. This spawns a hostile reaction towards the latter who become a 'folk devil' in the eyes of the former (see S. Cohen, 2002 [1972]; Garland, 2008; Goode & Ben-Yehuda, 1994). Analyzed in this way, the chav phenomenon has undeniable features characteristic of a moral panic. The term chav and the meanings currently attached to it emerged very recently in the British public realm, where it quickly became a widely-discussed and debated phenomenon in the news media, on web sites, and other public sphere institutions. Several commentators (e.g. *Netimperative*, 2004) suggest that the satiric web site *Chavscum* (and to some extent, *Popbitch*), which was set up in December 2003 (The Independent, 2004b), played a key role in constructing and diffusing the meanings attached to the term. Very much thanks to modern media such as the internet, the term diffused rapidly, and by the beginning of 2004, chav was all over the place: it was named the buzzword of the year by lithographer Susie Dent in a book published by Oxford University Press (Dent, 2004), and included in the *Oxford English Dictionary* and the *Collins English Dictionary* together with the adjectives chavish, chavtastic, and the closely related terms ned and ASBO (see below). The rapid diffusion of the term in the British public realm is illustrated in Table 3.1, which displays the number of articles mentioning the term in four major British newspapers.[10]

---

[10] This is by no means an exhaustive list. I have chosen those newspapers with reliable search engines, so as to reach a fair estimate of the number of articles mentioning the term. The list contains three broadsheets (*The Guardian, The Independent* and *The Times*) and one tabloid

As we can see, 'chav' is not mentioned until 2004, when there is virtually an explosion, or to use a humorous lay-term, a 'chavalanche' of articles mentioning the term. The numbers reach a peak in 2005, then decline but remain stable between 2006 and 2007, and finally, show a further decline in 2008 and 2009. This reflects the way 'chav' has become institutionalized in public and everyday discourse, but it also shows the volatility of moral panics—just like fads, the heightened public social reaction over a phenomenon eventually wanes (Goode & Ben-Yehuda, 1994). Only time will tell whether the institutionalization of the use of the term in lay-discourse will be long-term or disappear as quickly as it appeared. During my time in London (October 2007–December 2008), I frequently encountered the term in conversations.

Table 3.1. *The number of articles in four major British newspapers mentioning the term chav, between 2003-2009. Sources: Google News Archive Search, www.guardian.co.uk, www.thesun.co.uk, www.timesonline.co.uk*

Newspaper	2003	2004	2005	2006	2007	2008	2009
The Guardian	0	41	123	78	88	66	41
The Independent	0	34	52	46	62	39	26
The Sun	0	44	87	65	27	47	40
The Times	0	60	183	111	98	43	39

Yet, the phenomenon of young people dressed in street wear, associated with minor unlawful behaviour and low social status, has existed throughout Britain since at least the 1990s (Hayward & Yar, 2006). These youths have been given local names, such as ned in Glasgow, kev in London and Bristol, charver in Newcastle, scally in Liverpool, yarco in East Anglia and skanger in Ireland. Other names include bazza, divi, janner, kappa slappa, rarfie, ratboy, senga, spide, steek, stig and townie. Chav was a local term used in southern England, such as the Medway towns and the East End of London (see below), but with the wide dissemination and institutionalization of the term chav, it has become an umbrella term applied to white, young, street-wear-clad working-class persons all over Britain.

But despite the current spread of the term, chav has been used for much longer, and there are different folk theories about its origins and uses. One theory is that it stems from chavi or chavo, which is the Romani word for child that emerged in the mid-19th century. In *The Times*, one reader writes that

> 'chav' was used in the 1970s (and maybe earlier) by the Gypsy community in East Kent, and meant 'bloke' or 'mate'. As it indicated a traveller, it meant that if a non-traveller called somebody "chav", he was looking down on him. Hence its pejorative connotation (The Times, 2004).

(*The Sun*) but no middle-market newspaper (e.g. *The Daily Mail, The Daily Express*) for the stated reasons.

41

It has also been argued that chav is mainly a local term used to refer to people from the Medway towns in Southern England. Others argue that it is an acronym for '[Ch]eltenham [Av]erage', which refers 'to young people in Gloucestershire who lack the requisite qualifications to enter Cheltenham College, one of the foremost private schools in the UK' (Hayward & Yar, 2006, p. 16). Another folk theory is that 'chav' is 'a historical East End of London term for child' (Tyler, 2008, p. 21), while others say that, since chavs are associated with Southern England, the term comes from Chatham. Lastly, it has been argued that chav has been used among builders and construction workers in the London area in the same way as 'mate' or 'mush', and thus originally lacked derogatory connotations (Young, 2004). In sum, these folk theories suggest that it is only recently that chav has become attached to young, white people in streetwear, jewellery and so forth, who are labelled a folk devil.

The Creation of a Folk Devil

What makes chavs a folk devil? Two quotes from the respected conservative broadsheet *Daily Telegraph*, provide rather typical characterizations of chavs and how they are labelled a folk devil:

> Chav… [is] a suitably monosyllabic noun or adjective designed to illuminate that which is most appalling in the young, designer-label-obsessed underclass of early 21st century Britain.

> When you see a stunted teenager, apparently jobless, hanging around outside McDonald's dressed in a Burberry baseball Cap, Ben Sherman shirt, ultra-white Reebok trainers and dripping in bling (cheap, tasteless and usually gold-coloured jewellery), he will almost certainly be a chav.

> If he has difficulty framing the words 'you gotta problem mate?' then he will definitely be a chav. Very short hair and souped-up Vauxhall Novas are chav, as is functional illiteracy, a burgeoning career in petty crime and the wearing of one's mobile telephone around the neck.

> Chavs are most at home in run-down, small-town shopping precincts, smoking and shouting at their mates. A teenage single mum chewing gum or drawing on a cigarette as she pushes her baby, Keanu, to McDonald's to meet the chav she believes to be his father is a chavette (Tweedie, 2004).

> They are the sullen, pasty-faced youths in hooded tops and spanking-new 'prison white' trainers who loiter listlessly on street corners; the slack-jawed girls with mottled legs, hoop earrings and heavily-gelled hair who squawk at each other in consonant-free estuary English and frighten old ladies on buses. They are the non-respectable working-classes: the dole-scroungers, petty criminals, football hooligans and teenage pram-pushers (Lewis, 2004).

Chavs are first and foremost identified through their visual characteristics. As shown in Figure 3.1, chavs typically refer to young, white people adopting a particular way of styling their dress and appearance: they wear branded clothing, especially sportswear such a baseball caps, tracksuits and trainers, which are combined with 'bling' or jewellery, usually in fake or low carat gold. Boys typically have short-cropped coiffure, while girls, or 'chavettes', have their hair in ponytails combined with large hoop earrings and large amounts of mascara around the eyes.

Figure 3.1. 'Chavs'.
Sources: Hayes (2007) and CaptiveInnocencePhotography (2008).

These visual characteristics are intimately bound to a range of other features. White, young people in tracksuits, jewellery and so on, are categorized as particular types of persons, with certain lifestyles, behaviour, body techniques, speech, values and social background. Chavs are said to congregate in gangs and behave in a loutish manner. They are loud-mouthed, and they threaten and harass people. Male chavs are often associated with violence such as football hooliganism and with minor forms of anti-social behaviour such as vandalism, assault and muggings. As a consequence, references to chavs as yobs or constituting a 'yob culture' are frequent. And as we will further explore later in this chapter, chavs are also associated with Anti-Social Behaviour Orders, or ASBO's, a civil order first introduced by the newly elected Labour government in 1997. This means that chav culture, and particularly chav masculinity, connotes danger and violence.

Moreover, chavs are often categorized as ignorant, uneducated, uncultured and stupid. In the quotes we read about 'functional illiteracy' and how chavs have problems forming sentences. Chavs are seen as only interested in excessive, tasteless, mindless consumption and adopting a hedonistic lifestyle. They smoke, binge drink and live on a diet of cheap and unhealthy food, especially fast food. Chavs are also described as promiscuous and sexually irresponsible, and this is especially the case for chavettes, who are depicted as 'slutty'; they are said to have no control over their sexual activities, and bear children at an early age.

Chavs are said to roam spaces such as shopping centres and McDonald's, or just 'hang out' in the street. They live in deprived neighbourhoods, often council house estates with high rates of crime, unemployment and teenage pregnancy. Marginalization is also shown in how chavs are often seen as largely outside the labour market and on welfare. They are often described as using the welfare system paid for by hardworking ordinary people. As expressed in one of the quotes above, chavs are 'dole scroungers'.

Taken together, these categorizations create a highly stigmatized identity, a folk devil. People with the visual characteristics of being white, young and adopting a certain style of dress are categorized as chavs and 'marked' or 'inscribed' with certain devalued characteristics. The chav becomes a stereotype, a denigrated 'other' against whom strong moral and aesthetic boundaries are constructed. Note the adjectives used to describe chavs in the quotes above. They are 'sullen', 'pasty-faced', 'slack-jawed', 'cheap', 'tasteless', 'stunted', 'appalling', 'designer-label-obsessed', and 'dripping' in jewellery. These boundaries are often drawn through mockery, though it is often blended with what can be interpreted as contempt, disgust or even hatred. Raisborough and Adams (2008) argue that humour can be used as a device to create distance, so that the content of what is expressed can appear harmless ('it's just a joke'). Their point is that mockery in general, and not the least that directed against chavs, can serve to legitimize the use of a strongly derogatory vocabulary.

Moreover, the 'chav' as folk devil is constructed primarily around consumption and lifestyles, rather than the sphere of production (cf. Hayward & Yar, 2006), and is linked with economic and social marginalization. Chavs are categorized as lacking economic, social and cultural resources, and thus as occupying a marginal position in social and terrestrial space. As we will explore further in this chapter, this makes 'chav' a figure of the non-respectable white British working-class, which is also spatialized and sexualized. The latter is particularly the case of chav femininity.

Being a non-respectable figure of the working-class also means that the chav phenomenon incorporates two 'familiar clusters of social identity' (S. Cohen, 2002 [1972], p. viii), which historically have served the role of folk devil, and appear along gendered lines. One is young, violent, working-class masculinity (Boëthius, 1995; Hall et al., 1978; Hay, 1995; Zatz, 1987). The other is working-class welfare cheats, which includes a gendered social type, namely the single, unwed, young, working-class mother (Ajzenstadt, 2009; Brush, 1997; Naylor, 2001; Phoenix, 1996).

Finally, the classed nature of the chav phenomenon is also intimately bound with whiteness. A person adopting the visual markers associated with chavs—e.g. tracksuit, trainers, baseball cap, jewellery—is only labelled chav if she is white, or at least approximating a white appearance. An Asian or black person, although dressed in a similar fashion, can by definition not be categorized as a chav. Whiteness is typically the unmarked, largely invisible norm against which other racial categories are defined (Dyer, 1997; Ruth Frankenberg, 1993; Webster, 2008). It is when marginalized, as in the case of chavs, that it can become a marked, racialized identity— a 'dirty' form of whiteness.

There are similarities between chavs and other labels of marginalized whiteness in Western countries. Perhaps the most well-known and explicitly racialized is the American term 'white trash'. Early usages can be traced to the 1830s (Wray, 2006). Like chavs, white trash has been associated with features and characteristics such as unemployment, poverty, deprived spaces, laziness, danger, violence, criminality and is thus a label for the undeserving poor, distinguished on moral grounds from 'poor whites', a label for the deserving poor. In Australia and New Zealand, the term 'bogan' has been used to label certain white working-class people. The term entered everyday and public discourse in the 1980s (Oxford University Press, n.d.), and perhaps it has even more similarities than white trash with chav. Like chav, bogan is a stereotype constructed around adopting certain visual markers of dress and style—e.g. flannelette shirts, tracksuit bottoms, ugg boots and 'mullet' hairstyles—which are bound to a range of moral-aesthetically derogatory characteristics, such as socio-economic marginality including deprived spaces and places, unemployment and welfare dependency; violence and gangs; lack of taste, manners and hygiene; low intelligence and level of education; 'tacky' and pathologized lifestyles. And like chavs, bogans are the subject of much mockery in public discourse (e.g. on websites like *Bogan.com.au* and *Things Bogans Like*).

A Contested Public Issue

As McRobbie and Thornton (1995) note, characteristic of moral panics in contemporary fragmented and mediated social worlds are that they, *qua* public issues, are contested and debated. And this is certainly the case with the chav phenomenon. Indeed, if one Googles the term, most of the content on blogs, discussion forums, news media and other web sites depicts chavs as folk devils in a similar way as we saw earlier in the two quotes from *The Daily Telegraph*. In fact, the great volume of such strongly derogatory content, not the least when articulated by journalists representing 'serious' news media, suggests that in many contexts, such language is legitimate. But this does not mean that these statements have gone unchallenged. There are many voices critical of the negative representations of chavs, and there is a dividing line between those who embrace the ridicule and moral denigration of chavs, and those who oppose it. Thus, in the conservatively oriented newspapers *The Times, The Daily Telegraph* and *The Daily Mail*, one tends to find outright mocking and sneering comments, whereas left of centre broadsheet *The Guardian* and its Sunday edition *The Observer* tend to critique such language. Yet these differences are by no means absolute, as journalists within the same newspaper sometimes take opposing sides in the 'chav debate'.

In this section I will argue that this public debate has in many ways been about social class, and to some extent, race. Several scholars have noted that, despite the prevalence of social class in the contemporary moment, it has more or less disappeared from public discourse (e.g. Savage, 2000; Skeggs, 2004). Along the same lines, others (Lawler, 2005a, p. 800; Moran, 2006, pp. 19-20) have claimed that the classed nature of the chav phenomenon has not been acknowledged as such. It is true that despite the fact that chavs are commonly associated with unemployment, council housing and welfare dependency, some commentators argue that chavs are a youth tribe, which is not related to social class or socio-economic positioning. To quote one reader's letter published in *The Independent*:

> Being a chav is a cultural decision. [It] is wrong to portray it as a working-class phenomenon, and wrong to portray all working-class people as chavs. 'Chav' is simply a postmodern urban tribe, no different from goths, trendies or indie kids. The rivalry between the groups isn't based on inverse class war. Teenagers feel happy when they can identify with their peers, and a common gang enemy is useful in forming that bond (The Independent, 2004a).

Yet, although many disagree that chavs have any relevance to social class, the public debates have frequently been about class and social location. For many commentators, chavs are working-class people. For instance, *The Collins Dictionary*, one of the first to include chav as a dictionary term, defines the term as 'a young working-class person who dresses in casual sports clothing', and in *The Daily Telegraph,* chavs belong to 'the wrong kind of working-class culture: the non-working kind', i.e. 'the non-respectable working-classes' (Lewis, 2004). Similarly, one blog poster claims that chavs are 'the new working-class infection that's sweeping the nation with epidemic-like speed' (Mitch's Blog, 2004), by which, he states, not all but certain *kinds* of working-class people are chavs. In this way, chavs are frequently categorized as belonging to a rough, non-respectable fraction of the working-class.

Many critics have argued that the use of the term reflects middle-class snobbery, that it is a way of sneering at the working-classes. In this way, the denigratory discourse on chavs has been called classism, class racism and social racism. One case that was critiqued in this way, but also gained popularity and ample interest from the media was a video clip posted on *YouTube* entitled 'Class Wars' and made by current and former pupils of Glenalmond College, one of Britain's foremost public schools. Set to classical music and filmed at the school grounds, the video starts by showing two men dressed in tweed fish a young person in a baseball cap from the river, then kick and beat him with a stick, while one of them shouts, 'Look at him, bloody chav!' The rest of the video shows two hunters on horses, dressed in full riding costumes, and how they, together with their aides and a hound, go on a 'chav hunt'. The hunters toast each other with champagne, then set off to pursue people dressed in tracksuits, trainers and Burberry caps. The last part of the video shows the chavs trapped on a lawn with the camera showing a double-barrelled shotgun aiming at them. The chavs are shot down, one after the other, their bodies falling to the ground in slow-motion. The end sees two hunters poking a chav lying on the ground with their rifles, to check that he is 'dead'.

Another telling event occurred in 2008, when Tom Hampson, editor in chief of the *Fabian Review*, the journal published by the Fabian Society, a left-wing think tank, spawned much debate in British news media, blogs and discussion forums in an editorial as well as in an article in *The Guardian* co-authored with Jemima Olchawski. They argued that the term 'chav' should be banned, and that its usage 'is deeply offensive to a largely voiceless group and—especially when used in normal middle-class conversation or on national TV—it betrays a deep and revealing level of class hatred' (Hampson & Olchawski, 2008). Similarly, an article in *The Times* comments on the 'chav-bashing' performed by 'middle-class and toff[11] social commentators':

> It is perfectly okay to sneer at the white working-class male with his predilection for garish clothing in man-made fibres and tattoos, his rude grammar and utter lack of social etiquette and refinement. No quango or pressure group will censure you for a spot of chav-bashing (Liddle, 2004).

---

[11] Toff is British slang for an upper-class person.

But less acknowledged in previous research (e.g. Lawler, 2005b; Tyler, 2008) is that not only the middle-classes make distinctions against chavs, but many people who identify as working-class draw boundaries against the latter, denying them working-class status. Take this person's furious reaction to a blog post arguing that chavs are working-class people: 'Chav is an attitude, not a fucking social class! I'm working-class and I'm fucked off to the back teeth of being lumped into the Chav catagory [sic] because of my working-class roots' (Mitch's Blog, 2004). Or take the following blog post:

> The difference between chavs and the working-class are [sic] that the working-class actually work for a living, whereas chavs are the underclass, those who live off benefits and can't even be bothered to look for a job. The working-class are hard-working and have their own culture, of which I only really know the East London one, coming from that sort of area with a family descended from Cockneys. Chav 'culture' is trash, and its [sic] insulting to even compare the two (Hollyzone, 2006).

Similarly, on *Chavscum,* chavs are described as 'the peasant underclass that are taking over our towns and cities!' These accounts, I would argue, reflect the long-standing moral distinction in Britain between respectable and non-respectable or 'rough' working-class people (e.g. Bott, 1964; Stacey, 1960; Watt, 2006).

In some instances, the racialized nature of the chav label has also been brought to the surface in public discourse. Chavs have been associated with white trash, as in the following quote from *The Daily Mail*: 'Chavs are Britain's answer to America's trailer trash. They're white, they're dumb, they're vulgar. And they don't care who knows it' (Thomas, 2004). The racialized character of the chav phenomenon has been critically recognized by several commentators, such as in newspaper articles entitled 'Everyone hates the white working-class male' (Liddle, 2004) and 'White trash, the only people left to insult' (Collins, 2004). Indeed, I would argue that the fact that chavs denote marginalized, marked whiteness is an important factor in explaining the widespread legitimacy of the strong derogatory vocabulary articulated against them. If such discourse were applied to, for instance, gays or people of non-white ethnicity, it would most likely be strongly condemned for being sexist or racist. Chavs, on the other hand, as part of the non-respectable, *lumpen*, white working-class, are basically morally bad people and thus 'rightfully' deserve to be denigrated. This can be related to Chris Haylett's (2001) argument that political discourse envisioning a multicultural, modern Britain has simultaneously cast white poor working-class people as an unmodern, racist and backward 'other'. I would argue that this group has come to be further demonized and pathologized under the label 'chav'.

McRobbie and Thornton (1995) argue that contemporary, contested moral panics are often characterized by the public involvement of the folk devils themselves or people who claim to represent them.[12] Yet, in the debates about the chav phenomenon, what is striking is the *absence* of people identifying as chavs or claiming to represent them. This makes chavs, as Hampson and Olchawski (2008) note, a largely voiceless group in the public discussion. One conspicuous exception, however, is the well-known journalist Julie Burchill, who is from a working-class background. In a series of newspaper articles and columns as well as several books and a SKY One documentary entitled *Chavs!*, Burchill both identifies as a chav and champions it as a positive identity. She celebrates chavs' hedonism as an ability to have fun, enjoy life and fill it with glamour. To 'slag off' chavs just reflects the envy among middle-class people for lacking these characteristics (e.g. Burchill, 2005).

One possible explanation for the lack of representation in the public realm by self-identified chavs is the stigmatization of the term. As Skeggs (1997) argues, the pathologization of working-class femininity means that it cannot serve as a positive form of identification nor as the basis for any form of identity politics. And with chav used as a word of abuse for allegedly non-respectable white working-class people, the same logic is even more apparent. Of course, it may also be that people who are labelled chavs lack the economic, social and cultural resources to access public sphere institutions or, if they do, lack the cultural resources to verbally defend themselves and argue their cause.

In sum, the public debates about chavs—whether they are taken to belong to the non-respectable working-class, an underclass or no class in particular—have frequently been about social class and socio-economic positioning. Moreover, the racialized character of this classed label has to some extent been acknowledged. Here I argue that the legitimacy of the derogatory discourse around chavs stems from their status as non-respectable working-class whites. Lastly, chavs are overwhelmingly represented in negative terms, with very few self-identified chavs participating in the public discourse.

A Question of Taste

While the previous section focused on the explicit ways in which chavs have become a public issue about class, this and the next section deal with more subtle, implicit forms of symbolic boundary formation along class lines. In this section, I explore the classed character of the aesthetic boundaries—often constructed through mockery—drawn against the consumption and

---

[12] For a recent example, see Ajzenstadt's (2009) study of the moral panic around single mothers in Israel.

lifestyles allegedly adopted by chavs. In *la Distinction*, Bourdieu (1984 [1979]) argues that, due to their lack of economic and cultural resources, the working-classes embody what he calls a 'taste of necessity'. It is governed by material constraints and thus characterized by a lack of choice and expressed as a preference for practical, informal forms of consumption oriented to satisfying basic needs. Conversely, middle-class taste is formed through strategies of distinction vis-à-vis the working-classes' taste of necessity. By virtue of their greater economic and cultural resources and their *distance* from material necessity, the middle-classes' consumption behaviour is characterized by choice and thus embodies a 'taste of freedom', or a 'taste of luxury'. This is an elaborate, stylized form of taste, governed by an 'aesthetic disposition', and characterized by 'manners' and form. Here, working-class taste is coded as crude, vulgar and excessive, as opposed to middle-class taste, which is coded as refined, sophisticated and restrained.

What can Bourdieu's analysis tell us about 'chav taste'? Representations of chavs eating fast food, smoking cheap cigarettes, and drinking equally cheap alcohol, indicate a taste constrained and governed by material necessity. These consumption practices have also been subject to similar types of aesthetic boundaries as those identified by Bourdieu. For instance, many of the humorous 'chav tests' featured on web sites such as *Facebook* joke about chavs' cheap, vulgar, unrefined taste of necessity. On the web site *Chavs Test* (n.d.) yes-or-no questions, include:

> Have you ever gone to Pizza Hut on a date?
>
> Have you ever got a present from a petrol station store?
>
> Have you ever cut out and used money off coupons from magazines?

Every 'yes' answer to any of these questions raises one's 'chav rating', which is calculated after one has finished the test. These examples reflect the ways in which chavs adopt a taste of necessity very much constructed as a *lack* of taste.

But the lifestyles and consumption associated with chavs have also features that clearly contradict Bourdieu's analysis. Many aspects of chavs' consumption practices can be interpreted as stylized forms of conspicuous consumption, which, in Veblen's terms is a way to 'show off', to display status and wealth through consumption, often through connotations of 'glamour'. This is shown in numerous ways. One is chavs' alleged consumption of designer brands such as Burberry and Prada, as well as streetwear brands such as Adidas and Nike. For Bourdieu (1984 [1979]), the phrase 'designer-label-obsessed under-class'—used to describe chavs in one of the quotes from *The Daily Telegraph* discussed earlier—is a contradiction in terms. Material constraints shape taste so that a person with few economic (and cultural) resources never develops a preference for expensive designer label items.

Perhaps the clearest example of the conspicuousness of chav consumption is its association with the term 'bling' and its adjective 'blingy'. The term derives from 'bling-bling' which is used by African-American hip-hop artists wearing heavy gold chains to display wealth, status, success, and a luxurious, glamorous lifestyle. The term and its connotations have diffused and translated into a British context in the form of not only jewellery, but also 'blingy' clothing items and accessories with shiny or glittery materials, such as shoes in silvery or gold coloured materials and jeans adorned with glittery details.

Bling and designer brands are of course part of a whole style featuring tracksuits, trainers, and baseball caps, which makes for a highly stylized appearance. But 'blingy' features are also found in other forms of consumption practices. For instance, the cars chavs are said to drive, mockingly called 'chav chariots', 'chaviots' or 'chavmobiles' often refer to inexpensive cars which are adorned with add-ons. The Vauxhall Cavalier is allegedly popular among chavs and has therefore been called the 'chavalier'. As one poster on the web site *Urban Dictionary* writes:

> The only mode of transport for the chav of today, a chavmobile is a derogatory word for a home-converted vehicle of some description. Countless modifications may include huge subwoofers in the boot, a crude soft-top, spoilers from an F1 car, blue neon underneath the doors, spinning hub-caps, painted flames around the wheels or bonnet, a nitro-charged engine (homemade, of course) and multiple CD player. The trouble is, a chavmobile will usually be a fifteen year old Vauxhaul Nova or a Ford Fiesta that should have been scrapped after the accident.

Moreover, one of the ways in which chavs are labelled is through their own and their children's names. For instance, in an article in *The Observer*, Kevin Mitchell (2005) critically notes that footballer Wayne Rooney, has a 'chav name'. And chav celebrity couple (see below) David and Victoria Beckham named their two children Brooklyn and Cruz, respectively, which is considered chavy, in the sense that these are names that are glamorous in a tacky way. It has also been claimed that chav names are 'often spelled in an unusual way or including punctuation' (Asthana, 2007), e.g. Ashleigh, Chelseigh, Cortnie and Destinee. These are frequently the subject of ridicule. There are also web sites with 'chav name generators' where one can create a chav version of one's own or one's baby's name.[13]

In Veblen's analysis, conspicuous consumption is the display of distance from necessity *par excellence*, and the stylized character of much of chavs'

---

[13] For instance, on the web site *Company* (n.d.) I typed in my own name and got Romeo Grand.

consumption, clearly suggests that they embody aspects of a taste for luxury. But although in some respects transcending the logic of material necessity, as Bourdieu understands it (and thus pointing to the limitations of his analysis, that is, his overstating the constraining role of economic resources), the conspicuous aspects of chav taste are downgraded for displaying distance from necessity in an obvious, vulgar way lacking in sophistication. It is especially the noticeable ways of 'showing-off' one's status, which are denigrated. To display the brand label onto the jumper one wears, is conceived as having a 'showing off' and 'shouting-it-out' aspect which is crude, vulgar, unsophisticated, and therefore 'cheap' and 'over-the-top', as opposed to middle-class taste, which values the discreet, refined and subtle ways of, say, wearing a designer-label clothing item. Thus, chavs lack access to cultural resources which are approved by and legitimate among the middle-classes. The adjective 'chavy' is frequently used to connote the vulgar, excessive and crude taste associated with chavs, and it is constructed very much in opposition to the more middle or upper class term 'posh'.

This form of conspicuous consumption means that there is an aspirational aspect to the consumption practices among chavs, symbolizing a desire to climb the social ladder. On *Urban Dictionary*, someone has even coined the word 'chavspiration', which is defined as follows: 'From Chav Aspiration—chavspiration is the desire for deeply awful things, burbury [Burberry] knock-offs, asbos, footballer boyfriends etc'. The conspicuous and aspirational aspects of chav consumption are especially evident in the context of social mobility and celebrity culture. Some British celebrities, almost always from a working-class background, are labelled chav celebrities. They are in fields usually associated with a lack of highly valued cultural resources such as footballers, glamour models, pop artists, participants in reality-TV programs, soap opera actors and TV-presenters, including Katie Price (also known as Jordan), Peter Andre, Jade Goody, Victoria and David Beckham ('Posh and Becks'), Cheryl and Ashley Cole, and Wayne and Coleen Rooney. But while chavs in general are portrayed in explicitly morally denigrated terms—e.g. as loutish anti-social dole scroungers—chav celebrities are more commonly ridiculed for their tacky, excessive appearances and lifestyles. This means that the notion of chav celebrity is primarily constructed around aesthetic rather than moral boundaries. Chav celebrities are positioned as having loads of economic resources but a lack of cultural resources—the latter is often reflected in mocking remarks on not knowing the cultural codes or trying but not getting them right. Again, it is the conspicuous consumption that is denigrated.

Figure 3.2. 'Chav celebrities' Peter Andre and Katie Price.
Source: Mahoney (2007).

The Daily Mail regularly mocks chav celebrities. In the article, 'The Chav Rich List', one can read: 'They're the celebrities taste forgot—the chavs who flaunt fake tans, false boobs and mock Tudor houses'. David and Victoria Beckham are, according to the article, 'Undoubtedly the King and Queen of planet Chav' and described as 'the ultimate in nouveaux riches'. In the same article, Wayne and Coleen Rooney's £4.5 million mansion is known as the 'Chav Towers'.

The status of chav celebrities is also illustrated by the incident involving glamour model Katie Price, known as Jordan. Before a polo match arranged by Cartier Polo International in Windsor, she was refused to book a £6000 a table in the highly exclusive Chinawhite tent, which is ripe with A-list celebrities. Media reports repeatedly quoted an 'insider' who is said to have explained that this was because she was too chavy to be admitted to the tent. Price wrote a letter to *The Times* arguing that this was due to class snobbery against a working-class girl like herself (Price, 2008).

A Question of Morals

The aesthetic boundaries drawn against chavs usually have strong moral connotations. In this sense, although the aesthetic dimension has a relative autonomy—e.g. to say that someone's shirt is 'chavy' one usually means that it is tacky—it is often intimately tied to the moral dimension, and, as I have argued throughout, to social class. As we will see, there is also a gendered dimension to the moral boundaries constructed against chavs.

As we have seen, symbolic distinctions against chavs are often constructed through mockery, and moral boundaries are no exception. One example of chav humour is an email, a 'Christmas Card' portraying the 'Chav Nativity', also called the 'Chavtivity' that was widely circulated during December 2007. Shown in Figure 3.2, the nativity scene is placed in a vandalized bus shelter with Mary, Joseph and the three wise men in tracksuits. Joseph is preoccupied with his mobile phone (composing a text message, perhaps?) and very much looks identical to the man on the 'wanted' poster behind him, implying that he is the one hunted by the law. Mary, hair tied in a ponytail, is smoking. The gifts offered by the three wise men—presumably stolen—look like alcohol, a DVD player, and cigarettes. Portraying the 'trashy' chav family engaged in 'cheap', wasteful consumption, associated with crime, and living off 'respectable' society, the picture vividly expresses the moral-aesthetic distinctions constructed against chavs.[14]

Figure 3.3. 'The Chavtivity'.
Source: Metro (2007).

Another humorous representation of the chav family is studied by Raisborough and Adams (2008), who analyze the mockery of neds, a local term used for chavs in Scotland, in the comic strip *The Neds*—a recent addition to *The Beano* children's comic published by DC Thomson and Co Ltd. *The Neds* is about the family of the same name, its members being Ned, Nedette and

---

[14] The 'Chav Nativity' is a recurring concept. *The Daily Telegraph* reports that pupils in a school in Kent were given a script for the rehearsal of a chav Nativity play, 'where Jesus turns water into strong lager [Stella—one of the beer brands most favoured by chavs according to the stereotype] and the three wise men bear gifts of Adidas and Burberry clothes' (S. Adams, 2008). Moreover, there are several 'humorous' video clips of people performing 'chav nativity' plays on *YouTube* and other similar web sites.

their children Asbo and Chavette. They and other neds are seen dressed in tracksuits and Burberry, are often obese, and frequently portrayed as idle, lazy, feckless, unemployed and dependent on welfare. Thus, we can see how moral-aesthetic boundaries are drawn against neds depicted as a work-shy underclass. When first published in 2006, the comic strip was originally intended as a one-off, but due to its popularity, it has come to feature as an 'occasional guest' in the comic *BeanoMAX*. The comic strip was critiqued for its way of labelling and portraying neds, especially by Scottish politicians, such as the Scottish Children's Commissioner. The publishers responded by stating that it was conceived as 'harmless fun' and not intended to offend anyone (*The Daily Record* Feb 6 2006; *The Sunday Times* February 5, 2006).

As mentioned earlier, there is also a gendered dimension to the moral boundaries drawn against chavs. To reiterate what I said above, the chav phenomenon incorporates two historically familiar folk devils distinguished along lines of gender. As regards masculinity, one recurrent folk devil is the young, working-class, violent man (cf. S. Cohen, 2002 [1972], pp. viii-ix; Hall et al., 1978). Here, chav masculinity is often represented as violent and 'yobbish' and associated with vandalism, assault, muggings and football hooliganism. This means that the aggressive and loutish behaviour commonly associated with chavs of both genders more often takes on a particularly violent character among male chavs. The latter are often portrayed as threatening and picking fights with people on the streets, sometimes also mugging them. This is especially evident in the many video clips on *YouTube* featuring 'chav fights'. They frequently show chavs coming up to someone on the street and starting a fight, or show violence involving chavs taking place outside nightclubs. There are also many clips featuring people who dress up and impersonate 'loutish chavs', sometimes laughing while they're doing it.[15] Thus, in this context, chav violence here becomes something of an entertainment genre. One notable example was when *The Sun*, in an article entitled 'Yob-Smacked' (Patrick, 2009b) wrote that a video clip uploaded on *YouTube*, and watched by more than 30,000, had become an 'internet hit' and it provided a link to the clip on its homepage. The video described in the tabloid showed a 'yob' who

> is seen hurling abuse at a man on his doorstep and trying to goad him into a fight—unaware that his 'victim' is a martial artist. Amazingly, the man remains calm—until the yob kicks over a dustbin. He then floors the attacker with a lightning-fast jab, then stands over him in a fighting pose. But the gobsmacked yob's had enough and flees in Merseyside.

---

[15] It should be noted that not only chav males are represented as violent. There are also some video clips, on *YouTube* and elsewhere featuring 'catfights' between chavettes.

The following day, another *Sun* article (Patrick, 2009a) revealed the names of the protagonists in the clip, the 'yob' and the 'hero', and interviewed the latter. Jason Smith was described as a 'video hero', 'dad' and 'Gulf war veteran' 'with TWO black belts' (in jiu-jutsu and karate respectively). The 'yob', Les Andrews, was arrested and fined. The article also claimed that more than 200,000 people had already viewed the video clip on *The Sun's* homepage. The day after, in a third article (Patrick, 2009c), *The Sun* claimed that the 'thug' Andrews had rung up the tabloid and threatened to sue it for providing a link to the video clip.

This is a very good example of moral boundary formation distinguishing between the respectable 'us'—*The Sun* readers and the heroic Smith—and the morally depraved, aggressive chav yobs of which Andrews is an example.[16] The tabloid *The Sun* is well-known for being patriotic, and this incident was perfect material for it, with Smith, a soldier who had fought for his country and is married with a daughter cast as a symbol of moral virtue and superiority protecting his family against immoral yobs.

Moreover, even though the term chav is only used once in the three articles, in many of the comments made on blogs, on *YouTube*, on *The Sun* web site and elsewhere, Andrews is frequently labelled a chav. Here are some examples:

> Serves the fuckin chav scratter right. The community should take a leaf outta the karate guys book!

> wot a fucking fairy lol [laughing out loud] fucking stupid chav wot a fucking pussy

> This could be the video of the year! LOL I HATE chavs like this that think they are 'hard' and try and ruin other peoples lives. I love it how this chav literally crawled back out the garden, absolute scum.

> Typical fucking Chavs!

> Little pussy chav!!!

But the ridicule of 'yobs', such as Andrew, were sometimes coupled with, or replaced by, accounts suggesting fear and a sense of moral and social breakdown—that respectable society was being besieged by 'yobs'. For example, take the following comments: 'sad thing is about this video is people are living in fear of chav yobs ALL OVER THE COUNTRY and the police are doing NOTHING to help them'.

While chav masculinity is associated with violence and yobbish behaviour, the moral boundaries drawn against chav femininity are particularly

---

[16] Interestingly, in the three articles, the 'hero' is called by his first name, Jason, implying familiarity and informality, that he is someone the reader can relate to, whereas the 'yob' is mentioned by his last name, Andrews, i.e. in formal terms, implying distance. Thus, the 'us' and 'them' distinction is also emphasized rhetorically by how the protagonists are addressed.

sexualized and bound up with reproduction. Here, another familiar folk devil reappears, namely the single, working-class, 'dole-scrounging' mother. Chavettes as sexualized means that they are represented as promiscuous and 'slutty', basically sleeping with anyone, and thus the very opposite of the ideal of the respectable woman. This is the gist of many chav jokes, such as the following:

> Q: What's the difference between a chavette and a Ferrari?
>
> A: Not many people have been in a Ferrari!
>
> Q: What does a chavette have written on the back of her knickers?
>
> A: NEXT
>
> Q: What's the difference between a chavette and an ironing board?
>
> A: An ironing board's legs are difficult to get apart!
>
> (Jokes Forum, 2009)

The 'sluttiness' of chavettes is coupled with their being sexually irresponsible, e.g. not caring about using contraceptives, and therefore often associated with teenage pregnancy and motherhood. To take another joke:

> Chavette with 8 kids is asked by social worker, 'What are all their names?'
>
> 'wayne, wayne, wayne, wayne, wayne, wayne, wayne and wayne'
>
> 'Oh that's a nightmare, what do you call if you want them to come to the dinner table?'
>
> 'easy, just shaat wayne and they all cum runnin'
>
> 'Oh well what about bedtime?'
>
> 'Just shart wayne and they all cum runnin?'
>
> 'OK, OK what about if you want one in particular?'
>
> 'Oh then I have to call em by their last name!'
>
> (The Student Room, 2008)

'Sluttiness' and teenage motherhood are also strongly linked with the notion that chavettes have children for their cunning, selfish economic interests, namely to get benefits. Motherhood thus becomes a form of willing welfare dependency paid for by 'us', respectable citizens. This is reflected in the use of the derogatory term 'pram face' to describe single, teenage, chavette mothers (Tyler, 2008).

Representations of the chavette, have been diffused in popular culture via *The Catherine Tate Show* in the UK and through the internationally popular British TV-series *Little Britain*, in the form of the character Vicky Pollard, played by Matt Lucas. Vicky Pollard is a girl in her late teens who is very overweight, wears a pink tracksuit as well as several gold necklaces and gold rings, has her hair in a ponytail, and a large amount of mascara on her eyelashes. She lives on a council estate, goes on welfare, chain-smokes, shoplifts, has about a dozen babies, gets pregnant regularly, is fickle, aggressive, extremely foulmouthed and speaks very fast and incoherently. One example of her morally and sexually irresponsible behaviour is shown in an episode where she exchanges one of her babies for a Westlife CD. Vicky Pollard has frequently been used by journalists as a reference point in order to illustrate and explain what a chav is. For instance, a *Daily Mail* (2006) article is entitled 'Woman mugged by Vicky Pollard look-a-like', and features a picture of the TV-character ('chav queen Vicky Pollard'), despite reporting that there were two muggers, both teenage girls. Another case is 19 year-old Kerry McLaughlin living in North Tyneside, who was dubbed 'the real life Vicky Pollard' by the press. After 111 complaints by neighbours and 25 visits by the police she was issued a particularly powerful form of Anti-Social Behaviour Order (ASBO) banning her from entering her flat, and sentencing her to jail if she did (Metro, 2005).

These and other cases imply that Vicky Pollard has become one of the 'public faces' of the chav phenomenon. But this has also been contested. An article in *The Guardian* critiques tabloids' way of using Vicky Pollard, a fictional character and clearly a caricature and parody, in real cases (such as the one involving McLaughlin) as it thereby creates 'a stereotype that dissolves the difference between fiction and reality, and allows "real life" cases to be traduced into a media pigeonhole' (The Guardian, 2005).

In sum, then, the moral-aesthetic distinctions made against chavs create classed boundaries between a 'respectable' us and a trashy, marginalized, immoral them. There is also a gendered dividing line between violent, yobbish chav masculinity and 'slutty', single teenage mother chav femininity.

Chav Space

The chav phenomenon is not only about the stigmatization of certain kinds of people but also of the spaces and places associated with them. These 'chav spaces' denote a lack of economic and cultural resources, and are tied to what one could call an imagined geography of class. Chavs are said to live in marginalized neighbourhoods with high rates of crime, unemployment and teenage pregnancy. Council houses in particular play a central role. This can be seen by the fact that chavs are associated with the highly derogatory acronyms '[Ch]eltenham [Av]erage', mentioned earlier, as well as '[C]ouncil [H]oused [a]nd [V]iolent' and '[C]ouncil [H]ouse [V]ermin (Hayward & Yar, 2006, p. 16). Moreover, the lifestyles associated with

chavs are spatialized. Chavs are often portrayed as congregating in gangs—
not only in council house estates—but also in public spaces such as shopping
centres, street corners and bus stops.

Chavs' consumption takes place in spaces that are characterized by selling
cheap commodities and as having low status. For instance, on *Chavs Test*
(n.d.) one is asked: 'Have you ever shopped at Co-op, Iceland or Hyper
Value?' and 'Have you ever purchased a KFC family bucket?' Similarly, on
Urban Dictionary (n.d.), one can read: 'Chavs are retards who think that
they're rebels and also think that their local McDonalds [sic] is a 5-star re-
straunt [sic]' and 'Filth hanging outside McDonalds [sic] in large groups
attempting to look remotely intimidating'. Consumption in these chav
spaces—e.g. fast food eateries and cheap clothing chain stores—very much
embodies a taste of necessity discussed earlier.

But the representations of chav spaces have also a more conspicuous aspect, found in the practice of Christmas lighting. Chavs are said to illuminate
the facades of their houses generously with colourful lights often in the form
of figures such as Santa Claus, reindeers, and snowmen. As Edensor and
Millington (2009, p. 106) note, this very expressive, conspicuous practice is
very much opposed to the 'modest, chic white and blue lighting [that] illu-
minates middle-class housing areas'. Unsurprisingly, these 'chav bling' illuminations are subject to ridicule on a number of web sites (see Edensor
and Millington, 2009).

Figure 3.4. 'Chav Christmas decorations'.
Source: Hannah More Zider (2004).

Figure 3.4 is taken from a web page where different 'chav Christmas lights'
are rated. The picture received the 'chav score' 5 of 5 and is accompanied by
the following ironic text:

This is true chav genius—the house is impressive enough with Santas, Snowmen and Trees... but the prancing reindeers on the garage are a tasteful masterstroke. This must be a well-off chav, as he even decorates his neighbour's house into the bargain! (Hannah More Zider, 2004)

The stereotypical images of chav spaces are also present in the representations of particular locations. I here use Rob Shields' (1991) notion of place images, i.e. 'the various discrete meanings associated with real places or regions regardless of their character in reality' (Shields, 1991, p. 60; quoted in Watt, 2006, p. 777). In other words, place images denote the codes and narratives constructed around a particular place. The most prolific source on the internet for place images associated with chavs is the web site *Chav-towns*, which features posts on towns, cities, neighbourhoods and regions allegedly 'infested with chavs'. Towns or areas with a reputation for having a large chav population include Croydon, Dagenham, Milton Keynes and Cheltenham. This post on Swansea is rather typical of some of the representations of chavs that appear on the web site:

I've lived in swansea all of my life and i have to say of all the places ive been to, the chavs in my home town are the worst.

the most popular hangout is the city centre high st,the job centre is located here and its close to dyfatty flats, full of heroin addicts. walking down high st in the day is bad enough but at night you're taking your life into your hands,the city centre is full of chavs especially on a monday, 15 year old girls with those piercings above their lips ,pack out primark with their prams ,greggs bakeries are another favourite to get their brats their pasties,oxford st is full of them , gangs of chavs with prams outside the 99p shop and of course soccer sports,if it wasn't for chavs i dont think soccer sports would be open , the chavs go there for their tracksuits and nike air max trainers,and of course to buy the latest trainers in chav style for their babies.all the chav girls have yellow hair, elizabeth duke earrings, and about 40 rings on each fin-ger,guaranteed every sentence they speak ends in the word MUSH,im hoping to move out of this shithole soon as its really starting to get me down, me and my mates dont even drink much in the city centre any more, because of the amount of chavs,thank god for the new sa1 development, otherwise we'd have nowhere to go, any body considering visiting this pit don't bother, you wont be missing anything.

We can note here how the moral-aesthetic boundaries drawn against chavs take a spatial form as they are bound up with the meanings around which Swansea as a place is constructed. Thus, we can note how the more abstract notions of 'chav spaces'—e.g. here in the form of references to 99 p shops, Greggs, Soccer Sport and Primark—become contextualized in Swansea constructed as a 'chav town'. In sum, the codes and narratives constructed around chavs have an important spatial aspect. The spaces and places associ-ated with chavs become stigmatized and generally denote socio-economic marginality and a lack of cultural resources. In this sense, it is a symbolic construction of class that is spatialized.

Consequences of the Moral Panic

During and after a period of moral panic, the hostile social reaction against folk devils can lead to profound cultural and institutional changes, such the introduction of new laws and changes in norms, or a strengthening of existing norms (cf. Goode & Ben-Yehuda, 1994). In this section, I will explore the consequences of the moral panic about chavs by looking at three different contexts or cases: (i) new and existing forms of policing explicitly targeting chavs; (ii) the consequences of high end brand Burberry being associated with chavs; (iii) the usage of the image of the chav to market and sell commodities.

Policing the Chav

In the wake of the chav phenomenon, new and existing forms of policing have come to target chavs. One such form of policing deals with regulating access to public space. Shopping malls, pubs, night clubs and other public establishments (e.g. internet cafes) have started banning people in clothing that is associated with chavs, including baseball caps, hoodies and clothing brands such as Burberry and Prada. This is clearly a way of excluding an unwanted, potentially troublesome and low status segment of the population. And when the Bluewater shopping centre in Kent started to ban hoodies and baseball caps in 2005, this was endorsed by both prime minister Tony Blair and deputy prime minister John Prescott (The Times, 2005).

Moreover, a recent campaign by the Department of Work and Pensions is targeted at working-class people in general and chavs in particular. The campaign has been advertised widely on radio, television and on posters. During my time in London, I saw one poster, depicted in Figure 3.5, on a daily basis. As we can see, it is a black and white photo of a very large-sized woman—an extremely uncommon image on an advertisement in public space—with scraped back hair tied in a knot, large hoop earrings, and a telescopic sight zooming in on her, and above in huge red letters it reads: 'We're closing in'. The woman has what seems like a stern look on her face, her face is turned and it is as if she is feeling that someone is watching her. The woman who is allegedly an actual or potential benefit thief very much looks like a chavette—e.g. the trademark scraped back hair— and it is difficult not to think that this is deliberate.

Figure 3.5. Department of Work and Pensions campaign poster.
Source: Department of Work and Pensions (n.d.).

Chavs have also been associated with Anti-Social Behaviour Orders, or AS-BOs. ASBOs were issued by the Labour government in 1997 before the emergence of the moral panic surrounding chavs, and subsequently strengthened and broadened throughout the UK during 2003-2004. An ASBO is a civil order, issued 'to restrict the movement and behaviour of people deemed to be anti-social' (Millie, 2008, p. 379), but it may be transformed into a criminal offence if breached. The web site *Tackling Anti-Social Behaviour and its Causes* set up by the Home Office (Home Office, 2009) provides an explanation of anti-social behaviour:

What is anti-social behaviour?

The term anti-social behaviour covers a wide range of selfish and unacceptable activity that can blight the quality of community life. Terms such as 'nuisance', 'disorder' and 'harassment' are also used to describe some of this behaviour.

Examples include:

- Nuisance neighbours
- Yobbish behaviour and intimidating groups taking over public spaces
- Vandalism, graffiti and fly-posting

- People dealing and buying drugs on the street
- People dumping rubbish and abandoned cars
- Begging and anti-social drinking
- The misuse of fireworks
- Reckless driving of mini-motorbikes.

(Home Office, 2009)

It goes on to say that the legal definition of anti-social behaviour is found in the Crime and Disorder Act 1998. The Act describes anti-social behaviour as 'acting in an anti-social manner as a manner that caused or was likely to cause harassment, alarm or distress to one or more persons not of the same household as the perpetrator'. Crucially, the text is also accompanied by a picture of four teens wearing hoodies, engaging in anti-social behaviour, here drinking alcoholic beverages in public space (see Figure 3.6). We can clearly see that the four youths display the visible appearance of chavs.

Figure 3.6. 'Youths drinking outside'.
Source Home Office (2009).

The association between ASBOs and chavs is also made explicit in everyday speech. In common parlance, ASBO does not only refer to a particular civil order, but also to the kind of people onto whom such civil orders are issued. One can therefore *be* an ASBO. Moreover, as chavs are associated with delinquency, they are also often portrayed as ASBOs. Indeed chav is sometimes more or less synonymous with ASBO in the sense just described. For instance, we can see this on Figure 3.7, and on *Urban Dictionary* (n.d.) one can find two definitions of ASBO that are very blunt about this connection:

an essential qualification for all chavs and general idiots who think that; beating the shit out of random people walking down the street/ throwing bricks through people's windows/ generally displaying how few brain cells they have, makes them look 'hard'.

New British Government scheme to crack down on chavs and their behaviour. Acronym for Anti-Social Behaviour Order. Stops offenders from doing certain things, going to certain places and meeting certain people.

Figure 3.7 implies that chavs glorify anti-social behaviour, and that getting an ASBO is a status marker, and this is a view that comes across in several other cases. A more critical view of ASBO is expressed by Carole Callwalladr who in *The Observer* writes that 'Asbos are just the word chav made concrete, a vehicle for old-school class hatred made over to look all pretty' (Callwalladr, 2005).

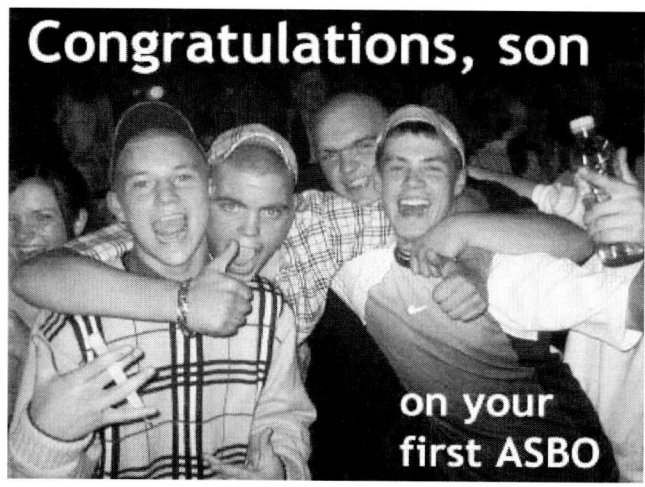

Figure 3.7. 'Congratulations, son on your first ASBO!'
Source: Anti Chav (2008).

Chavs in Me Burberry

In Figure 3.7 above two of the 'chav asbos' are wearing clothes with the beige, white, black and red tartan pattern which is the trademark of the high status brand Burberry. The brand, founded in 1856, has the status of a classic, luxury brand and its gabardine raincoats and its trade mark beige-white-black-red check pattern are considered classics. But by the 1990s Burberry was seen as old-fashioned and passé, and its main consumer segment were 'middle-aged, fashion-conservative men' (Tungate, 2005, p. 414). Consequently, the company went through major restructuring with Rose Marie

Bravo, appointed new CEO in 1996, a key architect in setting up a new business model. And crucially, the company also went through a fundamental rebranding process: the logotype was changed, Christopher Bailey became new design director and an advertisement campaign involving photographer Mario Testino and top models Kate Moss and Stella Tenant was launched. In all this, Burberry's trademark check pattern became a visible feature in its products and came to play a key role in the rebranding process. In a short time, Burberry had managed to change its image to a youthful, cool, luxury brand in touch with contemporary fashion. This also meant that the company's brand strategy became more inclusive, reaching out to a broader consumer segment. The company successfully retained the existing consumer segment and gained younger, fashion-conscious ones (Moore & Birtwistle, 2004; Tungate, 2005, p. Ch. 14).

Figure 3.8. Danniella Westbrook in Burberry check.
Source: *The Daily Mail* (2009).

Yet exploiting its trademark check pattern and 'opening up' the brand through producing more affordable items, such as Burberry checked baseball caps, attracted chavs. Another probable factor was the production of counterfeit items in Burberry check. But above all, the fact that the brand's identity had become distinctly displayed through the tartan pattern was certainly in line with the conspicuous, aspirational taste associated with chavs, which we have discussed earlier. Moreover, the media started to publish stories of chav celebrities wearing Burberry checked clothing. This increased the brand's visibility and might also have made it more desirable due to the status of these celebrities among some consumers. One defining moment was in April 2004 when Danniella Westbrook, former actress in the soap opera East-Enders, was pictured with her daughter and their pram—all in full-on Burberry check (see Figure 3.8). This has been described as disastrous for Burberry's image, as its check pattern became part of the public ridicule and sneering targeting chavs and chav celebrities such as Westbrook (cf. Kobayashi-Hillary, 2008).

As a consequence, in 2004 the Burberry check became strongly connected to chavs and thus associated with the stigmatized moral-aesthetic boundaries constructed around the latter. In Summer 2004, media reported about pubs starting to ban clothes with the Burberry checked items due to its popularity among chav football hooligans (Bothwell, 2005). In this sense, Burberry got 'hijacked' by chavs. And this had consequences. In 2005, Burberry experienced a slump in sales in the UK, but not elsewhere. The re-branding of Burberry with its emphasis on the trademark check seemed to have backfired. The company responded by cutting down its visibility. From featuring it on 20 per cent of its items, the check was slashed to 5 per cent. Among other things, the company stopped producing its Burberry checked caps, said to be a chav favourite (Bothwell, 2005).

Since then, Burberry has managed to rebrand itself again, successfully distancing itself from its association with their trademark check pattern. Indeed, in a British context, the check pattern has become so synonymous with chavs that it has come to signify the latter. On one blog, the word chav is jokingly said to derive from the Latin *chauvinistic burberrus* (Likilla, 2004). But time heals all wounds. In October 2009, *The Independent* reported that Burberry had again begun to produce some items that distinctly feature the tartan pattern. The article also ensured the reader that it was safe to wear such clothes again without being labelled chav (Harries, 2009).

In sum, Burberry's association with chavs had the consequences of lowering the company's status, negatively affecting its sales in UK. For chavs, it instigated dress codes barred chavs wearing the Burberry pattern from entry to public establishments.

The Commodification of Chavness

The moral-aesthetic denigration of chavs, and the role of mockery in constructing boundaries against chavs have created avenues for the production of commodities that cater to the alleged non-chav. As Paul Johnson (2008) shows, chav-related commodities and services marketed as 'chav chic' have become commonplace in British gay space. Here, chav masculinity takes on particularly sexual connotations that in other contexts are usually reserved for chav femininity. Masculine sexuality is combined with danger and violence in the form of magazines, telephone sex lines and pornography marketed as chav and scally. Johnson's argument is that the denigrated cultural symbols and practices associated with chavs are appropriated in middle-class dominated gay spaces where they are converted into valuable cultural resources, which, in turn, generate economic resources in the form of commodities and services.

British gay clubs also arrange 'chav parties' or 'chav nites' where people dress up as chavs. This practice is also found in many British university student unions. But while sexualised danger is the selling point in gay spaces, irony and humour is the general selling point in more hetero-normative contexts. Figure 3.9 shows four people dressed up for a chav nite. Their ways of posing for the camera suggest a reflexive stance of ironic distance, of performing chav in a 'humorous' way by drawing on some of the stereotypes about chavs circulated in the public realm. The young man in the middle grimaces towards the camera in a way that suggests he wants to display a mock 'hard' look, while having his arms around the two girls and holding a bottle of 'Stella' in his left hand. The beer brand Stella Artois is commonly associated with the chav stereotype. The two girls are heavily made up and have tied their hair in ponytails. They have also tucked pillows or cushions under their tops so as to look pregnant. The girl to the left combines a lot of cleavage with a pushed up bust, while the girl to the right poses with a lollypop in her open mouth while looking into the camera in an exaggerated way. Both perform 'slutty' chav femininity in a 'humorous', detached, ironic way.

Figure 3.9. 'Chav party'.
Source: seriouslymcmillan (2008)

Also, *The Sun* reports that Prince William dressed up as a chav on the ending day of services with his platoon: 'He donned a loose-fitting top and bling jewellery—then added an angled baseball cap and glare to complete his menacing lookalike of Lotto lout Michael Carroll [a chav celebrity who won £9.7 million on the National Lottery]. William even balanced a gleaming baseball bat on his shoulders to add to his intimidating stance'. (Larcombe, 2006) There is also a plethora of commodities, of chav merchandise, including several satiric books on chavs, such as Chav's Books series published by Crombie Jardine Publishing Limited, featuring *The Little Book of Chavs: The Branded Guide to Britain's New Elite*, *The Chav Guide to Life*, *The Little book of Chav Jokes*, and *The Little Book of Chav Speak*. Moreover, on the web site *Amazon,* one can purchase skateboard stickers printed with 'No chavs' and 'Chavs suck', 'Chav decorated' mouse pads illustrated with what is apparently supposed to be a chav (a cartoon of the head of a young man in baseball cap), 'Chav—Officially licensed pack of 4 metal button badges', Chav master game, baby clothing (a vest with 'chav' or 'upcoming chav' written on the front), 'Become a chav' gift pack (including, among other things, 'A seriously bling fake gold sovereign ring', 'England flag transfer tattoo', 'Chav couture poster—What to wear if you want to look like a real Chav', 'Chav your ride poster—Tips on making your car into a Chavmobile', 'Chav test—Complete the test to see exactly how chav you are', and 'Your very own ASBO—Simply complete the registration card inside the pack—along with your choice of ASBO offence—and we'll produce and send you this personalised ASBO to show to your friends!'

Lastly, the names associated with chavs have been central features in marketing products. In January 2009 Northumberland based Activities Abroad sent a promotional email to the 24,000 listed in their database. Here is an excerpt:

Hello [-----]

Chav Free Activity Holidays

According to the *Daily Mail*, children with middle-class names such as Duncan and Catherine are eight times more likely to pass their GCSE's than children with names such as Wayne and Dwayne.

This got us to thinking. Are there names you are likely to encounter or not encounter on an Activities Abroad holiday? After a bit of research we came up with two lists of names.

Unlikely	Likely
Britney	John
Kylie-Lianne	Sarah
Bianca	James

Tiffany	Charles
Dazza	Rachel
Chardonnay	Michael
Chantelle	Alice
Candice	Lucy
Courtney	Joseph
Shannon	Charlotte

Nuff said, innit? (Digitaltoast, 2008)

Thus, inspired by a *Daily Mail* article about how educational attainment is related to class and names, the company searched their database for the names of past customers and concluded that since people with names such as Wayne or Dwayne where 'unlikely' to be in this database, the company offers 'chav free holidays'. In an interview, the company's managing director Alistair McLean, said that he compiled the list of 'unlikely' names by making a web search on 'chav', and saw what names came up. He also claimed that not a single past customer of Activities Abroad had ever had any of the ten chav names listed in the email (BBC News, 2008).

In response to the complaint made by one the company's customers written on her blog, McLean responded:

> …I simply feel it is time the middle-classes stood up for themselves.
>
> We work hard to make a decent home and life for our families and we pay our taxes to contribute to our society and economy. Unfortunately, everybody else in our society seems to take from us whether it is incompetent bankers or the shell suited urchins who haunt our street corners.
>
> Last year Activities Abroad paid: corporation tax, income tax, PAYE, national insurance contributions, VAT and contributed to Aids projects in South Africa and other charitable organisations. We make a positive contribution to our economy and watch it all be frittered away by people who simply can't be bothered ('bovvered').
>
> So regardless of whether it is class warfare or not I make no apology for proclaiming myself to be middle-class and a genuine contributor to our society.
>
> (…)
>
> Do you encourage your children to go off and play with the shell suited, Lambert and Butler sucking teenagers who hang around our shopping centres at night?
>
> (Digitaltoast, 2008)

As we can see, McLean's account expresses the many stereotypical representations of chavs that we have discussed throughout this chapter. He positions himself and his customers as respectable, tax-paying, middle-class citizens who try to provide moral and social order in a society where those above and below exploit the fruits of their hard labour. Thus, the language of class conflict is apparent. McLean also justifies the content in the email by being written in a tongue in cheek manner, i.e. in a humorous way, and also proclaims that it is in parents' interests to be able to go on holiday without the presence of chav families and their loutish, tracksuit clad chav children called Wayne, Britney, and so on.

McLean's marketing strategy received much attention in the British media and became the subject of debate on many blogs and the comments pages of different news web sites. What is striking is that most commentators supported and agreed with McLean, though there were also a number of critical responses. One such response came from Paul Furner, managing director of Travel Republic, who called the 'anti-chav' attitude of Activities Abroad 'offensive', and added:

> We actively encourage bookings from everyone, irrespective of their name and its perceived social standing.

> In fact we're delighted to have 1600 Shannons, 1100 Courtneys, 600 Chantelles, 500 Kylies, 400 Tiffanys, 300 Candices and 200 Britneys on our database, and two Candices, a Chantelle and a Dazza among our staff (Oliver, 2009).

This statement was part of the company's own marketing strategy. During a two week period, it offered a 10 per cent discount to people with any of the 'unlikely' names listed in the Activities Abroad promotional email on condition that customers entered the promotional code 'DAZZA' when booking (Hide, 2009). In this sense, both travel companies have strategically used 'chav names' in their promotional activity, which has become widely debated in the British public realm, and thus has been very successful.

In sum, although chav culture is devalued and very much conceived as lacking taste and morals, it has been appropriated in (largely) middle-class contexts through humour or sexuality and turned into entertainment, and in this way, used to market and sell commodities and services. The denigrated, 'worthless' culture of the chavs becomes a valuable resource when appropriated by others. This can be related to Beverley Skeggs' (2004) argument that working-class culture is frequently exploited by the middle-class in order to generate economic value in capitalist markets. Conversely, but according to the same logic, when chavs appropriate high status items, these become tainted and devalued. When Burberry items became popular among chavs, the cultural value of the brand decreased, which in turn, led to a slump in sales in the UK, i.e. a decrease in economic terms.

Conclusion

In this chapter, I have explored the codes and narratives constructed around the term chav in the British public realm. I have argued that a moral panic has emerged where people with certain visual characteristics—they are young, white and appropriate a particular style—are labelled chavs, a label around which a range of highly derogatory moral-aesthetic boundaries are drawn, often through mockery. As a consequence, chavs have become a folk devil, a stigmatized social identity. A central contention here is that 'chav' is a figure of class contempt, relationally constructed through social class distinctions. Chavs constitute a *lumpen*, non-respectable, fraction of the white British working-class, against which middle-class and respectable working-class people distinguish themselves and construct their identities. In this sense, 'Class contempt... serves to project all that is bad and immoral onto the other, while reciprocally enhancing and confirming the goodness, self-regard and status of one's own class' (Webster, 2008, p. 294).

The 'chav' stereotype is typically constructed around consumption and lifestyles, which frequently are portrayed as crude, vulgar, tacky and excessive. Chavs are also associated with petty crime, welfare dependency, loutish and anti-social behaviour, and display an absence of moral education. This serves to construct chavs as *lack*—lack of cultural and economic resources. The images of chavs are also spatialized, often associated with deprived spaces such as 'chav towns'. Moreover, the moral boundaries against chavs have a gendered dimension, reflecting two folk devils familiar from the past: the young, violent, working-class male and the dole-scrounging young working-class mother. Female chavs are also depicted as 'slutty' and particularly sexualized compared with male chavs.

But although this derogatory vocabulary has attained widespread legitimacy, it has also been challenged and critiqued. The chav phenomenon has been contested and debated, with a dividing line between those who embrace the ridicule and moral denigration of chavs, and those who oppose it. This debate has to an important extent been about social class. Here, many commentators have argued that chavs forms part of the non-respectable working-class or an underclass. Thus, while it has been argued that class has largely disappeared from public discourse (e.g. Skeggs, 2004), the chav phenomenon has brought issues of class to the surface. The chav phenomenon also shows the tensions and divisions within the British working-classes, namely the longstanding distinction between respectable and non-respectable working-classes.

Moreover, I have argued that the widespread legitimacy of this demonizing discourse is very much due to 'chav' being a figure of non-respectable working-class whiteness. Such discourse would be considered politically incorrect if levelled against, for example, gays, or people who are disabled or of non-white ethnicity. But rather than constituting a potentially oppressed minority, chavs are conceived as immoral white people who deserve to be ridiculed. In this way, the chav phenomenon displays similarities with other stigmatized labels of marginalized whiteness, such as 'white trash' in the United States and 'bogan' in Australia and New Zealand.

In the following three chapters I will explore how the codes and narratives constructed around the term 'chav' are linked to the lives of the residents in Satellite Town, and how these stereotypes impact the ways in which the residents construct their identities.

4. Sense of Place

While the previous chapter focused on the cultural representations of chavs in the British public realm, we now turn from the national to the local context, that is, to Satellite Town and its people. This chapter is about the relationship between place and identity. It focuses on the dialectical interplay between 'external' and 'internal' processes of identification, with Satellite Town conceived as a place and space. I will proceed from the 'outside and in', and from the abstract to the concrete. I begin by exploring how Satellite Town and its residents are categorized from the 'outside' as an abstract space through statistics and also by studying the place images of Satellite Town in local newspapers and on web sites. We then enter Satellite Town and explore it 'from the ground', so to speak, but still from the 'outside', as a place or landscape through the eyes of the ethnographer. Finally, we study the construction of identity from the 'inside' by turning to the residents of Satellite Town and explore their 'sense of place' and their identifications or disidentifications with the area. I explore how people negotiate their sense of belonging and mobility in space as well as their sense of danger and safety in Satellite Town. Important here is how identifications with Satellite Town as a place are relationally produced through constructing symbolic boundaries against other places and spaces. In conclusion, I draw out the complex ways in which Satellite Town as constructed from the 'outside' and the 'inside' are interrelated.

Constructing a Marginal Space

Situated on the outskirts of one of South London's outer boroughs, Satellite Town was founded in the interwar period on what was farmland and woodland. But the core of what is present-day Satellite Town, e.g. the town centre, was built in the post-war period when the local authority bought the land and created a large council estate. I have chosen to call this area the Old Estate. During the 1960s, extensive construction of houses in a large area of unused property, became what is known as 'the New Estate'. It is smaller but more densely populated than the Old Estate and is generally considered to be the more deprived of the two (as we will see, this is also the image that appears from census data). And generally within Satellite Town, the New Estate and the Old Estate partly constitute separate neighbourhoods with their own identities.

I will now explore how Satellite Town is constructed as a space through statistics. Simon Charlesworth (2000) argues that demographic data of a locality doesn't say anything about what it's like to live there. Statistics give an '"official" and formalised sense of the place... the world as it is lived, does not emerge from the statistics' (p.35). Indeed, statistics of a locality tend to construct it as an abstract space seemingly devoid of living, breathing people. Nevertheless, statistics constitute important forms of categorization used by social scientists, policy makers and others to make sense of a locality, and are therefore one aspect of how its identity is constructed from the 'outside'.

I will mainly use data from the 2001 Census (Office for National Statistics, 2001), which includes data on the two wards that constitute Satellite Town. In the census, the population in Satellite Town amounts to slightly more than 21,000, of which more than half live in the New Estate. The great majority—about 90 per cent in the Old Estate and more than 80 per cent in the New Estate—are classified as white, which is higher than London on the whole (71.15 per cent), including the borough within which Satellite Town is located (less than 70 per cent). But there is also a significant presence of people classified as Black Caribbean and African, with about 5.8 per cent in the Old Estate and around 10 per cent in the New Estate.

Satellite Town's history as a council estate is reflected in the census data. Although many residents have bought their flats, still around half of the residents in the New Estate and about a third of those in the Old Estate live in council housing. This is a very high figure, compared with the numbers in London and England (17.12 and 13.21 per cent). Moreover, about a third in The Old Estate and a quarter in the New Estate own their property. In London and England the numbers are 33.51 and 38.88 per cent, respectively.

With regard to household composition, the proportion of single parents in Satellite Town is high. Single parent households with dependent children amount to around 13 per cent in the Old Estate and around 20 per cent in the New Estate, compared with 7.60 and 6.42 per cent in London and England, respectively. There is a large proportion of children and young people in Satellite Town in general, and the New Estate in particular. For instance, the census shows that the age groups 0-4 and 10-14 each make up about 10 per cent of the population of the New Estate, as opposed to the London and UK numbers of 5.96 and 6.97 per cent respectively.

The Census uses the NS-SEC schema[17] to measure the class composition of Satellite Town. The results from the census shows that people with 'large

---

[17] The NS-SEC schema is based on the Goldthorpe (2007, Vol. II, Ch. 14) schema (see Rose & O'Reilly, 1998; Rose & Pevalin, 2003). It is a deductive, nominalist schema where groups of occupations are labelled into certain 'classes' based on their working conditions and pro-

employers and higher managerial' occupations are about twice as common in London and England as in Satellite Town (4.41 and 3.50 per cent respectively). And 'higher professional' occupations are held by less than 2 per cent of people in Satellite Town, compared with 7.67 and 5.11 per cent in London and England, respectively. Similarly, a greater proportion of residents in Satellite Town hold 'routine occupations' (about 11-12 per cent) compared with London and England (5.79 and 9.02 per cent). The same goes for 'semi-routine' and 'lower supervisory and technical' occupations. Thus, Satellite Town is constructed as a classed space with a high proportion of blue-collar occupations and a low proportion of white-collar occupations.

The class composition of Satellite Town is also indicated in the census data on educational attainment. More than 40 per cent in the Old Estate and about 45 per cent in the New Estate have no post-compulsory educational qualifications compared with 23.73 and 28.85 per cent in London and England, respectively. Conversely, the number of people with the highest educational level, 'qualification level 4/5',[18] are far below ten per cent of the population, with the New Estate scoring slightly lower than the Old Estate, while London has as many as 30.99 per cent and England is at 19.90 per cent.

The unemployment levels, according to Census data (Nomis, 2001), are around 7.5 per cent in the Old Estate and slightly more than 11 per cent in the New Estate, which is higher than on a borough and a national level (6.2 and 5.8 per cent, respectively). Moreover, economic activity—72 per cent in the Old Estate and 65 per cent in the New Estate—is lower than on both borough (77.9 per cent) and England (76 per cent) level. One can also note that full-time employment among female one-parent households with dependent children, about 15 per cent in the Old Estate and more than 10 per cent in the New Estate, is far lower compared with London and England as a whole (24.61 and 21.61 per cent respectively).

According to 'experimental' ONS-data (Office for National Statistics, n.d.) on life expectancy by birth on ward level from 1998-2003, the numbers for the Old and New Estates—77.2 and 77.3 years respectively—are lower than on a borough (78.5 years), London and England level (both 78.3 years).

With regard to crime statistics, data on reported crimes per 1000 inhabitants recorded by the Metropolitan Police, show that Satellite Town, and especially the New Estate, has generally lower crime rates than the borough and London as a whole (Metropolitan Police, n.d.). Comparing the crime rates in Satellite Town with those in the borough as a whole during the pe-

---

duction units. Thus, there is no ambition to study class as real social groupings and the schema might therefore, at best, work as a proxy of class.

[18] 'Level 4/5 qualifications cover: First Degree, Higher Degree, NVQ levels 4 and 5; HNC; HND; Qualified Teacher Status; Qualified Medical Doctor; Qualified Dentist; Qualified Nurse; Midwife; or Health Visitor' (Office for National Statistics, 2001).

riod October 2008–October 2009,[19] one can note that while the rate of reported sexual offences is about the same as in the rest of the borough with around 1 per 1000 inhabitants, the number of robberies amount to around 3 as compared with 4.4 in the borough as a whole. Moreover, the reported rates of theft and handling as well as drugs offences are slightly lower in the Old Estate and much lower in the New Estate compared with the borough average. The same goes for the numbers of reported cases of fraud or forgery with 2 in the Old Estate and 1 in the New Estate compared with 5.6 in the borough as a whole.

In some respects, however, Satellite Town rates higher than the borough average. The burglary rates are slightly higher in the Old Estate though slightly lower in the New Estate than on a borough level. And reported rates of cases of violence against the person are slightly higher in the Old and New Estates compared with the borough as a whole. But what is most notable is that there are particularly high rates for criminal damage, 20-21 in the New and Old Estates, to be compared with the borough average of 12.9.

In the Index for Multiple Deprivation 2000 (DETR, 2000), which combines measurements of employment, income, health, education, skills and training, housing, access to services and disability, the 8414 wards in England are ranked, with 1 being most deprived and 8414 least deprived. Here, the Old Estate score in the lower regions of top 1200 and the New Estate is in the top 500, fairly close to the 600 mark. Interpreting this hierarchical form of categorization displayed in the index, the Old Estate is located in the 14th percentiles and the Old Estate in the 7th percentiles of the most deprived wards in England. The deprived status of Satellite Town is also reflected by a range of policy initiatives. During the period 2001-2008, the borough in which Satellite Town is located received money from the Neighbourhood Renewal Fund, which was targeted at the most deprived wards in the borough, including the New and Old Estate. Moreover, Satellite Town was classified as an Education Action Zone in 1998 to improve the educational standard in the area. Lastly, the New Estate has received a Single Regeneration Budget (SRB) targeted at unemployment and low achievement among its young people.

One can also mention that voting turnout in local and general elections in Satellite Town is in the lowest 10th percentiles in Britain. Here, one can also note that the British Nationalist Party (BNP) has a strong presence in the area, especially in the New Estate. In sum, through the census and other forms of statistics, Satellite Town, and especially the New Estate, is relationally constructed as a deprived space. Interpreting the data presented here, one can create the following narrative: Satellite Town is a largely white area with a high unemployment rate, a high proportion of council house estates,

---

[19] For this time period I have not been able to obtain detailed statistics for London on the whole.

single parents, and young people. Note, however, that crime rates are lower than the average, although the rates of criminal damage are very high. But life expectancy is lower than the England average and there is low voting turnout with a rather strong electoral support for the BNP. Comparing the two wards in Satellite Town, the New Estate generally comes across as the more deprived.

Images of a 'Chav Town'

In contrast to the abstract space that appears in statistics, representations of Satellite Town from the 'outside' on web sites and in newspapers provide more contextualized accounts of the locality and its residents, that is, certain place images (Shields, 1991). As we learnt in the previous chapter, place images denote the codes and narratives constructed around a particular terrestrial space. What is striking is the amount of morally loaded, derogatory place images of Satellite Town, categorizing it as a 'chav town'. Indeed, when visiting the web site *Chavtowns* on 24 September, 2008, Satellite Town was mentioned in 32 posts. And the comments made on articles featured in the web editions of the two local newspapers are telling in their number of negative place images. For instance, an article about the council discussing the problem of the lack of food stores in Satellite Town and a possible solution being a direct bus line from Satellite Town to one of the larger supermarkets outside the estate, is met with numerous derogatory comments:

> As for the lazy Satellite [Town] residents (not all of them) we are sick to death with their moaning and their take, take, take attitude. They act like the world owes them something! I'm sorry but it's not our fault you got knocked up at 15 and have no idea who the father is.
>
> Are these people for real. Get the bus or taxi with your benefits.
>
> Stand by for the Chav special.

Similarly, one poster writes about people in Satellite Town as 'dole merchants', another about 'their noisy and abusive kids!' and yet another calls Satellite Town 'chav central' and a 'dump'. And an article about a young man in Satellite Town finally getting employed after applying for a host of jobs is met with several derogatory comments of which the following sums up the general tone: 'I am surprised someone from Satellite Town actually is looking for work. I am just writing what everyone is thinking. lol [laughing out loud]'.

Moreover, Satellite Town is also tied to images of violence and antisocial behaviour (which, as we saw earlier, is very much contrary to the picture presented by the statistics). For instance, on a discussion forum on *Facebook*, one poster writes: 'Even the grannies have got knives up here!!!' On another web site someone writes: 'Satellite Town is widely known as Chav Central. It's used by the police as a dumping ground for South London's social misfits'. And a short article in one of the local newspapers about a young man who was shot in the back in Satellite Town is followed by a long discussion in the comments section. In it, it appears that the young man was a drug dealer and shot by people from a rival gang. But the discussion is just as much about Satellite Town, which is derogatorily portrayed as a place with criminal people. One poster even writes: 'More guns & drugs for Satellite Town please, this way the scum will eradicate each other faster'.

As we can see, these place images portray Satellite Town as a 'chav town' full of teenage mothers, loutish kids, violence, criminality and anti-social behaviour. Its residents are portrayed as lazy, work-shy, irresponsible dole scroungers having no qualms about letting 'us' respectable citizens pay for their lifestyle. One can therefore paraphrase Goffman (1963) and say that Satellite Town has a 'spoiled place identity' (cf. Watt, 2009, p. 2887). Thus, a web page presenting Satellite Town quotes a recent council planning document calling for measures to counteract the view that 'if you come to live in Satellite Town, you've failed'.

So far, we have only seen Satellite Town through representations in statistics and place images on the web. It is now time to experience it 'from the ground' through ethnographic methods.

Entering Satellite Town

Throughout its history, Satellite Town has been isolated from the rest of the borough and other neighbouring areas. One major factor is that it is located on the periphery, or outside, of the other areas in the borough, surrounded on most sides by green belts—open fields and greenery—and thus with very few direct geographical connections with other areas. The other major factor has been poor transport services. An elderly woman and resident of Satellite Town for about 40 years told me that up until the 1960s, there was only one bus per hour to the main town of the borough in which Satellite Town is located. But transport communications have improved significantly since then, especially during the last ten years. Of course, that doesn't change the way Satellite Town is geographically cut off from other areas. As one commentator, allegedly not from Satellite Town, wrote on an internet discussion forum: 'Whoever designed Satellite Town should be shot—the place is an island in the middle of nowhere. [I] Swear it was designed to keep poor people out of town and isolated'.

We will now experience Satellite Town through the eyes of the ethnographer. Perhaps, needless to say, it is a partial, outside view of Satellite Town conceived as a place or landscape. Satellite Town is a small place—perhaps not even big enough to be called a town. An elderly woman who has lived in the New Estate since it was built and is a frequent visitor of one of the 'chip shops' in the town centre (she went there almost every day with her best friend), told me: 'It is perfect. It's smaller than a town but bigger than a village'. In her view, Satellite Town is not too small like a village, but small enough to give the area a sense of intimacy and homeliness. But of course, size is always relative. One evening, I was early to a session at Northside so I decided to take a walk in the New Estate. Approaching a line of shops, I accidentally met Steve, one of the youth workers who lives in the New Estate. He was on his way to buy supper at a fast food eatery and I accompanied him. During the next ten minutes, he met and chatted with several people he knew. Afterwards, on our way to Northside, he turned to me and said: 'I'm meeting everyone today!' 'Well, it's a small place', I answered, but Steve just looked at me and said: 'What are you talking 'bout? It's the biggest estate!' Seen from this perspective, it is certainly true that Satellite Town is rather large for a council estate.

But from an outsider's perspective, Satellite Town is a small place. A newcomer is quickly spotted, especially in the town centre, and it doesn't take long before one begins to recognize people one has seen before. Shortly after I moved to Satellite Town, I went to one of the hairdressers in the town centre. The owner, who had lived in Satellite Town for 25 years, was an outgoing person and often greeted people who came by the shop. He told me that he instantly identified me as 'a new face' in the neighbourhood.

Moreover, Satellite Town also felt 'small' in the sense of feeling 'non-urban', having certain village-like or countryside-like features. What struck me when I arrived there was that its geographical distance from the more central parts of London also meant that you came to quite a different living environment, to a place that looked and felt different, more rural, compared with those central parts. In more centrally located parts of South London, houses sit tightly together, streets are narrow and bristle with people, roads are crammed with cars, the pace is fast and there are sounds and noises everywhere. Satellite Town contrasts with this in many ways. Although houses are built closely together in some areas, there are still many substantial open spaces and a fair amount of woodland. Except for areas with heavy traffic, it is usually rather quiet, and the pace is slower. But while the silence, the lack of people, the greenery and open spaces sometimes left me in a peaceful state, more often the landscape appeared desolate, and gave me an empty feeling in the stomach. This was particularly true of the open spaces, which did not give me any sense of community or homeliness but rather one of emptiness—of cleared, soulless land.

Most of Satellite Town consists of terraced houses, in the Old Estate often in red brick. There are also a few larger houses and grim-looking high rises with flats. As I wrote in Chapter 2, when I first entered Satellite Town I was surprised that this allegedly marginal area had such pretty houses, and this impression stayed with me. Looking at some of the well-kept small lawns and flowerbeds outside the houses and the new shining cars gave a rather well-off impression, a far cry from the stereotypical place images of 'chav towns'. A Swedish friend, who came to visit when I lived in Satellite Town, expressed his surprise when entering some of the parts of the Old Estate: 'This looks like a middle-class neighbourhood', he said.

The New Estate, however, has a rather more run-down feel to it, as many of the terraced houses are smaller, look more worn and generally sit more tightly together. The absence of a town centre also gives it a more desolate feeling, although there are two streaks of shops in the area, each with a pub, a few take-aways, an off licence and a few other shops such as a dry-cleaners, a key maker and a barbershop. There was also a small food store, though it had closed down by time I arrived in November 2009.

The town centre in the Old Estate very much forms the heart of Satellite Town. Unsurprisingly, people in all ages work, pass through or 'hang out' in the town centre during the course of a day. During day time, it is frequented by many young people and mothers, often young, too, walking with their prams or holding their children by hand, as well as some elderly people. As evening approaches or during weekends one sees more families. And, generally, while most residents in Satellite Town are white, one frequently comes across black people and sometimes people who appear to be from the Middle East or South Asia.

As described in Chapter 2, the town centre is basically formed around one long, angled street. On one side is a parking lot with a small lawn next to it. The line of shops looks rather rundown as some shop windows and front areas don't look like they have been maintained for a long time. A persistent local issue is how to regenerate the town centre.

If one walks from one end to the other on the town centre street, one does not need to take many steps to pass a fast food eatery, take away or café. They include a fish n' chip shop, a Gregg's pasty shop, two shops selling deep-fried chicken, a Chinese take away, an Indian eatery, a coffee shop which turns into a fast food eatery in the afternoon, a kebab shop and a café I will call Town Café. Here, I spent many afternoons. Town Café serves among other things all day breakfasts, hamburgers, pork chops, liver, omelettes and desserts. Making a short tour through the town centre, then, it is more than clear that there are no coffee shops with Wi-Fi, skinny lattes, pecan nut cake or smoothies in sight.

There are two food stores in the town centre, and in Satellite Town on the whole. One is a small, and therefore rather pricey, food store, and the other is an Iceland, a store chain specialising in frozen foods (hence the name) and generally quite inexpensive prices. There is also a butcher and a greengrocer. Other shops and institutions include a police station, a bank, a post office, a solicitor's office, an estate agent, a few card shops, a few off licences, two bookmakers, a funeral store, a florist, a clothes store, two barbershops, two pharmacists, a pet shop, a dry cleaners, a tanning salon, and an internet unit sponsored by the council. And next to the town centre, is a library, a leisure centre and a community centre. The latter also hosts a pub for those who hold a membership.

A market is held twice a week on the lawn next to the parking lot which lies opposite the line of shops at the town centre street. The lawn fills with stands lined closely together selling everything from food, clothing, jewellery and house care. The dominant feature is the stands selling different types of discount clothing, including children's clothes, conventional 'mature' type of male and female clothing, as well as more youthful clothing, such as tops, skirts, and shoes of different types, e.g. ugg boots, plimsoles and high heels. There are also two stands selling jewellery. One sells cheap imitations of the gold and silver jewellery sold at the other stand. In the food category, there is a fruit and vegetable stand and a butcher's, both rather conventional, as is the fast food stand. Then there is a shop selling foodstuff—such as sweets, chocolate, spices, ketchup, pasta—and house care items at low prices.

Elements of a local style

In this section, we investigate the ways of styling clothing and appearance— what I call visual markers of taste—worn by people in Satellite Town. Our goal is firstly to explore in what ways these visual markers serve to position the people in Satellite Town in wider codes and narratives, and thus how clothing and style is bound to identity construction. (The respondents' own identifications with, and boundaries against, different markers of taste will be explored in the next chapter). Secondly, although there were many differences and variations of clothing style and appearance, I would argue that many residents appropriated elements of what I call a local style. This local style was particularly apparent among young people. Many young people, especially those in their early teens or younger, wore streetwear clothing, such as tracksuits, baseball caps, 'hoodies' (hooded jumpers) and trainers. The tracksuits were often loosely fitted, and some girls wore ones that were more femininely coded, e.g. in pink or baby blue, with flared legs and in a velour fabric.

Having said that, casual clothing items were also quite common, either as mixed with street wear clothing, a school uniform or making up the whole look. Respondents in their late teens, especially girls, more often wore jeans, tops and sweaters than streetwear. And instead of wearing trainers, many girls also wore ugg boots (soft sheep skin boots), plimsoles (cloth shoes with rubber soles) or ballet flaps (thin, small shoes with flat toe). The latter were often in glittery gold or silver (but sometimes black or white), and sometimes this was also the case with the ugg boots. Glittery items were quite common and included scarves, belts, details on the back pockets of jeans, and eye shadow. Some of the girls combined several glittery items, such as Sharon, aged 13, who was a frequent visitor to one of the youth clubs; she used to wear silvery glitter eye-shadow, with which she matched her silvery-white ugg boots.

Boys often had very short cut hair ranging from almost completely shaved to a few inches long. Sometimes they had had patterns made in the hair, e.g. a zigzag pattern or a 'double edge-up', i.e. edging-up the hair at the hair line creating a line that goes parallel to the hair line. Several of the younger male respondents had 'cut corners' in one or both eyebrows, i.e. a little part of the eyebrow(s) shaven off. The female respondents typically had long straight hair hanging down over the shoulders or worn in a pony tail. The latter came in several variants. Makeup was also an important feature in girls' styles. This often included visibly accentuating the eyelashes with eyeliner and sometimes using white or silvery eye-shadow.

Most young respondents wore jewellery, usually in gold or a less expensive material. Girls often wore hoop earrings and boys wore stud earrings. It was very common to wear rings, such as sovereign rings, and it was not uncommon to have a ring on two or three fingers on each hand. Necklaces or bracelets were also rather common, with some youths wearing pendants, often in the form of one's initials or sometimes shaped as a cross.

Thus, many young people adopted highly stylized and elaborate dress and appearance. But many of these stylistic features were far from restricted to them, but general features of a local style that was popular for all generations. The tracksuit, for example, was not only a frequent feature among children and young people, but also among the elderly and middle-aged. Similarly, ponytails and hoop earrings were not confined to young girls but were also worn by middle-aged women as well. Sometimes when I saw young and older people together, the similarities in some elements in their style of dress and appearance were striking. Conversely, seeing the continuities and similarities, one should obviously not overlook the differences and distinctions among people of different ages.

Another feature in Satellite Town was the practice of wearing jewellery over generations from small children to elderly. Once, in one of the cafés in the town centre, I saw a baby in a pram wearing a small, gold bracelet on her right wrist. As the bracelet was far too big for her tiny wrist, it had been tied together with the ends hanging loose, like a gold-string. Similarly, I saw many older residents wearing jewellery. One evening in Town Café an elderly couple, probably in their 60s, were seated in front of me having dinner. Both had appropriated a carefully stylized appearance, in which jewellery played an important part. The woman had rather short-cropped silvery hair, drawn backwards and wore a white, tightly fitted cotton jumper open at the shoulders and upper arms but with seams holding it together. The man had short hair and wore a brown jacket with the collar turned up, the inside of the collar in the Burberry tartan pattern. The man wore a large ring on each of his ring and middle fingers. The woman wore several thin necklaces, designed in slightly different ways (e.g. in terms of the thickness of the chains). On each of her wrists, she wore five or six thin bracelets, and she had rings on all fingers. Lastly, she wore large hoop earrings, with large letters in the middle forming the word 'MUM'. Though the woman wore an unusually large amount of jewellery, it was far from unique.

I have argued, then, that particular ways of stylizing one's appearance through clothing, jewellery, makeup and hair styles constitute a local style in Satellite Town, particularly apparent among young people but to some extent crossing generations. But, as we saw in Chapter 3, some of the visual markers in this local style are also elements in the stigmatized stereotype formed around chavs in the public realm. In this sense, many residents of Satellite Town risk being positioned in the codes and narratives constructed around the term. It is important to note, however, that although there is a local style, many people do not appropriate it. One example is the man, probably in his 70s, with a walking stick, wearing a checked hat, brown boots, beige chinos and a light gray jacket, who sat and looked through a magazine for model engines in the library.

'Strong Sense of Community'

I now turn to the people—and particularly the young respondents—of Satellite Town and their relationship to and identifications with the place. There is a rich, longstanding body of scholarship about identifications with place. It goes back to the classical scholars' analyses of the alleged breakdown of traditional communities with the advent of modernity, as conceptualized by Durkheim (1984 [1893]) in the distinction between organic and mechanical solidarity, and by Tönnies (2001 [1887]) in the distinction between *Gesellschaft* and *Gemeinschaft*. The latter's notion of *Gemeinschaft*, often translated as 'community', forms the classic statement of place-based solidarities characterized by mutual trust and understanding, and a shared sense of belonging and fate forged among people in the family and neighbourhood. This idea has served as the basis for a vast body of case studies produced in the so-called community studies tradition, which had its high point in the 1950s and 60s (see Crow, 2002). In a British context, it has seen the production of a series of seminal ethnographies of working-class communities, such as Dennis, Henriques and Slaughter's *Coal is Our Life* (1969 [1956]), Frankenberg's *Village on the Border* (1957) and Elias and Scotson's *The Established and the Outsiders* (1994 [1965]).

In present-day globalized and deindustrialized conditions, however, this approach has very much become outdated (Savage et al., 2004; though see Crow, 2002, 2008). As we saw in Chapter 1, the community studies approach has been undermined by globalization theory and the critique of traditional ways of conceptualizing place, on which this type of research, if only implicitly, is founded. This renders the idea of attachments and solidarities through face-to-face interaction within bounded locales largely obsolete.

Another argument is that traditional place-based communities, particularly among the working-classes, have broken down in the wake of deindustrialization. This is not the least the case in the north of England, a region hit particularly hard by this process. Simon Charlesworth's (2000) ethnography of his hometown Rotherham in South Yorkshire follows a narrative progressing from something akin to a past industrial golden age to a pitch-black postindustrial present. The closing of industries (particularly mining pits) and the high unemployment that followed has turned a once industrial space providing people with dignity, worth and a sense of belonging into an atomized space where people lack hope and meaning, their only solace being in consumption. Charlesworth describes it as 'a social experience that is, by its very nature, fragmented, dissolute, polysemic, ambiguous and yet nevertheless desolating' (p. 60). A similarly grim view is presented in Royce Turner's book *Coal Was Our Life* (2000). The title paraphrases Dennis, Henriques and Slaughter's previously mentioned study (1969 [1956]), and in it, Turner visits former mining areas. His interviews with residents convey feelings of fragmentation, loss and despair over the death of old communities.

Similar processes are observed by Wacquant (2008) in his comparative work of 'advanced marginality' in the United States and France. He argues that the French *banlieue*, traditionally characterized by strong cohesion and sense of working-class identity, have now been replaced by individualization, distrust and conflict. And the American 'communal ghettos', which were places of pride and attachment as well as sites of collective action and identification, have now collapsed and transformed into lawless, atomized 'hyper-ghettos'. A loss of community can also be read into one of Bourdieu's later works, *The Weight of the World* (Bourdieu, 1999 [1993]), with its recurrent narratives of pain, suffering, loss, displacement and alienation.

The following account tells a different story from those of postindustrial fragmentation on the one hand, and of 'post-place community', on the other. One strong impression from my fieldwork was that Satellite Town has, as one respondent put it, 'a strong sense of community'. One woman, who has lived in Satellite Town for decades and worked for a long time at Northside, said that everyone knows everyone here. She told me that after the funeral for a person from the neighbourhood, there was a spontaneous gathering for the deceased in Northside featuring many people from the neighbourhood. She described it as a sad but beautiful ceremony. Similarly, a middle-aged man who owns one of the shops in the town centre, said: 'I've lived here for 25 years. It is one of the best places in England. The air is clean'. And he spoke warmly about the great sense of community of the place where everyone knows everyone, and of the beautiful green surroundings.

The notion that 'everyone knows everyone around here' was repeated to me during the fieldwork, and social interaction was often bound up with a sense of familiarity. This could be shown in the everyday, rather slow paced context of the town centre, where I often saw people chatting with someone they met on the street. This familiarity could particularly be observed in the public establishments in the town centre such as the market, the barbershops and the eateries. At Town Café, where I spent much time, young people, elderly and families, such as mothers with their children, dropped in for a bit to eat or for some coffee. Some of the regular customers could linger for hours. People among the staff were often acquainted with the customers, and it was not uncommon to hear friendly greetings and small talk between staff and customers. There was generally an informal atmosphere to the place and many of the customers were acquainted with one another. Town Café was a place where you could go to and meet people you knew and where you could just hang out. It had, at times, an atmosphere similar to a living room. I quickly became acquainted with most of the people on the staff and it did not take long before a few of the regular customers started to greet me, asking me how I was doing. When I came back to Town Café after having been away for two weeks, I met two regulars who said they had been wondering what happened to me. 'We thought you had been kidnapped!', one of them joked.

To illustrate the sense of familiarity and homeliness in Town Café, I will tell what happened one afternoon. One of the regulars, a balding, elderly man in glasses, entered wearing a short cotton jacket. His face lighted up when he saw me and he greeted me by asking 'you alright'. Sitting down at his table, he then saw Sally and Bridget, two other regulars sitting at the other end of the room, and he asked, 'You want coffee, ladies?' 'Got one here. Thanks, darling', Sally answered and turned to Bridget, 'He's *so* nice'. Such mundane, friendly interaction was not uncommon in Town Café.

I experienced similar aspects of familiarity among people who frequented the other eateries in the town centre, such as the kebab shop. One telling example of this was also the first time I went to one of the two pubs in the New Estate to watch a football match. It was a Saturday afternoon and the rectangular room where they showed the match was quite empty and had a rather sleepy atmosphere. At the bar sat two girls in their late teens or early twenties, each holding a bottle of beer. At the table to the right, sat a middle-aged couple, with a pint each, and to their right, a boy of maybe four was standing while playing with a toy car, a Porsche, on the table. When not playing with the toy car, he ran to and fro between the couple and one of the two girls at the bar, sometimes hugging her. The girl at the bar must be the boy's mother, and the couple at the table must the girl's parents, I thought to myself. To the left of the couple, sitting at the same table, was an elderly man, at least 70, with pale skin and thin face, with a pint in front of him. Perhaps he was the father of either the man or the woman sitting next to him, I reflected. The impression I got was of four generations next to one another in the pub: the small boy, the two girls at the bar, the middle-aged couple and the elderly man.

At the end of the room a big TV-screen was showing the football match, and to its left was a dartboard. In front of me, a middle-aged man sat alone, casually watching the game, nursing a pint. A group of about 10 people sat at the large table close to the TV-screen. Among them was a girl in her late teens with her two small children, sometimes sitting in her lap, sometimes walking or running around. The rest were men of different ages though most of them looked like they were in their 30s. On the table, I could see a few pints and several beer bottles.

Everyone in the room was white except one of the girls sitting at the bar who looked like she was of mixed race, born to a black and a white parent. People chatted sporadically, glanced at the TV-screen, sometimes commented on the match, sometimes raised their voices. I could occasionally see people throw a glance in my direction where I was sitting in the corner, but in general, I was tactfully ignored. The atmosphere was very informal and relaxed but with a hint of boredom. This felt even more like entering someone's living room than Town Café. But this time, I did not feel at home. There were elements of social distance. I was a stranger, an outsider.

The market is a longstanding feature of the activities in the town centre and also one of the places with a role in creating a sense of community and thus part of the identity of the town centre and Satellite Town as a whole. On a sunny day, I can see why, the market buzzing with activity, full of people walking along the stands, chatting, perhaps eating a sausage roll or something else bought from the 'chippie' stand. During such times, the town centre seems to come alive and the rundown feel to the shop fronts temporarily disappears from view.

The fact that Satellite Town is a small place where everyone knows everyone, meant not only familiarity, but there were also intimations of more negative aspects such as informal control and that information, such as rumours, spread quickly. As two young respondents, Tom and Britney, said in an interview:

> Tom: You really, like, know everyone in Satellite Town if you lived here as long as us.

Britney: In Satellite Town, everyone knows everyone's business. If there's one bit of rumour going around, it's around in Satellite Town in two minutes [everyone laughs]. That's how bad it is.

Tom: Especially with Britney...

Moreover, the inclusive aspect—the sense of community among residents of Satellite Town, is also coupled with an excluding aspect, with forming boundaries against outsiders. I was told that in some public places and contexts, people do not like strangers. That said, I never experienced any explicit forms of exclusion or hostility, though perhaps some social distance, as when I visited the pub described above. The strongest sense I got about this hostility against strangers was on two other occasions when I went to watch football in the local pubs. One Sunday, I left my flat to find a pub showing a football match. I walked to the town centre since I knew that the community centre hosts a pub. I was late, the match had already started. As I approached the community centre, I saw a middle aged man walk out of there. He was rather tall with a lined face and short hair and he walked with a straight posture. I asked him 'Do they show football, the United game in there?' The man did not seem to hear me at first, and when he turned to me he did not look particularly inviting. He had a serious look on his face, as if he didn't want to be disturbed. 'You have to be a member to get in there', he said. 'But do they show the game?' Apparently they do, so I asked him what the score was, and he said that Man U was winning 1-0 and Chelsea was playing 0-0. He continued walking, and as there was no point in my going to the community centre if I couldn't watch the match, I turned and walked back the same way I came, ending up walking beside him. I asked him if there was any other pub nearby where they might show the game. He said that there was one pub a 10 or 15 minute walk up the road, then turned to me and asked: 'Do you live here?' 'Yeah, I live on [name of street] at [name of high school]', I answered. Then he asked me where I came from. When I told him he said, 'Oh Sweden! Yeah, I thought it sounded like that', and smiled. From initially seeming a bit reserved, he now seemed much friendlier, as if he'd opened up. Then he said to me: 'You know, I'm not saying this to be rude, but people in places might not like strangers. They don't know who you are, some people might... I'm not saying this to be rude, but with good intentions. But if you tell them you're from Sweden...' I thanked him for his advice and he asked me if I was a student, and then told me about his son who was at college. We also chatted for a bit about football before saying goodbye. 'Nice to meet you', he said as we parted.

So, the man basically told me that I could get into trouble if I went to any of the pubs in Satellite Town because they would see that I was an outsider, but that people might accept me if I told them I was Swedish. Thus, being a foreigner, a European outsider rather than a British one, the man clearly considered was to my advantage. This might mean that, for instance, a British middle-class person would have had a higher risk of encountering hostility.

On another occasion, I went to one of the local pubs in the New Estate to watch the Champions league final between Manchester United and Chelsea.[20] Before the match, I popped by to say hello at Northside. When I told the staff I was going to the local pub, everyone seemed to react with disbelief, as I could see by their facial reactions and sceptical smiles. Darren laughed and said: 'Good luck! You're gonna end up with a bottle in the head!' Mike, standing nearby with a pool cue in his hand, looked amused. 'Why's that? Why's it dodgy?', I asked. 'It's very *cliquey*. That's what I've heard', Darren, who had lived his entire life in the New Estate, answered and added that he had never gone there. Indeed, having been to the pub before, as I described above, I could understand what Darren was saying, since I had felt unwelcome on my first visit. Everyone suggested that I go to the other pub in the New Estate. But against their advice, I stuck to my plan and returned to the pub I had visited earlier. When I arrived, about ten people were standing outside smoking. Entering the pub, it was packed with people there to watch the match, in contrast to my previous visit. Most of the attendees were men and almost all were white. Someone next to the bar was taking bets. One could give money to a middle aged man, who then wrote down the bet on a small piece of paper—a homemade betting slip. Many people were congregating around the man to place their bets before the game started.

Far from experiencing any hostility, I was met with much friendliness; many people chatted with me. In return, I was very sociable and friendly myself, talking to people whenever I got the chance—about the match, about the teams, but also other sorts of small talk—e.g. with one girl who was angry with her cheating boyfriend. The only time I felt a trace of suspicion or social distance was when I was chatting and joking with two boys and two girls in their late teens or early twenties; a couple of people sitting at the nearby table, who knew the girls, looked at me with what seemed like reserve. But all in all, it was a memorable evening, I remember with warmth.

In this section, we have seen that face-to-face interaction in the locale of Satellite Town plays a part in creating a sense of familiarity, togetherness and mutuality among residents. Such a sense of familiarity and density of social networks are also evident among the respondents' accounts in MacDonald and his colleagues' (MacDonald & Marsh, 2001; MacDonald et al., 2005) work in the marginalized neighbourhoods in Teesside, the North East of England. Similarly, Mike Savage and his colleagues' study of Cheadle in Manchester, note 'strong culture of neighbouring' and overall 'strong sociability', particularly among male respondents (Savage, Bagnall & Longhurst, 2004, p. 108-109). We have also seen that the sense of inclusion and cohe-

---

[20] The Champions League is the most prestigious international competition for European football clubs.

sion among residents is coupled with suspicion and hostility against 'strangers'. This reflects a well-known distinction in British community studies (e.g. Elias & Scotson, 1965; Frankenberg, 1957; Stacey, 1960; Strathern, 1981) between 'established' and 'outsiders'.

Danger and Safety in Satellite Town

At Northside just before a session. I was chatting with the staff in Gary's office, as Gary asks: 'How's your British English, Elias? Can you impersonate British English?' I laugh and say I feel too self conscious to do that in front them. 'But is there like a South London accent or a Satellite [Town] accent?', I ask. 'Some people say [so]. The two ladies that come here on some Wednesdays'. Gary talks about the outreach workers who visit Northside about once every week. 'The younger one, she says that she can hear that we speak with an accent. A Satellite [Town] accent'. Then Peter says with a mischievous grin: '"Give me your wallet!" *That's* Satellite [Town] accent!' Looking pleased, he repeats the joke.

Peter's joke draws on the notion that there are a lot of muggings in Satellite Town, which is connected with the widespread place images of the area as associated with social problems, crime, violence and danger. These were recurring features in the young people's accounts—and contrary to the rate of reported crimes, which were generally lower in Satellite Town than in London as a whole, as we saw earlier.

When I asked the respondents if they liked living in the area, many of them mentioned violence and social problems, like, stabbings, muggings and vandalism. One boy, aged 16, said he didn't like the area because there were too many 'crack heads' walking about on the streets, but added that as long as you just minded your own business, you would not get into trouble. And the sense of danger, violence and social problems in Satellite Town comes across very clearly in the interview with Dan, who works part-time in one of the food stores in the town centre.

> Dan: We get a lot of trouble there.
>
> Elias: With shoplifters, or?
>
> Dan: Shoplifters, alcoholics come in (okay) stealing beer, [and] we have to stop them. If they try to smack a punch at us, the security guard comes along. One time, like last week or two weeks ago, a gang came along, threatened a security guard, and a security guard obviously he rang up some boys as well and (sure, sure) he had a bit of a fight and he got sacked. It's rough.
>
> Elias: So even if you've got some security...
>
> Dan: It's still rough.

Elias: 'Cause, I didn't think they'd do anything when [you've got security]...

Dan: I still feel safe though, because I know nearly... I know *everyone* around here. So many people, they say 'I'm a big man', but (yeah) I know, I talk to a lot of people as friends and stuff (sure, sure) [so] I feel pretty safe. Most people that come in that are drunk, I know.

Despite the occurrence of threats and violence, Dan says he feels safe as he is well-known in the neighbourhood and has a lot of friends, which serves as a form of protection. As we will see, this is a recurring theme in people's accounts. I also encountered several instances where respondents or people they knew had been the victims of assaults. One of the pictures I showed the young people during the photo elicitation interviews was a sheet of paper with five pictures of Satellite Town.[21] The pictures are of buildings and surroundings, but do not feature any people. This makes for a rather peaceful atmosphere, something which was pointed out and contradicted by the young people, as in the following excerpts from my interviews with Mike and Ryan.

Elias: Okay, cool. So, what do you think about when you see these pictures?

Mike: See, *there* [points at one picture], it looks like a nice little town. But it's *not* a very nice little town, there's a lot of violence around here. I don't get... no trouble comes to me, so I'm alright innit.

Elias: Okay. What kind of violence happens?

Mike: Too many stabbings and stuff. Not that much around here. Still, there's quite a lot [in] the papers [when] you read it. (okay) Like in [name of area] and that.

Elias: Do you know anyone that has been, like, stabbed?

Mike: There is that boy I met with Brandon, I know a little bit but not as much as Brandon, he got stabbed in [name of area].Elias: What do you think about when you see this picture, I mean?

Ryan: It looks much better than what Satellite Town is now.

Elias: You think?

Ryan: Yeah.

Elias: In what way does it look better?

Ryan: Lot of people running around it, like, that terrorize shops and that (alright). [name of a fast food shop] used to get terrorized, cause it's an Indian shop innit (okay). That's why, and like people used to terrorize Satellite Town, still terrorizing Satellite Town (yeah?). In this picture it looks much better, like a place to live in, but I would not recommend to live in it.

(...)

---

[21] The pictures are not shown here to protect the anonymity of the area.

Elias: What did they do in the shops?

Ryan: Like, just like... like throw cans and that in there and, like, terrorize the people.

For Mike, Ryan and others I talked to, the peaceful atmosphere in the pictures I showed them was false; it said nothing about the reality of the place. As Britney said: 'In them pictures they'd made Satellite [Town] look clean'. Several respondents told me about the 'attitude problems' people have in the area. As Dan puts it: 'It's 'cause there's quite a lot of young people in Satellite Town. You're gonna get it. Everyone's gonna think they're big ones'. I myself experienced these 'attitude problems' in some situations and we will explore this issue in some depth in Chapter 6.

The general image of Satellite Town as marginal and with social problems was also reflected in the talk among members of staff. They regularly told stories about young people who have been in trouble, or suspended from school, and who had complicated family relations. At Greenwood, one male respondent told a member of staff that his sister had been mugged of her mobile and beaten by a group of girls and boys (apparently it was a friend of hers who had turned against her). Since her brother had reported the mugging to the police, he was afraid that the gang was going to attack him.

Let me retell the most dramatic event during one evening at Northside. It was eightish and I was 'floating' around the area at the entrance with Gary from the staff. Alex and Luke entered and started talking to Gary. I listened standing a few meters away. I couldn't hear everything but discussed the matter with Gary later on and also during the debrief with the rest of the staff after the session. The boys said that they were mugged the night before on their way home from a friend's place. One of the three muggers pointed a pistol against Alex's back. They took the boys' wallets and mobile phones but for some reason didn't take their gold bracelets. During the debrief, one of the staff members suggested that maybe it was a warning, that the real target was Alex and Luke's friend whose place they had just been visiting. Apparently, the mugging was drug related. Their friend dealt drugs, which was what made the three muggers come to his home in the first place. They waited outside his home and followed Alex and Luke, seeing them as easy targets. The robbers forced Alex and Luke back to their friend's place and when they got there, took their friend's PlayStation and jewellery. Someone the boys knew arrived later with his Doberman, but the muggers had by then departed. Mike, a member of the staff laughed. 'What help is a dog against a gun? All you need [to do] is [to] shoot it down'.

Both Alex and Luke were regulars and well-integrated at Northside, and neither were perceived as particularly 'rough' people. Luke was 13 and quite polite and rather tall for his age. Alex was 16 and good-humoured and sociable person who was 'quick' and talked fast. He went to college and worked part time in his father's business.

The boys asked Gary not to tell anyone. Later in the evening, they told Joey, who then told everyone else. Joey apparently knew the robbers. Luke was quite shaken, more so than Alex. Luke was the one who had felt the gun against his back and his dad was the one who called the police to report the mugging. He was also nervous about going to the police the following day to make a statement. He was afraid that there might be repercussions.

During the debrief, some members of the staff thought there might be a gang fight. Mike seemed to be familiar with such incidents. He was very involved in the discussion, he often made comments and asked about details of the mugging. He seemed sceptical that reporting to the police would lead to anything. He said that when so and so (he mentioned a few names) were mugged under the threat of guns, nothing had happened.

In the bus on my way home after the session, I was struck by what I ex-perienced as the calm, matter-of-fact and detached way the staff seemed to respond to and discuss the matter. One staff member even said: 'Why do we even care so much about this?' arguing that the incident was not relevant for the debrief since it didn't take place at the youth club. Rather than express empathy, another answered: 'Cause it's us that will have to take care of the consequences'. My interpretation of their reactions was that incidents like muggings, though not common, were not the kind of extraordinary events that shocked and surprised people as they shocked and surprised me. Rather, muggings and violence were common enough to be part of life in Satellite Town.

In the case of one respondent, Katie, the bad reputation of Satellite Town affected her in negative ways.

> Elias: So do you feel safe around in Satellite Town?
>
> Katie: Yeah, it's where I've lived here all my life. It's sort of, you don't really think about [that]. People that... some of my friends that live far away, come into Satellite Town and are worried, and it's like you feel ashamed to live here. That they're scared of coming.

As she said this, Katie looked down and blushed—as if she were ashamed and embarrassed. Here, the negative place images of Satellite Town affected Katie's relationship to the place as well as her own self-identity as she, *qua* resident, had become associated with it.

But although they mentioned violence, muggings, dangers and other so-cial problems, most respondents said that they felt safe. The stated reason for this was that they knew 'everyone' in the area. As Dan says: 'I could walk down to my Chinese shop late at night—at eleven o'clock at night to get my Chinese [food]. And nothing happens'. Here, the community aspect, notions of trust and informal social control were evident. When I talked with Aaron about muggings, he said:

Aaron: Yeah, it happens everywhere (sure, sure). But, [in] Satellite Town, normally [there] is no mugging not unless people come from outside of Satellite Town (yeah-yeah). Satellite people usually don't start on other Satellite people, 'cause it's a small place. Everyone knows each other.

In such a small place, where one is known, one 'cannot hide' but risks becoming accountable and this would affect social relations with people. It was this kind of informal social control that was perceived to be a source of safety. But some of the young people pointed out to me that certain areas in Satellite Town were more dangerous than others, they were hot spots frequented by gangs and targeted by the police, and thus in the words of one respondent, 'kinda dodgy at night time'. Still, some of the respondents also felt safe in these places, like Mike when I asked him if it was equally safe or dangerous everywhere in Satellite Town.

Mike: No, there's certain areas.

Elias: Okay. Which ones are less, or more, dodgy?

Mike: See, [name of park], that's a bad, that's a violent area for most people. For me, that's a *good* area, 'cause I know *everyone* around there.

Elias (laughs): But if you don't know anyone?

Mike: Yeah, that would be a violent area.

Elias: So why is that? Gangs?

Mike: Yeah, yeah, yeah. And hard pitch. Hard pitch. Hard pitch. A violent [area].

Elias: Okay. Hard pitch?

Mike: A football pitch across the road from Northside.

Again, safety is all about being known and approved by other people, and not being an unknown outsider. Social ties are a useful resource and in a Bourdieusian sense, function as a form of social capital. But the people's understandings of danger and safety in Satellite Town is multi-layered and sometimes expressed in ambiguous and even contradictory ways. There was a tension in many of the accounts emphasizing, on the one hand, the safety of the place since 'everyone knows everyone', and on the other hand, talking about all the danger, violence and other 'dodgy stuff' going on there. But when I talked to Mark about these place images of danger and violence, he said: 'I think it's more gossip and rumours'. In the same vein, Steve who works at Northside, first said, 'There's a lot going on [in Satellite Town]. People get stabbed and stuff', but then added: 'You have violence and stuff happening *everywhere*. It's not worse than any other place, really'. I heard similar accounts on a few other occasions.

These accounts can also be coupled with the fact that people also drew boundaries against other areas considered dangerous, more so than Satellite Town. At the start of the fieldwork I lived in Brixton, and almost every time I mentioned it, people told me how dangerous it was there; it was also shown in their facial expressions. Mike who, worked at Northside and lived in a neighbouring area to Satellite Town, said, 'It's pretty rough, probably a bit worse than here [Satellite Town]', but added, 'It's not as bad as in Brixton'. Another boy said with emphasis: 'Brixton is the worst place in England!' And one girl told me that her 'mum's friend' had been mugged in her car while stopped at a traffic light, waiting for it to turn green. 'Someone opened the door, took her bag, took her phone and everything, just left her there'. In accounts like these, Brixton was used as a reference point for a truly dangerous place, far worse than Satellite Town. By drawing boundaries against Brixton, Satellite Town emerged in a more positive light.

Another telling example of drawing boundaries against other areas was when, after a session at Northside, I spoke with Gary in his office about my plans for the immediate future. I told him about going to Sweden for a week and then moving from Satellite Town to somewhere in South London, to an area like Catford. When I said Catford, Gary went 'Ooohhh!', his mouth O-shaped, and smiled. However, he then added: 'But you never know, maybe that's just how it's made out to be. Maybe they say the same things about us. Satellite Town's had a bad rep for years'. Sometime after this, I told Gary and Mike that I'd moved to Peckham. 'So you moved out to *Peckham*! You've chosen the dodgiest spots. First Brixton and now Peckham', Gary said and laughed. Again, we have strong boundaries drawn against other places. But we also note that, as in Mark's account, Gary problematizes the relationship between the images and reality of these places by stating that Catford might not be as bad as its reputation suggests.[22]

Belonging and Mobility

The notion that Satellite Town is a small place with a countryside feel to it, where the pace is slow, social relationships have strong aspects of familiarity, trust and safety but also of danger, was also reflected in the young people's accounts about their sense of, and attachment to, place. Very few respondents stated that they saw their own future in Satellite Town. The only one who explicitly expressed a wish to stay there was Abbey, who said: 'It's

---

[22] As Brixton and Peckham are areas with a large Afro-Caribbean and Black African contingent respectively, and Satellite Town a largely white area, one reader of this chapter asked me if the respondents' negative place images of the two aforementioned areas were racialized. My answer is that no intimations of race were made in these situations but that additional research is needed to investigate this issue further.

my home. I know everyone'. A few others answered like Mark: 'I'll probably move away... But if I end up in Satellite Town, I don't really mind about
that'. And like Mark, most respondents saw their future trajectories as living
elsewhere, outside of Satellite Town, often naturally as part of getting a job.
As opposed to Mark and Abbey, several said that they wanted to leave Satellite Town, some because it was 'boring' and others wanted to live in a sunny
place like Spain. But very few said that they wanted to move to an urban,
inner city area. Thus, Katie who said she found it 'boring' and 'hated it' in
Satellite Town, and did not want anything but to leave the place, had no
ideas whatsoever of moving to a big city like London, as was apparent when
I showed her a picture of the City of London and asked what she thought
about it.

> Katie: It doesn't appeal to me (no?). No. My aunt lives in central London
> (she does?) and I hate... I like it going there for weekends and things, but I
> could never live there permanently.
>
> Elias: Why not?
>
> Katie: Too many tourists, and it's just like, no greenery, and it's... *crap*,
> really.

In a similar sense, Britney and Tom stated that they wanted to live in London, but not the inner, urban parts:

> Tom: I'd love to live in London.
>
> Britney: I'd love to live in London. Not like actually central, *central* London,
> but on the outside.
>
> Tom: Along the river Thames.
>
> Britney: Yeah, that'd be nice, if on the outside of the busy part.

For most respondents, the urban, busy, fast paced, crowded places without
greenery such as those associated with the inner areas of London held no
appeal. Rather, their sense of place was shaped by having lived in Satellite
Town, with its very opposite characteristics of small size, slow pace, lots of
greenery and open space. One critical aspect was also about, as Mark put it,
the 'community thing', apparent in Satellite Town but lacking in the big city.

> Mark: Yeah, I'd rather live in a busier, community thing like that. But, the
> difference between *this* [picture of the City of London] and then obviously
> this one [a picture of the town centre in Satellite Town]. So this is more
> community based stuff, whereas here [City of London], it's like, you're on
> your own kind of thing (yeah). It's more...private.
>
> Elias: So would you like to have more [of] this private or would you like to
> have a community thing as well?

Mark: I like the fact of the community thing, but it's just if whether everyone does actually get together, or if it's like gangs and stuff like that.

Elias: Sure. You mean that people know each other (yeah), you can say hi to people...?

Mark: When I walk down the road I can say hello and stop and have a conversation with someone, whereas if you're in a busy place like London (yeah), you're not necessarily gonna know someone who could.

(...)

Mark: I think [what] best suits my personality and my taste would be Satellite Town and around here obviously 'cause I've grown up here, and this is what I know (sure). So that's kind of influenced it a lot, but (yeah-yeah) I think I would prefer to live in a community based area like this rather than somewhere in the city.

The interviewees stressed that in Satellite Town, they belonged to a community where people knew and engaged with each other, whereas central London was more anonymous, 'private', a 'you're on your own kind of thing'. But as we saw, Mark did not want to live in the type of 'community thing' with gangs and 'stuff like that', i.e. 'bad' forms of familiarity and social ties in localities such as in Satellite Town. Wanting to leave Satellite Town to get away from the violence, gangs, muggings and other social problems associated with the place was a recurring feature in the interviews.

Katie: I like to be around people, but I'd like to have a big house. Sort of like Satellite Town, but without... the trouble.

In this sense, Katie and others expressed a notion of wanting to live in an area similar to Satellite Town, with a strong sense of community, intimacy, greenery but without the social problems.

As regards mobility in space, being located in the outskirts of, and cut off from the more central parts of London, Satellite Town not only appears at a cultural distance, but also at a fair spatial distance from those central parts of London for most of the young people. This affected their spatial mobility. Anthony, a youth worker at Greenwood, told me: 'Some of these kids have not even been to central London. They're fourteen, fifteen and have never been there their whole lives'. Thus, he told me that the youth centre tried to take them there on daytrips. This was reflected in the interviews. Though none of the respondents said that they had never been to London, two female respondents, 13 and 15 years old, stated that they had visited London once, and most respondents rarely went to London. Rather, for most respondents, the capital of the borough in which Satellite Town is located, was the place where one went to go shopping, to go to bars and clubs, and engage in other activities. Thus, there was rarely any reason to go to London other than when there was a special occasion, such as a football match, concert, school trip, or holiday trip.

> Abbey: London is like, you go [there] when it's your birthday or Christmas.
>
> Rebecca: It's kinda like a daytrip. Everyone's like: 'Shall we go to London?' 'Yeah, let's go [to] London!'

Thus London is a distant place, both culturally and spatially. But this is not to say that the respondents were immobile in space. A few respondents had friends and relatives in other parts of the London area whom they visited. One boy travelled throughout London with his work, and a few respondents had relatives there whom they visited regularly. Moreover, many respondents said that they regularly went abroad on holiday, typically to sunny spots in South Europe, such as Greece, Ibiza, Canary Islands and Cyprus. But they rarely travelled elsewhere, except for a few respondents who had relatives living abroad in places such as Ireland and the United States whom they sometimes visited. Someone also mentioned school trips to France and Germany. One notable event was also during an informal interview with one of the older boys who used to frequent one of the youth clubs. He told me that, some time ago, his former girlfriend wanted them to go to Thailand for holiday. 'But I got scared so I never went'. His movement in space was constrained due to fear of travelling to an unknown place.

Conclusion: Ambiguous Place Images

In this chapter I have explored the dialectics between 'internal' and 'external' identifications, with Satellite Town conceived as a place and space. As we have seen, these spatialized identifications are strongly bound to social class distinctions. Through statistics, Satellite Town, and especially the New Estate, is conceived as a deprived space—a largely white, working-class space with a high unemployment rate, high proportion of council house estates, single parents and young people. But note that the rate of reported crimes is generally lower than in London as a whole.

In public representations in local newspapers and on the internet, Satellite Town is positioned in the codes and narratives constructed around the non-respectable figure of the white working-class that is the chav. In these place images, Satellite Town is derogatorily labelled a 'chav town' full of dole scroungers, teenage mothers, loutish kids, violence and anti-social behaviour. Thus, contrary to statistics, Satellite Town is portrayed as a crime-ridden area. In short, the area has a 'spoiled' place identity. Moreover, aspects of what I argue is a local style in Satellite Town, particularly appropriated by young people, also feature as elements in the public discourse on chavs. In this way, Satellite Town and its residents are positioned from the 'outside' in the stigmatizing public representations of chavs and the spaces and places that they are said to inhabit.

As regards identity from the 'inside', most residents of Satellite Town draw on similar negatively loaded place images of their home town and express an awareness of its bad reputation. They make frequent reference to violence and muggings in the area. This means that some respondents, at least partly, acknowledge the spoiled identity of Satellite Town that is constructed in public discourse. But although they are positioned by and draw on some of these negative place images, their social relations in, and images of, Satellite Town also have *Gemeinshaft*-like features such as strong social ties, familiarity and interpersonal trust. Moreover, despite the recurrent accounts of violence and criminality, knowing 'everyone' in Satellite Town means that respondents generally say that they feel safe there. Thus, social relationships function as useful resources or social capital. But there is a tension in respondents' accounts between negotiating place images of danger on the one hand, and place images of safety and familiarity on the other hand. This ambivalence is akin to the one experienced by the working-class council house tenants in Camden, interviewed by Watt (2006) and the children in deprived inner city council estates studied by Reay and Lucey (2000).

Moreover, accounts of community are far from rose-tinted as some residents display exclusionary tendencies such as suspicion and hostility against 'strangers', reflecting the dichotomy between 'established' and 'outsiders' (Elias & Scotson, 1994 [1965]). Symbolic boundaries are also constructed against other areas, such as Brixton and Peckham, both considered more dangerous.

But the young respondents are not 'established' in the traditional sense of born and bred locals who feel a sense of permanent attachment to Satellite Town. With the exception of Abbey who clearly conceived of Satellite Town as her home, most respondents' expressed readiness, indeed assumed that they would in the future, move to other areas; this is more akin to Mike Savage's notion of 'elective belonging'. Here, 'Belonging is not a fixed community, with the implication of closed boundaries, but is more fluid, seeing places as sites for performing identities' (Savage et al., 2004, p. 29). In this way, one chooses the places around which one builds attachments. And these choices, *qua* performances of identity, are structured by taste, and thus linked with access to, and deployment of, cultural resources. As regards the respondents, their sense of elective belonging was strongly shaped by living in Satellite Town with its small size, greenery and open spaces, slow pace, sense of familiarity and safety, but also of danger and violence. Many respondents wanted to live in an area akin to Satellite Town but without the danger and violence they associated with the place. This also meant that the urban, central parts of London appeared at both a cultural and spatial distance for most respondents who rarely went there. It was conceived as an anonymous, busy, crowded space lacking 'community'.

Thus as we can see, the boundaries between inclusion and exclusion, between 'external' and 'internal' identifications in Satellite Town are complex and sometimes ambiguous. Satellite Town's history of being a council estate, geographically and socially isolated, may partly explain some residents' suspicion of and hostility toward outsiders, but also their 'strong sense of community'. Robert MacDonald and his colleagues (MacDonald & Marsh, 2001; MacDonald et al., 2005) found similar patterns of familiarity and close social networks in the deprived Teesside neighbourhoods they studied. Satellite Town's status as isolated estate can also be related to Colin Webster's argument that in Britain, council estates 'mark the *prime* spatial location of marginalized white ethnicity'. This entails a 'spatial segregation by class' (Webster, 2008, p. 305). And like Satellite Town, council estates are frequently stigmatized (Hanley, 2007; Hastings, 2004; Reay & Lucey, 2000). The dialectics of identification with Satellite Town, then, is a story of the spatialization of class.

A paradox in the material is the difference between the comparatively low rate of reported crimes and the widespread place images among residents and in public discourse of Satellite Town being a violent, 'dodgy' area. One explanation could be that some crimes are never reported. This may be due to informal social control, e.g. for fear of repercussions or the unwritten code that one doesn't 'grass' on people one knows. In short, conflicts are preferably managed without involvement from the police and judiciary. Another explanation could be that these place images are classed stereotypes that are typically given to an area labelled as a marginalized council estate and 'chav town' with a young population and a high population of teenage mothers; they just don't reflect the actual crime rates.

Another issue is that the accounts and observations of people's identifications with Satellite Town presented here, are in many ways contrary to the narratives of atomization, loss, despair, suffering and displacement—in short, the very absence of 'community'—in the wake of deindustrialization, as reported in the work of Charlesworth (2000) and others (Bourdieu, 1999 [1993]; Turner, 2000; Wacquant, 2008). Why would there be such contradictory empirical findings? Focusing on Charlesworth's work, one reason may be the different impacts of socio-economic transformations. Deindustrialization hit the north of England particularly hard, with rampant unemployment in many areas including Rotherham where Charlesworth conducted his study. The effects were far smaller in the South East (Kirk, 2007, Ch. 2). One of Charlesworth's central arguments is that the hopelessness, despair and poor prospects characterizing present-day Rotherham have their roots in these dramatic socio-economic transformations, which affected Satellite Town far less.

Moreover, I have argued that Satellite Town's status as a socially and geographically isolated council estate may strengthen social cohesion. Lastly, another difference between this and Charlesworth's study lies in empirical foci. While much of the research reported here portrays everyday social interaction in public space, Charlesworth focuses on personal testimonies, many of which seem to be made by people he knows. But his selection of empirical material is rather one-sided. His powerful narrative is pitch-black throughout with no place for nuances, complexities or contradictions in the respondents' testimonies. As Angela McRobbie notes in her review essay of Bourdieu's *The Weight of the World*, a one-sided focus on pain and suffering results in an analysis 'stripped bare of all these things that co-exist with suffering... Even the poor and the dispossessed partake in some forms of cultural enjoyment which are collective resources which make people what they are' (McRobbie, 2002, p. 136).

Finally, this chapter has also made a case for face-to-face interaction in the spatiality of Satellite Town in constructing and reproducing notions of 'community'. This means that in the study of residents' identifications with and symbolic boundaries against Satellite Town conceived as a place the analysis is not simply on the ways in which community is 'imagined'; I also show how these symbolic constructions of community are bound up with social relationships and interaction situated in this locale. In this way, my account has served as a correction to the tendency to overstate the turn toward deterritorialized symbolic boundaries in the wake of globalization, which we discussed earlier.

5. Markers of Taste

In the previous chapter, we studied the dialectics of identity formation in relation to Satellite Town conceived as a space and place. This chapter turns to the young respondents and how they construct their identities in relation to style and appearance. The chapter focuses on how these aspects of identity are discursively articulated. Central here is the exploration of style and appearance as 'markers of taste' and the ways in which these may be morally loaded. I am particularly interested in how the notion of chav is understood by the respondents. This means that I explore how they identify with or disassociate from, and how they categorize others, in relation to style and appearance as markers of taste, particularly the notion of the chav. Important here are the aesthetic boundaries the respondents draw against others. We will investigate if these boundaries are morally loaded.

Throughout the chapter, I show how, from the perspective of the young people, the figure of the chav appears, is pushed away and resisted, or applied as a categorization of others. A central contention here is that many of the styles and tastes appropriated by the respondents, and their identity construction in relation to markers of taste, reflect their class positioning, i.e. their access to social, cultural and economic resources. This, in turn, reflects the working-class culture predominant in Satellite Town: there is a dominant taste in the locality of Satellite Town, reflecting its status as a working-class space. And crucially, the methods by which the styles and tastes are expressed position some of the respondents in the codes and narratives constructed around chavs. But as the latter entails a stigmatized form of categorization, the respondents disidentify with it; they draw symbolic boundaries against the term and use it to categorize others. The classed character of the respondents' notion of taste is also shown in that symbolic boundaries are drawn against forms of middle-class taste.

In what follows, the first two sections explore the respondents' conceptions of and relationship with the term chav. I then investigate their understanding of tattoos. In the fourth section I compare the respondents' understanding of the chav phenomenon with those of another youth cultural formation, namely emos. The fifth section investigates the respondents' understandings of middle-class markers of taste. Lastly, I make some concluding points.

Identifying Chavs

In the previous chapter we saw that many respondents, and particularly young people, in Satellite Town displayed highly stylized forms of dress, what I would argue constitutes a local style, i.e. one that is characteristic in the locality of Satellite Town. Moreover, some of the stylistic elements, in terms of dress, hairstyles, make-up and accessories adopted by the respondents, are elements in the public discourse of chavs, and thus risk positioning many of the respondents in the stigmatizing public codes and narratives constructed around the term. Similarly, we could see in Chapter 4 that in public discourse, Satellite Town and its residents are positioned in the codes and narratives constructed around chavs and the spaces and places that they inhabit, particularly so-called 'chav towns'. It is therefore vital to explore the respondents' thoughts about chavs.

During my stay in London, I frequently encountered the term chav in conversations, yet hardly ever during fieldwork in Satellite Town, at least not spontaneously in normal conversations. The only time I recall hearing it was when Gary, the caretaker at Northside, said of a particular nickname of Satellite Town, that it was a 'chavy' way of calling the area. 'Why is it chavy?' I asked. 'It has a proper name, why not use it', he replied. In the photo elicitation interviews, however, 'chav' came up spontaneously only a few times, but as we will see, very frequently in response to some of the pictures I showed the respondents.

'That's a Typical Satellite Town Girl'

Katie was 17, one of the regulars at Northside, and part of the group of older members with the highest status there. Many aspects of her style departed from what one could call the dominant taste in Satellite Town. She had long straight light-blond hair and wore a checked blouse, skirt, and sandals, though she also appropriated some aspects of the local taste; her sandals, for example, were decorated with small glittery pieces. Compared with most other respondents, she was also generally more mobile in space, visiting inner city London to a greater extent than most of the other young people to whom I talked. She also expressed a clear desire to move from Satellite Town when she was older. One of her relatives, whom she regularly visited, lived in central London, and she preferred to go shopping on Oxford Street in central London, rather than in the main town of the borough where Satellite Town is located. 'I like high street fashion rather than designer fashion', she said and mentioned Top Shop, River Island and Miss Selfridge as clothes store chains she liked. During our interview, I showed her a picture of a person's hands which are full of golden rings and bracelets (Figure 5.1).

Figure 5.1. Jewellery.
Source: Chavscum (n.d.).

Katie: [emphatically but in a low voice, hardly audible on the recording] *Disgusting.* [In a normal tone] I like jewellery but I would never wear it like that.

Elias: Yeah, okay. This is a bit much. So you wouldn't wear, like, one sovereign ring?

Katie: I wouldn't wear a sovereign [ring], for a start.

Elias: Why not?

Katie: It's just chav jewellery.

Elias: Yeah-yeah, but it's quite common around here in Satellite Town, isn't it?

Katie: *Exactly!* [laughs]

Elias: So do you think that there are a lot of chavs [in Satellite Town]...?

Katie: Oh *definitely!*

As we will see, like Katie, many respondents drew symbolic boundaries against certain visual markers, such as sovereign rings, and categorized them as 'chavy'. And Katie's contention that Satellite Town was a place with many chavs was expressed by others, such as Dan, Katie, Rebecca and Mark.

Dan was also 17 and a frequent visitor at Northside. He usually had a toned down dressing style, often casually dressed in plain clothes, such as jeans and T-shirt, and he had rather short brown hair, but longer than was the norm and very different from the almost shaved coiffures popular among many boys in Satellite Town. He was also different in that he identified with Christianity. He was considered a good football player and he told me he might even go for professional if the opportunity arose. One picture I showed Dan and the other respondents was of a girl in pink tracksuit, trainers, hair in ponytail, big hoop earrings and golden jewellery sitting in a bus stop while smoking and holding a mobile phone to her ear (see Figure 5.2). This picture also featured in Chapter 3 as an example of a stereotypical image of a chavette, a female chav. The purpose of showing this picture in the interviews was to explore the respondents' views of the visual representations of chavs circulating in the public realm.

Figure 5.2. Girl at bus stop.
Source: CaptiveInnocencePhotography (2008).

Elias: What do you think of her style?

Dan: Eh… As I would say: chavy.

Elias: Okay. So, what's chavy about this picture, I mean?

Dan: Yeah, like, wearing all that jewellery (yeah), doing all that make up [inaudible]. Girls wearing really baggy clothing.

Elias: Yeah, and the sneakers too, I guess.

Dan: Also, that's a typical Satellite Town girl.

Elias: Is it? Alright.

Dan: That's how most of Satellite Town girls are.

As we can see, Dan identifies the girl as a chav through her ways of styling her appearance, then adds that the picture depicts 'a typical Satellite Town girl... how most Satellite Town girls are'. Again, we have a clear notion that Satellite Town is a place with many chavs. But we can also note that both Dan and Katie's respective styles differ from the one that is typically adopted by young people in Satellite Town, and this might explain why they draw distinctions against others in the area and call them chavs.

And generally, most people identified the girl in Figure 5.2 as a chav on the basis of her visual attributes—tracksuits, trainers, jewellery, cigarette, sitting on the street. One example is Aaron, friends with Katie, and like her, 17 year old and part of the group of high status kids at Northside. He lived in the New Estate just a few minutes away from the youth club and was one of its core members. He was well-liked among the staff and the other young people at Northside. He had a straightforward and good-humoured manner and a rather lively way of gesturing and moving his body. From a Caribbean and white British background, he had sharp features, was very short with slightly curly black hair and usually wore diamond studs in his ears. He often wore a 'hoodie' (hooded top) or a T-shirt which he almost always combined with tracksuit bottoms and trainers. During the interview Shane, one of the younger boys, and Katie joined in but mostly sat listening in the background. I showed them Figure 5.2.

> Aaron: Chav.
>
> Elias: Why is it a chav, I mean?
>
> Aaron: She's wearing tracksuits and trainers [inaudible]. She's putting no effort into her looks. I like a girl to put a bit of effort into their looks and she ain't doing that.
>
> Elias: Yeah, yeah? So what's...?
>
> Aaron: Big earrings.
>
> Elias: Big earrings? So, you think it's too much?
>
> Aaron: It's not enough. [inaudible] is that she's wearing tracksuits, trainers, big earrings. She hasn't really done her hair.
>
> (...)
>
> Mark [walks by, stops, looks at the picture then turns to Aaron]: Do you know what she looks like? Nikki Bennett [a girl in Satellite Town both of them know].

When identifying the girl as a chav, Aaron also makes a moral judgement. 'She's putting no effort into her looks'. 'She hasn't really done her hair'. As a chav she lacks ambition to style her appearance in a proper way. Rather, her dress is a bit scruffy. Mark's comment is interesting in that, to him, the girl on the picture resembles a girl he and Aaron know.

Rebecca, 15, was born to an Irish mother and a Jamaican father. Tall for her age and of slightly larger size than the norm, she had a 'pineapple' haircut, worn with a hair band. She wore a yellow tracksuit, trainers, and a big rectangular bracelet in silvery metal on her left wrist, rather different in style from the gold chains usually favoured by Satellite Town residents. She was articulate and very forthcoming about being interviewed. I interviewed her together with Abbey, also 15, and one of the core members at Northside, who often talked to and socialized with Gary and other staff members. Born and bred in the New Estate, she expressed a strong sense of belonging to the place, considering it her 'home' and where she knew 'everyone'. Somewhat larger size than the norm, she used to wear tracksuit, trainers and a gold necklace around her neck with a gold pendant in the form of an 'A', short for Abbey, and gold or silver earrings. She had her straight, light brown hair in a knot. Like previous respondents, both Rebecca and Abbey identified the girl in Figure 5.2 as a chav, then added:

> Abbey: Slag.
>
> Elias: Slag? Okay.
>
> Rebecca: She does dress like one...
>
> Abbey: Look at her big, dangling earrings, the cigarette, the bracelet...
>
> Rebecca: And the Nike trainers [are] out of fashion! [laughs]
>
> Abbey: ...And the tracksuit.

For Rebecca and Abbey, then, the girl on the picture symbolized a slag, a gendered, sexualized and highly morally loaded term, which we saw in Chapter 3, is frequently applied to female chavs.

One of few respondents who didn't categorize the girl on the picture as a chav was Tommy. Like his friends Katie and Aaron, Tommy was also 17 and amongst those with the highest status at Northside. He was mid-sized, had a straight posture and quite robust, muscular physique. His hair was short cropped at the sides, and a bit longer on the top of his head, and he often had a stubble. He usually wore a T-shirt with a gold chain necklace, tracksuit bottoms and trainers. Always playing football during sessions, he said that he trained hard to become a pro footballer and wanted to get away from 'this shithole', i.e. Satellite Town, his dream being to go to New York. Thus, it seemed to me that the stakes were high: he was working as hard as possible to create a new, successful life away from Satellite Town. I showed him Figure 5.2 and asked him what he thought about 'the style of her clothes'.

> Tommy: Nice, man. It's nice, sexy stuff for a chick, yeah (alright). It's nice. Nice [inaudible] her hair. She's got some nice makeup and jewellery. She's got nice trainers.

Thus, rather than classify her as a chav and draw symbolic boundaries like most of the other respondents—in fact, he never mentioned the term during the whole interview—Tommy found her stylish and attractive.

106

'Propa Chav like Him'

A general observation throughout the interviews is that the respondents, when interpreting the term chav, drew on similar codes and narratives as those circulating in the public realm (see Chapter 3). When shown pictures featuring the visual markers associated with chavs, almost all of the respondents also readily identified these with the term, which always had negative connotations. And, as in public discourse, the term was often given several, albeit connected, meanings. This means that there were often several layers to the respondents' understanding of the term, with aesthetic boundaries bound up with visual markers, but more morally loaded distinctions expressed as the interview proceeded. We could see this in different responses to the girl portrayed in Figure 5.2, and we will see this in the respondents' definitions of the term chav.

> Katie: A chav is like... Do you know if someone that wear tracksuits all the time, that wear fake designer clothes and everything has to be designer, (alright). That have jewellery everywhere.
>
> Elias: Is it always fake?
>
> Katie: Yeah, it's someone who tries to make them self look like they've got money but in the wrong way.

Thus to Katie, being a chav was associated with a conspicuous display of jewellery and 'fake' designer clothing. 'A big chav thing last year was, like, everyone wore Burberry. Fake Burberry hats, Burberry jackets and all things like that'. About the trade with counterfeit designer clothing, she said, 'Back of the lorry, 25 quid, you know', and laughed. In Chapter 3 I showed that this conspicuous and aspirational character of chavs' consumption and lifestyles is a common feature in the codes and narratives constructed around them in public discourse.

Dan initially identified chavs with visual markers, but then added another symbolically loaded aspect.

> Dan: A chav is basically, like, a young person who hasn't got a job, isn't in college, and relies on his parents.

For Dan, chavs are not only young people appropriating a certain style, they also have a socio-economic status of dependency—of being outside of the occupational and educational systems. The appearance of morally loaded layers also became apparent during the interview with Rebecca.

> Rebecca: The definition would be: it's like a council house, aggressive and violent (okay, okay). But, like, we'd describe a chav as like with big hoop earrings, hair to the side, Burberry tracksuit, stuff like that.

To Rebecca, the acronym, [c]ouncil [h]oused [a]nd [v]iolent, provides the formal definition of the term, but she partly distances herself from this morally loaded definition, and identifies chavs via the visual markers we have become familiar with throughout this book. Yet, later in the interview I showed her a picture featuring a teenage boy in a hooded top, pointing his arm towards the camera, his fingers shaped as a pistol.

> Rebecca: Yeah, he would be more like a chav, like a yob.
>
> Elias: A yob. Alright. What's a yob?
>
> Rebecca: Like a hoodlum, like, I don't know how to put it.
>
> Elias: [feigning ignorance] Yob, yeah, I'm not sure if I know the word. I mean...
>
> Rebecca: [to someone else in the room, I then see it's Abbey] How do you describe a yob, a hoodlum?
>
> Abbey: Like him [laughs][points at the person on picture]. Proper chav like him. He thinks he's like a gangster.
>
> Elias: Like a gangster?
>
> Abbey: A wannabe.

Rebecca, now joined by Abbey, classified the boy as a 'yob', 'hoodlum' and 'wannabe gangster' and thus associated him with minor forms of anti-social behaviour, aggressive display and violence. As we saw in Chapter 3, this is a gendered stereotype and a recurrent feature in the construction of male chavs in the public sphere who are portrayed as violent, loutish white working class males in gangs. Similarly, we saw that Rebecca and Abbey classified the girl in Figure 5.2 according to another gendered stereotype attached to female chavs, namely the slag.

Another picture (Figure 5.3) I used in the interviews depicted a group of white boys in tracksuit, baseball caps, trainers and short cropped coiffures, sitting on a fence in public space—the stereotypical image of the chav 'yob' gang, which like Figure 5.2 also featured in Chapter 3.

> Elias: Alright, what about this picture?
>
> Aaron: Chavs.
>
> Shane: [Inaudible] getting a lot of trouble.
>
> Aaron: Just... Losers.
>
> Elias: Yeah, why?
>
> Aaron: [Points at one of the boys in the picture] That guy, he looks like he's twenty, and he's hanging 'round on the street.

Figure 5.3. Group of boys.
Source: Hayes (2007).

Aaron draws moral boundaries against the boys. They are 'losers', sitting idle, 'doing nothing' in public space. We will return to Aaron and this interview excerpt in the next section.

Disidentifications

Thus far we have explored the respondents' understandings of chavs, which, as I have argued also exist as elements in the public discourse on chavs explored in Chapter 3. As we can see, most respondents categorized the people in the pictures as chavs, and all of those who did, disidentified with the label. And although chavs were identified through particular visual markers, the latter were often also morally loaded. It is also important that, although all the respondents drew boundaries against chavs, some of them like Mark, Dan and Katie identified Satellite Town as a place that was home to many of them. The question, then, is: do these people who are categorized as chavs identify with this label? This was discussed in the interviews with Dan and Katie.

Elias: Would they consider themselves chavs?

Dan: They don't like to be called chavs. That's probably because they can't face the fact that's what it's called [to look like they do].

Elias: Alright, alright. So, no one here would wear that kind of style, I mean?

Dan: Ehm. Some people might like to show off.

Elias: But I mean, do people call themselves chavs?

Katie: No... Yeah, some people do, (yeah-yeah) and are proud of the fact, but I wouldn't class myself as a chav.

This was also shown in other respondents' accounts, namely that most people who are labelled chavs by others disassociated with the term. It can be noted, however, that both Dan and Katie claimed that 'some people' may identify with the label to 'show off' (Dan) or even be 'proud' to be called chavs (Katie). Moreover, while Aaron drew strong distinctions against chavs, two of his friends, Katie and Mark, identified him as a chav. Katie was present (but mostly listening in the background) during the interview with Aaron. I then interviewed her on her own, and showed her Figure 5.3 again.

Katie: Aaron can call them [the boys depicted in Figure 5.3] losers, but he used to be like that (okay). We all used to sit on the street because there's nothing else to do.

What Katie is saying is that she, Aaron and their friends used to hang around in public space just like the boys in the picture—the same boys whom Aaron called chavs and losers. This implies that Katie thought Aaron was a bit hypocritical on the subject. Later in the interview, Katie mentions that there are many chavs in Satellite Town. I then ask her if there are any people who dress like chavs at Northside that night.

Katie: [turns around and looks out into the adjacent room] Who dresses like a chav? [inaudible] example of chav... Aaron's quite chavy. Tracksuits, big jewellery.

Elias: Yeah-yeah, but would he say that himself? [Katie shakes her head] Do you think he would be... [offended]?

Katie: Probably, yeah! [laughs]

Elias: But he didn't like, I mean, when I showed the picture of... let's see... of this girl [shows Figure 5.2]. He said, 'Yeah, she looks like a chav', and then said 'No, I wouldn't go out with her. I don't like her style because she looks like a chav'.

Katie: Yeah, that's 'cause he's fussy [smiles].

Elias: Is he fussy [laughs]! So you think it's because he has high standards about girls?

Katie: Well, no, but if he was to talk to her, he would get on her [laughs].

Katie categorizes Aaron as 'quite chavy', but says that he would probably find it offensive to be called chav. And again, she implies that Aaron is not completely honest when he said that he did not find the girl on Figure 5.2 attractive while in reality he would 'get on her' given the chance. Thus, according to Katie, Aaron likes girls more than he admitted in the interview.

Like his friend Aaron, Mark was also 17 and one of the core members at Northside. He used to come in once or twice almost every week, and was generally very well-liked among members and staff at the youth club. Mark's own style clearly set him apart from the common way of dressing in the youth clubs or indeed Satellite Town as a whole. His hair, coloured black, was often a bit straggly on the top of his head. Sometimes he wore a hairclip to make the hair lie down, a femininely coded stylistic touch. He usually wore skinny jeans, T-shirts and Converse basketball shoes. Mark spoke with a deep and low voice. He came across as very relaxed. This interview excerpt starts at the point when I showed Mark the picture of the girl depicted in Figure 5.2.

Elias: What do you think about when you see this picture?

Mark: [Looks at the picture for several seconds] Yeah [laughs]. That's the ideal chav, really.

Elias: Yeah, yeah? But would she call herself chav?

Mark: I don't think she would. I don't think they call themselves chav, like, people here like Aaron (yeah). I call them a chav (yeah), but they don't call themselves, 'cause I'm not a chav and they get quite offended (okay) by it.

Elias: So, how come?

Mark: I don't really know. I think it's seen as insulting stereotype with dodgy tracksuits, smoking, caps. Stuff like that (yeah). You don't need to be stereotyped into saying that.

Elias: Sure, sure. So you use it? You don't see it as anything negative?

Mark: Not really. It's just classes and categories that people fit into, really.

Elias: Sure, but what is a chav? Is it just a way of dressing, or is it something more?

Mark: [inaudible] ASBO orders, drinking on the street, getting pregnant at a young age. Stuff like that. That's the stereotype of the chav.

Elias: Okay, so I guess that's why Aaron gets offended... [laughs]

Mark: Offended [laughs].

Elias:...When you call him chav [laughs]. But is it true, you think, to some extent? Or is it just a few people who do that?

Mark: Yeah, it's just a few people, like, in Satellite Town you get a certain people that get pregnant at young ages and that. Obviously, when you call Aaron a chav he gets really offended. The minute I call him a chav: 'Shut up, I'm not a fucking chav, you emo!' [smiles]

Mark's account is reflexive, multi-layered but also somewhat inconsistent. He recognizes that the term chav is bound up with a derogatory stereotype. However, for him, chav is a descriptive term that captures an existing phenomenon, and in this sense calling his friend Aaron a chav is not something he sees as necessarily a denigration. In this sense, Mark argues that one can use chav in a 'real' way that is not stereotypical. Yet, he admits that he understands why Aaron gets angry when he gets called a chav as it has negative connotations. Then, in turn, he says that some of the denigratory features of the chav stereotype, like teenage pregnancy, are not simply stereotypes but actually existing phenomena among 'a few' or 'certain' people.

Sometimes, the respondents disidentified with chavs using very finely tuned criteria. This was evident when Abbey and Annie discussed the group of boys in Figure 5.3.

> Elias: Do you like their style?
>
> Abbey: They look kind of cheap. Chavy.
>
> Elias: Why is that?
>
> Annie: 'Cause they're wearing, like, tracksuit bottoms, hats, things like that, like tracksuit tops. But I sometimes wear them.
>
> Elias: Yeah, I mean, what's...
>
> Abbey: That's the fashion.
>
> Annie: They got different...
>
> Abbey: That's the fashion for boys innit.
>
> Annie: They got different stuff on. They've got Nike...
>
> Abbey: Yeah.
>
> Annie: Adidas...
>
> Annie and Abbey: McKenzie...
>
> Annie: All in one.
>
> Elias: Alright, they're kind of mixing [brands]...
>
> Annie and Abbey: Yeah.
>
> Elias: So you should have everything by the same brand?
>
> Annie and Abbey: Yeah.

The girls make aesthetic distinctions against the boys' clothing style. Wearing tracksuits, baseball caps and trainers, they look 'cheap' and 'chavy', as Abbey puts it. But then Annie acknowledges that she herself wear these kinds of clothes. So how come the boys' but not her own way of dressing is 'chavy'? She says that the way she and her friends dress is different, because they follow the current fashion whereas the boys in the picture don't; they mix clothes of different labels. To mix brands like that is considered 'chavy'. Rather, one should stick to one brand in your entire outfit. We can see here the ways in which a distinction between chavy and normal is created in very finely tuned ways

The boundaries between taste and distaste were similarly shifting when it came to jewellery. Several respondents wore and expressed a taste for jewellery. But they sometimes also associated it with chavs and 'chavy' things, and thus as something against which they drew boundaries. As we saw earlier, sovereign rings where described as 'chav jewellery' by Katie. And both Dan and Katie pointed out that it is 'chavy' to have jewellery shaped in the form of your own or someone else's name or initials. Dan also said that he did not like wearing jewellery because it was about 'showing off', a way of displaying status and wealth which did not go well with his toned down style and Christian values. Yet some time after the interview I saw him at the youth club with a gold chain on his wrist. Thus, like Katie, Dan drew boundaries against the dominant style and taste, and adopted a style that departed from this dominant style, but not completely, as he appropriated some aspects of it. His taste was shaped by living in Satellite Town. Moreover, when I interviewed Abbey, this time with Rebecca, they identified chavs by, among other things, wearing jewellery. Abbey was wearing a gold necklace with a pendant shaped in the letter 'A'.

> Elias: But I mean, like, jewellery—when is it chavy or not chavy? I mean, you know, like... [pointing at Abbey's necklace].
>
> Abbey [to Rebecca]: Do I look like a chav you think?
>
> Rebecca: No.
>
> Abbey: Chav is...
>
> Rebecca: Too much.
>
> Abbey: More blingish, like.

As we can see, Rebecca and Abbey make a distinction between chavy and non-chavy, associating the former with excessive, vulgar taste—'too much' and 'bling'. The notion of bling is, as we learned in Chapter 3, about conspicuous display of jewellery and other glittery pieces. Thus the 'right', non-chavy way of wearing jewellery is to not do it in an exaggerated, 'over the top' fashion. This is also reflected in the interview with Abbey and Annie. They told me that one or two rings on each finger look 'nice', but to wear more than that they considered 'too much' and thus chavy.

In sum, all of the respondents disidentified with chavs—drawing strong aesthetic and moral boundaries against the term. Chavs were always 'others'. As we have seen from Chapter 3, this may hardly be surprising as the chav has become such a classed, stigmatizing signifier with strongly negative moral-aesthetic connotations. The term has very little to serve as the basis for a positive identity, which explains why the respondents avoided and resisted being positioned as chavs. This is very similar to the white working-class women in Beverley Skeggs' (1997) ethnography in North West England and their relationship to the term working-class.

But sometimes, the boundaries between the visual markers associated with chav and those adopted by the respondents were difficult to draw, with the latter using finely tuned criteria to avoid being positioned as chavs. Moreover, respondents like Katie, Mark and Dan also said that those 'others' whom they classified as chavs, most likely disidentified with the term as well. 'Some' people in Satellite Town and elsewhere were said to adopt the label 'and were proud of the fact' (Katie) or used it to 'show off' (Dan). That some people identify with the term may be due to a form of deviance amplification, a concept Howard Becker (1997 [1963]) uses in his classic study of marijuana smokers. Those who are marked with the stigma that the label chav entails may react by identifying strongly with the label and embracing the outsider status it entails.

Tattoos as Inscriptions of Love

During the interviews I showed the respondents pictures of people wearing tattoos. Most of the respondents liked tattoos and wanted to get one when they turned 18, the legal age in Britain. Several respondents also wanted to tattoo the names or faces of family members. I showed Abbey and Annie Figure 5.4 depicting two pictures, each featuring a person with a tattoo on the small of the back.

> Elias: Would you like to have tattoos like this?
>
> Abbey: Yeah, I would like to have them, but I'd like to get, like, if I was to have kids when I'm older, their names and their faces.
>
> Annie: That's what Tom's mum got. She's got her husband there and her kids there [pointing at different parts of her body].
>
> (...)
>
> Abbey: Gavin got 'Mum' tattooed on his arm. That is so cute!
>
> Annie: What?
>
> Abbey: He got 'Mum' (alright). He got tattooed mum on his arm. It's so cute! My brother was there with him when he got it all done. My brother wants to get one as well.

Accounts like these express Les Back's (2007: Ch. 3) contention that tattoos in white British working-class culture are 'inscriptions of love'. As he puts it: 'Love is given a name; it is incarnate. But this commitment is not made in elaborated speeches. It is performed rather than described' (Back, 2007: 82).

Back's point is that the practice of tattooing the name or symbol of a loved one is largely absent from British middle-class culture, which, indeed puts more emphasis on the 'described', the verbal.

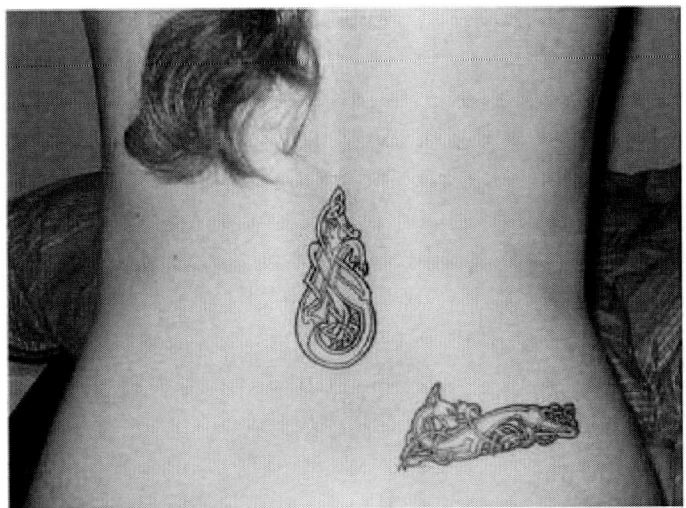

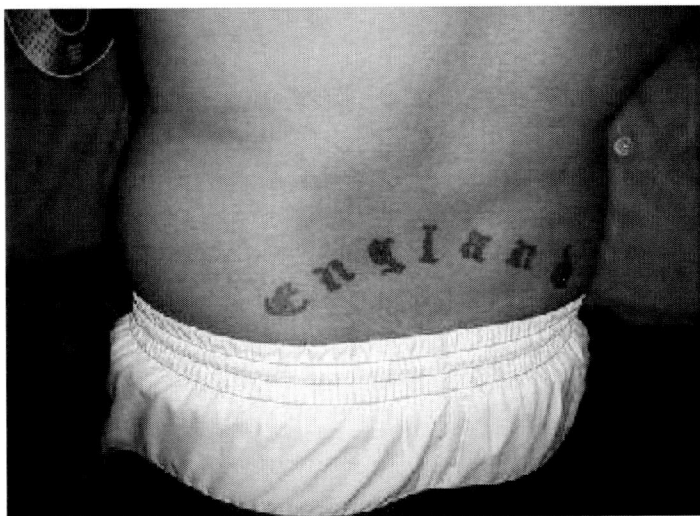

Figure 5.4. Tattoos.
Source: Flickr (n.d.).

But for the general importance and taste for tattoos among the respondents, certain ways of styling and wearing tattoos were identified as chavy and thus regarded with distaste. Indeed, they were tainted by being associated with chavs. For Rebecca, a tattoo on the small of the back was described as a 'chav stamp'. And Mark's account of the tattooed man featured in Figure 5.4 is also telling.

> Mark: Them tattoos... [Looks at the pictures for a several seconds] I think they're quite chavy tattoos (...) ...it's just tacky and chavy.
>
> Elias: It's tacky?
>
> Mark: Yeah.
>
> Elias: Because it kind of shows...?
>
> Mark: Yeah, I dunno, it's just that, it's kinda of a chavy thing to do (is it?). You might as well have a bottle of Stella tattooed to the back of his neck or something.

The strongest sense in which associations with chavs affected the respondents' relationships to tattoos I got when I interviewed Katie. I showed her a picture of a couple having their partner's name on the small of their back, the man having 'San', and the woman 'Andy' (see Figure 5.5).

Figure 5.5. Tattooed couple.
Source: Chavscum (n.d.).

Katie: I would never wear that.

116

Elias: Have you never had like a name or anything? No, no?

Katie: Only if it feels like... I'd have family. But I'd never have a boy's name.

Elias: So you'd have your mum's name or something?

Katie: Yeah, I'd have my mum's name. But not in a chav way, like [inaudible] name in Hebrew.

Elias: What's a chav way to have a...?

Katie: To have 'Mum' and 'Dad' on a tattoo.

Elias: But in Hebrew?

Katie: In Hebrew.

Elias: So you wouldn't have, like, jewellery with her name or 'Mum' or something?

Katie: Oh no!

Elias: Okay [laughs at her reaction]. And not names and not your initials or anything?

Katie: [Shakes her head]

In Katie's conflicting account we can both see the value imbued in tattooing the name of a loved one and the symbolic power of the stigmatizing chav discourse. She wants to inscribe the name of her mother on her skin. At the same time, she draws strong boundaries against it, as she recognizes that tattooing the name of someone is classified as chavy. To distinguish herself from chavy ways of wearing tattoos, and thus resolve this contradiction, she wants to have her mother's name tattooed in Hebrew instead of English. In this way, Katie manages to avoid being positioned in the chav category while still maintaining her wish to tattoo the name of her beloved mother. The alternative for Katie would be to fully distance herself from this allegedly 'chavy' practice, but that might be difficult as it would entail breaking with a deeply emotional and historically rooted practice.

This way of negotiating the boundaries between 'chavy' and 'non-chavy' through very minute distinctions we also saw in Abbey and Annie's accounts as regards the wearing of tracksuits and jewellery. Small distinctions, then, make all the difference.

Emos, Goths and Mark the 'Chemo'

The respondents' accounts of chavs can be usefully compared with those of other youth cultural forms. During my research, several respondents talked about 'emos' and a few mentioned 'goths'. These two terms are sometimes related, and I will focus on the respondents' accounts of emos. An acronym of 'emocore' or 'emotional hardcore', emo is based around a form of music that is usually described as a hybrid of punkrock, pop, indie and sometimes metal, which, as its name implies, always has an emotional current. 'The behaviors, attitudes, and values expressed through the music involve emotionally turbulent themes often associated with adolescence such as despair, nostalgia, heartbreak, hope, and self-loathing' (Bailey, 2005). Emo kids appropriate a style, which also here to some extent is a hybrid of other music-based youth cultural forms, such as those mentioned above. Typical elements of emo style include 'black stovepipe jeans, dyed black hair and side-parted long fringes' (Phillipov, 2009).

During my time in Satellite Town I only came across people adopting stylistics features associated with emos on a few occasions. This was also reflected in some of the interviews, such as the one with Rebecca:

> Elias: Are there, like, many Goths [in Satellite Town]...?
>
> Rebecca: There are a couple of Goths, and a couple of emos.
>
> Elias: Because I've hardly seen anyone around here in Satellite Town.
>
> Rebecca: There's really not a lot around here. More chavs really.

Like other respondents, Rebecca associates Satellite Town mostly with chavs rather than emos. Similarly, Dan said that there were few emos in Satellite Town, but more in central London and in the main town of the borough. And during my fieldwork in the youth clubs, the only person I encountered who looked like an emo was Mark. As described earlier, his hair was coloured black and straggly on the top of his head, and he usually wore a T-shirt and skinny black jeans. I sometimes heard others refer to him as an emo, like when I showed the respondents a picture of a boy in black straggly hair, makeup and t-shirt with 'Fight for your right' printed on it (Figure 5.6).

> Abbey: That is a punk. That is what you call an emo.
>
> Tom: That's Mark.
>
> Rebecca: Nooo!
>
> Tom: Mark. 'Fight for your right' [reading what is written on the t-shirt].
>
> Abbey: That ain't Mark. Mark is so nice. Those people scare me. I can't walk by [inaudible] them. They scare me.
>
> Rebecca: I don't think. I think...
>
> Tom: They do scare me. Even [name of shop in main town] scares me.
>
> Rebecca: I think they're fine!
>
> Abbey: I think... I think they like death too much. That's what scares me.

Tom: They wanna know when they're gonna die.

Abbey: They want to know what it's like to die, but why would anyone wanna know that? That scares me.

Rebecca: I'd like to know what it's like to die. [laughs]

Tom [To Rebecca]: [Mock-scared] Get away from me!

Rebecca: I'm curious! I'd like to know what heaven's like, what hell's like.

Figure 5.6. Emo boy.
Source: Ask Lo Pan (n.d.).

Tom and Abbey identify the boy in the picture as an emo, then both draw moral boundaries against the term. They associate emo culture with a morbid and abnormal fascination with death and dying. Tom also classifies Mark as an emo, though Abbey and Rebecca disagree—Abbey because 'Mark is so nice' unlike the scary, morbid emos. Rebecca has nothing against emos and shares their interest in 'what it's like to die'. When I interviewed Mark himself he had a few things to say about the meaning of emo.

Mark: I have different sets of friends. I have friends here, and then I've like emos and goth friends down in [main town of borough]. Different sets of friends that don't really mix [laughs].

Elias: Would you consider yourself, I dunno, emo or something?

119

Mark: I've been called chemo.

Elias: Chemo? [laughs]

Mark: I'm like, in between. My chavy friends call me emo, and my emo and goth friends call me chav.

(...)

Elias: Really? Okay. But Emo is not a negative thing?

Mark: People who don't understand it say it's just rock music, screaming, slicing wrists and stuff like that and suicide. There's a lot more to it than that.

Elias: Okay, what would you say it is then? I don't know anything about emo, actually.

Mark: Tight fashion. Fashion's very tight and that [laughs]. Tight jeans and shirts and stuff like that (okay). Really crazy and out of the box of what people would think is normal (yeah), like big hair and long fringes on boys and stuff like that.

(...)

Mark: A couple of weeks ago, I bought a pair of pink trainers just 'cause I knew everyone else got a thing [against it] [Elias laughs]. [Inaudible] they're girls trainers. It's just about being different, really.

As we saw earlier, Mark categorized Aaron as a chav, which he, unlike Aaron, did not necessarily conceive as derogatory. In this excerpt, Mark says that he is called chav by his emo friends in the main town outside Satellite Town. He also was called chemo—a hybrid of emo and chav—by others, a term he also uses to refer to himself. Thus unlike other respondents, Mark partly identifies with the term chav, and does so in a way which is largely free from negative connotations. Yet, in other contexts, we have seen that Mark has used the term in a derogatory way, as when he talked about chavy tattoos.

Moreover, it is clear that Mark and others' understanding of emo culture is quite different from their conception of chavs. Emo is a term and concept based around a particular form of music, and used by emos themselves as a collective form of identification. Mark is attracted by the emo style as it allows him to distinguish himself from 'normal' people and practices—'it's about being different' and perform in 'out of the box' ways. While Tom and Abbey drew symbolic boundaries against emo culture, Mark defended it against what he saw as misconceptions. My argument here is that in this context, emo culture has more features characterizing a subculture than chav culture, which, rather than based around a specific form of music, is primarily a derogatory label applied to others but not to oneself. And unlike emo, chav is a classed category bound up with socio-economic marginality, such as council housing, unemployment and petty crime.

Against Middle-Class Taste

While most respondents drew symbolic boundaries against visual markers associated with chavs, they also made distinctions against middle-class forms of visual markers. One example was when I lived in Satellite Town and Kristoffer, a friend and colleague from Norway, came to visit. He arrived late in the evening and I met him on the bus on the way to my flat. Entering the bus, I saw him standing next to the doors, holding his luggage. He wore a beige leather jacket, very tight navy blue pinstriped cotton trousers, a knitted hat and pointed brown leather shoes. Just next to him stood two girls in their early teens, wearing light-coloured tracksuits and trainers. We greeted each other and started chatting. He told me (in Norwegian) that throughout the whole trip, the two girls had looked at him, and especially at his trousers, while smirking and exchanging glances. The two girls were mocking, or 'taking the piss out' of, Kristoffer's way of styling his clothing and appearance. It was also clear that Kristoffer's dress and style deviated from the norm in Satellite town. During my fieldwork in Satellite Town, I saw very few, if any, people with a style similar to or approximating the one adopted by Kristoffer.

Figure 5.7. Jarvis Cocker.
Sources: Albion (2009) and Superfuture (2009).

Similar distinctions were apparent when I showed the respondents two pictures of pop artist Jarvis Cocker, who originally became famous in the mid-1990's as the singer of the now disbanded indie band Pulp (see Figure 5.7). He is generally portrayed in the media as a person with a sophisticated, albeit quirky or 'arty', sense of styling his clothes and appearance. He also holds a degree in fine arts and film from Central St. Martins in London. The two pictures are examples of editorial fashion photography that has high status in the market for fashion photography (Aspers, 2006). In a wider British context, then, these pictures possess high cultural capital and are objects of legitimate culture, to use Bourdieusian parlance. But the sense in which these pictures embody 'good taste' is, of course, highly contextual. When I showed the pictures to the respondents, none of them seemed very impressed. For instance, take Aaron's and Katie's accounts:

> Aaron: Nerd.
>
> Katie: Looks like a freak... Sort of a paedophile.

Similarly, when I interviewed Abbey and Annie:

> Abbey: He needs to get a haircut 'cause his hair looks kinda greasy. And his glasses... He needs to go to Specsavers.
>
> Elias: Okay [laughs].
>
> Annie: And then put his dictionary away.
>
> Abbey: And he needs to 'fix up, look sharp'[23] [everyone laughs].
>
> Elias: So you think it looks a bit scruffy.
>
> Abbey: Yeah.
>
> Elias: And he needs new glasses as well?
>
> Abbey: Yeah.
>
> Elias: What do you think is wrong with them?
>
> Abbey: They're too big for him, like, they make his eyes look bulgy. Like, I don't know, he should just go to Specsavers.
>
> Elias: Okay.
>
> Annie: And get a new coat.
>
> Elias: You don't like the...?
>
> Abbey: No, that's for girl's innit [points at the fur collar].

Cocker looks like a 'nerd', 'freak' and 'paedophile'; his hair looks 'greasy', the glasses are too big and he wears a girls' coat. In a fundamental sense, the visual markers in these pictures are morally and aesthetically 'wrong' to the respondents. Moreover, Abbey's reference to the eyewear chain Specsavers is instructive. Specsavers, a high street retail chain, is the largest in the UK, and very much denotes middle-brow taste. For Abbey, Specsavers signifies a good place to buy spectacles. Thus, while Cocker's spectacles may denote

---

[23] Abbey is referring to the title of a track by London rapper Dizzee Rascall.

high-brow taste in the wider symbolic economy of taste, they are here bound up with distaste as opposed to 'normal' spectacles from Specsavers.

Another picture I showed the respondents was of Anne Hathaway, a famous American actress who had starred in recent major Hollywood film productions (see Figure 5.8). The picture was taken from *The Devil Wears Prada* (2006), a film centring on the people working in the editorial office of a prestigious high fashion magazine, modelled after American *Vogue*.[24] Less 'arty' than the pictures of Jarvis Cocker, the picture is chosen to reflect a more 'mainstream' and glamorous type of high status taste. Again, most respondents were unimpressed, and neutral or indifferent at best.

Figure 5.8. Anne Hathaway in The Devil Wears Prada.
Source: Straight from the heart (2009).

One example is Tommy, who had the following to say when he saw the picture:

> Tommy: Actress. She's not beautiful. (No?) Nah, I don't really... I don't think she's very beautiful at all. [Inaudible] what's she's wearing is her jewellery. Her hat doesn't suit with what she's wearing.

Tommy's account of Hathaway has similarities with the one made earlier by Abbey and Annie of Cocker. To Tommy, Hathaway's style was poorly executed, with mismatching combinations of items, and in general, he did not find her attractive. Rather, his type of style was, as we saw earlier, the one

---

[24] Patricia Field, a famous stylist and designer, was responsible for the costume design.

worn by the girl in Figure 5.2 which he found 'nice' and 'sexy'. Abbey and Annie's reactions to Hathaway were also telling.

> Elias: Do you recognise this girl? What do you think of her style?
>
> Abbey: She looks kind of rich because she's wearing Chanel.
>
> Elias: Yeah, but do you like this style?
>
> Annie: No!
>
> Abbey: No! It's a bit teacher.
>
> Elias: [laughs] Okay so it looks too...
>
> Abbey: Sophisticated.
>
> Elias: Alright
>
> Annie: Looks like [inaudible] church [everyone laughs].

For the girls, Hathaway looked 'too sophisticated', adopting a style that is tidy and dull bringing associations to church and teachers. But it is important to note is that the respondents generally distinguished between the meanings of jewellery in this picture and 'chavy' ways of wearing jewellery. In Rebecca's words: 'I don't think it looks chavy, I think it's more like a fashion statement'. Or as Dan put it:

> Dan: That style, I don't think that's showing off. I think it's fashion. That's being in the fashion. Being in the fashion... everyday life.
>
> Elias: What about all her jewellery, I mean?
>
> Dan: That's not... It's a different kind of jewellery. That's not gold, that's not bling—showing off. That's fashion.
>
> Elias: So it's kind of different. Do you like this style or do you think it's...?
>
> Dan: I think this style is better than being a chav. Definitely.

Both Rebecca and Dan, then, made a distinction between Hathaway's style of wearing jewellery and chavy style in that the latter denotes excess and conspicuous display while the former is a fashion statement. This was also expressed by Katie, who *contra* many of the other respondents, liked Ann Hathaway's style, and not the least, her necklace.

> Katie [looking at figure 5.8]: Oh yeah, definitely. Chanel necklace.
>
> Elias: So you don't think it's chavy or too much?
>
> Katie: That's *classy*.

Katie instantly recognized Hathaway in the picture and identified the necklace as made by Chanel. To her, the necklace was the very opposite to chavy, that is, sophisticated rather than vulgar and excessive. This can be explained by the fact that she had adopted a style and taste which in many aspects departed from the dominant one in Satellite Town, and was somewhat more in line with Hathaway's. In general, however, the respondents drew boundaries against middle-class taste.

Conclusion: Tainted Markers of Taste

In this chapter, I have explored how the young respondents construct their identities in relation to visual markers of taste. The *leitmotif* throughout the respondents' narratives has been the symbolic power of the 'chav' discourse. When interpreting the term, the respondents drew on similar codes and narratives as those circulating in public discourse (as explored in Chapter 3). They often used the same language of contempt, where 'chav' is a non-respectable figure of the white British working-class characterized by a *lack* of cultural and economic resources. It was therefore a stigmatizing label against which the respondents drew strong moral-aesthetic boundaries and they actively disidentified with it. They used 'chav' to refer to others and never to themselves. Some respondents, like Mark and Katie, identified Satellite Town as an area were chavs were common. They also categorized their friend Aaron as a chav, though he himself strongly opposed such classification. And generally, respondents claimed that those they labelled chavs, like Aaron, also were likely to disidentify with the term. It was said that only a few might think that it was 'hard' to refer to themselves as chavs, though I never met any who did.

But the visual markers appropriated by many of the respondents—whether we are talking about wearing tracksuits, baseball caps, jewellery or tattooing the name of a loved one—risked positioning them in the stigmatizing 'chav' discourse. The notion of 'chav' thus encroached on their lifestyles. This proximity to 'chavy' practices could cause tensions for the respondents when they negotiated their identities, as it sometimes entailed identifying with markers of taste associated with chavs while simultaneously disidentifying with the term. This led some respondents to draw very fine distinctions between 'chavy' and 'normal'. Perhaps this was shown most forcefully in Katie's relationship to the practice of tattooing the names of family members, which she clearly valued. But these inscriptions of love had become associated with chavs. They had become tainted markers. This explains her wish to tattoo her mother's name in Hebrew instead of English, as she conceived this to be a non-chavy way of inscribing the name of a loved one onto your skin.

Similar forms of disidentification among young people labelled chavs were reported by Mark Rimmer (2010) in his ethnographic work on youths in a deprived council estate in Newcastle, as well as by McCullough and his colleagues in interviews conducted in Edinburgh and Newcastle (McCulloch et al., 2006; Rimmer, 2010). Rimmer's respondents also used the term to categorize others. Moreover, these accounts can be related to the white working-class women in Beverley Skeggs' (1997) study and their under-standings of the term working-class. She argued that the women actively denied or resisted being categorized as working-class, since it was perceived to be a stigmatizing label, signifying poverty, unemployment, danger, dirt and vulgar taste. This pathologization of working-class femininity, Skeggs argues, means that it cannot serve as a positive form of identification. This is even more apparent as regards the notion of chav. As a figure of non-respectable working-class people, it has become a word of abuse used to categorize others rather than oneself. Thus, the respondents' accounts reflect a more general phenomenon of people disidentifying with working-class labels and markers.

Moreover, this means that the respondents' meaning of 'chav' is very different from their understanding of 'emo'. For Mark and others, emo is a term with positive connotations to certain forms of music, values and lifestyles, with which he and other emos identify. These collective identifications with the term and concept 'emo' means that emo culture has characteristics usually attributed to subcultures.

However, evidence from the north of England indicate that youths who are labelled chavs, although disidentifying with the label, may perform other collective forms of affinities and identification, and thus display some sub-cultural features. The young people labelled chavs in McCullough and his colleagues' (2006) study identified with their place of residence and the groupings or 'gangs' to which they belonged. Similarly, Rimmer's (Rimmer, 2010) estate youths identified with 'new monkey' music, a mix of house and techno. This also served to strengthen their bonds and affinities with the estate and its history. Another example is the underground scene that has formed around the hard house music called 'donk' among working-class youths often categorized as chavs and often from deprived areas in northern England (VBS.TV, 2009).

Lastly, Anoop Nayak (2003, 2006) conducted ethnographic research of 'charver kids' in a deprived area in Newcastle. An important argument is that these youths form a subculture. In addition to adopting a certain style of appearance, they listened to jungle and rave music. And despite frequently being derided and stigmatized by others,

> in boldly exhibiting their subcultural style the *Charvers* were also overturn-ing these negative inferences in what may be considered an act of 'symbolic creativity' (Willis, 1990). In short, their stylistic activities were a celebratory statement of their 'underclass' identity and 'hardness' (Nayak, 2003, p. 90).

This implies that charver is a term with which young people identify. Nayak presents empirical material from one respondent, a 12 year-old called Nicola, who identified as a charver 'in certain situations' (p. 93) and who 'resisted' denigrations of charvers made by others. But in most of the respondents' accounts, charver was a derogatory label applied to others.

In the context of Satellite Town, however, the markers of taste associated with chavs are not features in what can be called a subculture, but rather constitute, as Annie put it, 'the fashion' in Satellite Town. Wearing tracksuits, trainers, jewellery and certain types of make-up or hairstyles, is less a statement of subcultural affiliation than an expression of popular taste in this working-class space. As we saw in Chapter 4, some elements of style, such as hairstyle and jewellery, were not limited to only certain groups of young people but were worn by people of all ages in Satellite Town. This demonstrated that the respondents' markers of taste were first and foremost expressions of personal identity rather than forms of collective identification. But these stylistic elements of working-class taste prevalent in this space have been tainted by their associations with chavs. As a consequence, it was much easier for the respondents to distance themselves from the chav label on a *discursive* level, than on the level of social practices, including their tastes and lifestyles. Even while disidentifying with chavs, they might still be positioned in the codes and narratives constructed around the term. This shows that the respondents could not simply choose their identities since they were structured by class and constructed in relation to the categorizations made by others. As we can see, this is very different from the post-subculturalist notion of freely chosen lifestyles unconstrained by class, which we discussed in Chapter 1.

Moreover, the respondents not only 'othered' chavs, but many of them also drew strong symbolic boundaries against visual markers of middle-class taste. Although these middle-class markers in the wider British (or indeed 'Western') context, embodied 'good' or legitimate taste, in the local context of Satellite Town, they clearly signified poor taste. This emphasizes that there is a social as well as spatial distance between working-class markers of taste appropriated in Satellite Town and those embodying middle-class taste.

6. Putting up a Front

This chapter turns from the discursive aspects of identity construction, which we studied in the last chapter, to the young respondents' embodied, and often tacit, performances of self in social interaction. The chapter explores how the respondents construct their identities through performances in face-to-face encounters. We are interested, not simply in people's behaviour *per se*, but as it is situated with one or more other people in specific time-space contexts. Thus, identity as performed cannot be reduced to be inherent in the actor and changed according to her will, but also depends on the properties of the social situation and is therefore to some extent always beyond her control. Identity is constructed in the dynamic of performances between differently positioned individuals interacting in the spatiality of Satellite Town.

If we recall from Chapter 1, when interacting with others, actors perform their identities through impression management (Goffman, 1959), which is conducted, often routinely, through verbal and non-verbal means such as manners, dress and body techniques. In this chapter, I extend this framework by making use of some further concepts from Goffman's toolbox. Identity as performed also revolves around maintaining and constructing 'face'. Face, Goffman says, is 'the positive social value a person effectively claims for himself by the line others assume he has taken during a particular contact. Face is an image of self delineated in terms of approved social attributes' (Goffman, 1967, p. 5). In this sense, a person's face is closely tied to her relative status vis-à-vis other actors in a social situation. Moreover it is bound up with her sense of self-respect as well as the respect of others in a given situation. And 'face-work' entails the expressive activity of upholding or maintaining one's face, particularly in relation to perceived symbolic threats to face. It is therefore an important aspect of impression management.

Moreover, in order to understand the dimensions of respect and social status in performances, particularly as connected to face and face-work, I also use the concepts of deference and demeanour (Goffman, 1956). Goffman conceptualizes deference as 'a symbolic means by which appreciation is regularly conveyed *to* a recipient *of* this recipient' (1956, p. 477). In this sense, deference is a central means by which respect towards others is expressed. Performances of deference can involve different methods, such as through greetings, compliments, gifts or inquiries into the other person's well-being. It is also important to note situations in which a person *withholds* deference, and how these are to be interpreted.

Demeanour refers to 'that element of the individual's ceremonial behaviour typically conveyed through deportment, dress, and bearing, which serves to express to those in his immediate presence that he is a person of certain desirable or undesirable qualities' (Goffman, 1956, p. 489). Expressions of demeanour symbolize a person's self-respect; a person who is sloppily dressed comes across as someone who is badly demeaned and thus who is morally failing to care properly for himself. Of course, the interpretation and value of a person's demeanour depend on the social context. Someone might perform with 'bad' demeanour in order to challenge or resist certain norms of behaviour, or to instil fear and respect in others and thus be identified as a 'tough' person. The relationship between deference and demeanour, Goffman notes, is one of 'complementarity' but not 'identity' (1956, p. 492). Thus, they are usually dependent on one another, but need not be.

Throughout this book, the formation of identities in Satellite Town has been analysed through the interpretative lens of social class, and this chapter is no exception. Firstly, performances of identity are bound with class on the level of the respondents' endowment of social, cultural and economic resources, which position them in the working-class. Secondly, the meanings of identity performances depend on the spatio-temporal contexts in which they are situated. Here, class processes take spatial form as performances are situated in the locality of Satellite Town, a working-class space. As I will show, identity performances in Satellite Town are to an extent structured by allegiance to certain cultural codes particular to this space.

Moreover, I focus on certain types of performances and situations in this chapter. A substantial part of the analysis will revolve around the interactions among the boys. In this context, I will explore how some of the performances are particular to the young male respondents, and in this sense tied to a working-class masculine identity. Here, I will also include my own interactions with the young people and my masculine performances as sources of data.

In what follows, I start by exploring some of the modes of self-presentation among the young people. Here, I draw out and distinguish between 'friendly' and 'tough' forms of display performed by the respondents. These are first and foremost distinguished by different ways of showing deference. I then study the performances typical among the boys and how these are expressions of masculine identity. I particularly focus on the importance of putting up a 'tough' masculine front and how it is connected to social status, including the pecking order existing among boys. In the third section, I further explore the meaning of keeping up a 'tough' front and its relationship to masculinity by studying how it is related to challenging the authority of the youth workers and the institutional context of the youth clubs. I do this by interpreting an incident I experienced with a 14 year-old boy called Nicky. In conclusion, I identify the wider implications of the themes we have explored.

Modes of Self-Presentation

Before I started working at Northside, I chatted with Jane, a long-term resident in the New Estate and administrator at the youth club. I told her briefly about my PhD project. 'You're brave, working with young people. I like many of the young people, but some of them are awful', she said and laughed. But my initial impression from the youth clubs was of the relaxed and friendly atmosphere of these spaces. I found this particularly true at Northside, which was frequented by people such as Aaron, Dan, Katie, Abbey, Mark and Rebecca, all of whom we met in last chapter. They and many other young people displayed 'friendly' modes of self-presentation, that is, performed in ways following common norms of propriety, particularly by showing deference. These displays of deference in casual encounters were shown in numerous ways. I will use the performances of Aaron and Katie as illustrations.

Aaron had a cheerful and straightforward way with people, and often used lively gestures when he wanted to explain something. Often smiling, he had an 'open face', looking straight at you when speaking. In so doing, he displayed a positive sense of acknowledgement, of showing recognition of the person with whom he interacted. Thus, once when he joked with me saying, 'Elias, a real bad ass!', I could not take offence, as it was said in such cheerful tone, devoid of spiteful undercurrent. Katie was also a cheerful person. Her deference behaviour was to a large part embodied in her feminine manners and body techniques, as in the way she greeted people in her high but soft voice with a smile and a little wave with the hand. Or when she was sitting at one of the tables in the table tennis room working on a small pillow. She was cutting out the letter A from a bit of cloth she was going to sew on to the pillow. I asked her what she was going to write. 'Adam', she answered. 'Adam?' 'That mixed race boy with the jacket', she said and pointed at a boy in the adjacent room. 'He's my friend. I've already made a pillow to Carl'.

While these observations may seem trivial (people were nice, so what?), they should be understood in relation to other forms of performances common among young people in Satellite Town. In Chapter 4, we saw that even though most respondents claimed that they felt safe in Satellite Town, many of them associated the area with violence, muggings and social problems—a 'rough' and dangerous place with gangs and other people 'causing trouble' or 'terrorizing Satellite Town'. In relation to this, Katie said that 'everybody [in Satellite Town] seems to have an attitude problem'. Dan provided an explanation: 'It's 'cause there's quite a lot of young people in Satellite Town.

You're gonna get it. Everyone's gonna think they're big ones'. For him, the large number of young people created competition and conflict.

Some of the young people displayed the 'attitude' Katie was talking about, which can be conceptualized as different ways of putting up a front— of displaying what could be called 'tough' manners. These were often inconsistent with common rules of propriety, like refraining from showing deference. One way of putting up a front was to adopt a 'cool' stance, of displaying what is usually coded as distance and reserve, and sometimes also arrogance or boredom. It was important here to maintain expressive control and to show restraint rather than excitement. Johnny, aged 14 and a frequent visitor at Northside, often put up a 'cool' front. He seldom looked directly at people, often had a serious expression on his face and rarely smiled. This could make him appear bored and dismissive of those around him.

Johnny usually participated in the highly popular football games in the gymnasium. These sometimes became quite heated affairs, for example, when one's own or the opposing team scored. People would cheer or show their frustration. Johnny seldom changed his expression and would continue to look unfazed. His restrained or cool demeanour was often coupled with the withholding of deference towards others. For instance, one evening when I was playing badminton with three other boys in the gymnasium, I saw Johnny entering and greeted him with 'You alright'. He ignored me, looking elsewhere and continued walking into the hall with slow strides. Thus he refrained from showing a routine form of presentational deference by returning a greeting.

Having said that, he sometimes let down his guard, like on his birthday, when he behaved like a happy child. On that occasion, he was really cheerful and smiling, running back and forth throughout the youth club. In these situations, it became even more apparent how reserved he usually was. This shows the situational nature of identity performances, of how social interaction is bound up with, and depends on, time and place.

Performing 'cool' was generally more common among boys but performed by some girls as well. For instance, Annie could in some contexts display such 'cool' manners. During an interview with Abbey, Annie came by and joined in. She was by far the most reserved subject I'd interviewed to that point. She looked straight at me without blinking or moving her face. Or she ignored me, leaning forward and resting her elbow on the table while looking away as if she couldn't care less about what I was saying. She did this to provoke me, but rather than a hostile act, she did this mostly to tease me. When she interacted with Abbey, however, she dropped her guard and displayed 'friendly' manners. They laughed and joked. But after a while, she also opened up to me, and fully participated in the interview. This turnabout was induced to a great extent by the fact that I was also interviewing her friend Abbey.

In sum, the performances among the young people could be idealtypically distinguished between 'friendly' and 'tough', an important part characterized by different types of deferential behaviour. But these performances cannot be conceived as personal characteristics inherent to the respondents. Rather, they are highly contextual, depending on time and place as well as on the relationship between the interactants. As we saw in the example of Johnny, and explored further in this chapter, some youths could display 'tough' manners in one situation but perform in 'friendly' ways in another.

Performing Masculinity

I will now focus on some of the performances specific to the boys and how they served as expressions of masculine identity. I will explore how masculine identity performances are bound up with the status order among boys. I will also study the role of body techniques and embodied forms of taste in performing masculine identity. But first, I will look at the characteristically masculine ways of putting up a front or 'tough' performances. While 'cool' manners where performed by both girls and boys, more aggressive or hostile forms of display were largely performed by boys. One such display occurred one evening at Northside. I was standing at the door with Gary. Many people arrived in groups and entered the youth club at the same time, leaving Gary busy with handling the 50p entrance fee. Suddenly, I saw that a boy in his early teens was about to enter without paying. I fixed him with my gaze, its intended non-verbal meaning being, 'Don't think you can get in without paying'. When he saw me looking at him, he stopped, turned towards me with pushed-back shoulders while stretching out his chest. With a serious expression on his face, he returned my gaze and said: 'Why are you looking at me like that!?' I continued looking at him with the same expression for several seconds. The boy turned to Wayne, gave him a 50p coin and then walked in. I was surprised by the force with which he reacted, and also by the fact that a boy in his early teens was 'squaring up' against an adult like myself who was physically much taller and stronger. A very similar incident happened a few weeks later in the pool room. I and a boy, coming from different directions, accidentally touched each other's backs. It was a slight touch. When I turned around, he was squaring up in front of me, shoulders pushed back and chest stretched, in a similar way to the previous encounter. He tilted his neck slightly, as he looked me in the eyes. It was as if he was prepared for a fight. Surprised, I smiled at him to communicate that I didn't bump into him on purpose. He turned and continued walking. Again, I was surprised by the sudden, emphatic reaction.

In both situations, the boys interpreted my behaviour—the first time a stare, the second time a nudge—as expressions of disrespect, and thus as threats to face. They responded, or challenged me in return, by performing aggressive, hostile face-work. Protecting their self-respect, the boys upheld a tough demeanour, showing that they were people who don't let anyone put them down and fail to show them proper deference. Such masculine identity performances in 'man to man' situations sometimes took place in the youth clubs and could threaten to evolve into fights, though this rarely happened as staff or other young people usually were able to calm things down. And in general, putting up an aggressive front and craving deference was central to some of the boys' performances of identity. I will further explore this through some situations at Northside involving Tommy, whom we met in the previous chapter. After a session, I said to Gary: 'Tommy seemed to be upset tonight'. I had walked past the gymnasium and seen Tommy talking in a high voice with Gary. 'Which one of the times?' Gary asked, and told me that the boy often became upset. 'He takes it all very seriously. Even if it's just playing around, to him it's serious', Gary said. I then remember a few weeks earlier when he went in to the table tennis room and told everyone how easily he would beat Ryan, a tall, polite boy of 14 with brown stripy hair and flushed cheeks. During the game, however, Tommy made some easy mistakes and immediately lost his good-humoured, assured mood and seemed to get frustrated.

But the most profound way this came across was in an incident that took place in the gymnasium during a game of football. Tommy had broken the rules and brought a soft drink into the gymnasium. As a consequence, David, a member of the staff, banned him from the gymnasium for the remainder of the evening. Tommy seemed very upset: 'Look, I'm seventeen years old! He's treating me like I'm a mug!' He repeated this several times. Gary tried to calm him down and put a hand on his shoulder. Tommy pulled back his shoulder and upper body away from Gary's hand to show that he didn't want to be touched. But his anger was not addressed to Gary, but to David: 'You [Gary] wouldn't have done it [banned me]. You would've given me a chance. But *he* [pointing at David] is treating me like I'm a mug!' Later on as the session was about to end, Tommy walked through the premises and said goodbye to everyone and shook the hands of the boys and male staff before heading home. He had a very firm handshake. It is notable that Tommy also often greeted people with a handshake when he entered the youth club. While a few of the older respondents sometimes did this as well, most greetings and good-byes, where informal of the 'you alright' or 'see you later' variety.

I want to make two points here about performing masculinity. The first is that Tommy's self-image and self-respect were undermined. In short, he lost face. He was both one of the oldest boys at Northside and one of those with the highest social status. As he pointed out, being 17 years of age, he considered himself old enough to be treated like someone who could take responsibility for himself. By banning him, David did not show deference to this fact, and therefore treated him 'like a mug'. David's putdown made Tommy come across as a person with bad demeanour. Humiliated, he responded by performing furious face-work. Secondly and related to this, his serious manner of performing the formal (at least in the context of the youth club) ritual of presentational deference in shaking everyone's hands before leaving, was a way to show respect and thereby giving off the impression of being a respectable person. By doing this, Tommy was upholding good demeanour.

Dress, body techniques and non-normative masculinity

For many boys in Satellite Town, performing masculine identity entailed certain 'manly' body techniques and ways of appropriating visual markers of taste embodied in dress and appearance. One typical masculine body technique, especially among those displaying 'tough' demeanour, was to stand or walk with the upper body slightly slouched, the arms hanging wide at the sides, with the legs quite far apart. The masculine character of those body techniques were further emphasized through embodied forms of taste and style, for instance, by adopting short-cropped hair, wearing a thick gold necklace, a big sovereign ring or baggy streetwear clothing. The latter was especially apparent among the younger male respondents, who although smaller than the older respondents, tended to wear tracksuits of a similar size. As a consequence, boys with a slim build could look quite 'big', and in this sense more masculine.

When I interviewed Dan, he associated some forms of dress, namely the practice among some boys of wearing two pairs of tracksuits or having a cut in the eyebrow, with 'gang members'. He categorized them as 'the people who think they're hard' or 'the sort of people who wear jewellery... it's 'their kind of fashion'. As for Dan himself, in the previous chapter, we learnt that he had a more toned down, casual clothing style. He explained that to 'show off', that is, dress conspicuously, was not in line with his Christian values and therefore not part of his demeanour. This could also be shown in Dan's body techniques which were not as expressly masculinely coded as those adopted by many other boys.

Another boy who deviated from the norm was Mark. As I mentioned in the last chapter, he was well-liked among the young people and staff at Northside, and generally well-integrated into Satellite Town where he had many friends, some with high status like Aaron and Tommy. As we learned in the last chapter, Mark identified himself, and was categorized by others, as an emo or 'chemo', that is, 'a cross between a chav and an emo'. He also had many friends that he categorized as chavs. With his black-coloured, straggly coiffure and black skinny jeans he clearly looked different from most other youths at Northside. And like Dan, he also adopted different body techniques, which sometimes were somewhat femininely coded. For instance, sometimes when he was walking or running it was sometimes like strutting. This was accentuated by his tall and slender physique. He was also open about being bisexual, something he could mention calmly and matter-of-factly in conversations with his dark, low voice. Thus, he appeared very confident and open about his own sexuality, and it was clear that it was not out of place for him to say such things. It did not come across as a major issue.

Moreover, Mark could also display femininely coded manners. For example, one evening at Northside, Mark and Charlotte sat next to one another on the sofa in the pool room. They said nothing. After a while, Charlotte, who had seemed low most of the evening, leaned over and hugged Mark. He hugged her back, holding her for a while, consoling her. This public display of friendly affection, of showing a 'soft' side, could be seen among all female friendships but not ones involving boys. In general such public display of emotions were rarely displayed by boys, and only if it involved 'snogging' a girlfriend. This is in line with research identifying emotional detachment as an aspect of masculinity (Bird, 1996; McGuffey & Rich, 2008).

I have argued in this section that embodied forms of taste and style as explored in the previous chapter are bound up with performing masculinity. The dominant form of masculinity in Satellite Town often entailed wearing streetwear clothing and appropriating explicitly masculinely coded body techniques. But to deviate from the norm did not necessarily mean social marginalization or low status, as is shown in the case of Mark.

Masculine Performances and Social Status

In this section I will explore how masculine performances of identity are related to social status, that is, the relative prestige according to which boys were ranked vis-á-vis one another. This created a pecking order among boys. Tommy was one of those with the highest status at Northside and this was shown by the fact that he could dominate situations, particularly when younger members were involved. He often did this through 'tough', aggressive forms of display. For instance, one evening, we had arranged for the members to play badminton in the gymnasium where football usually was played. This sparked complaints among several boys, and Tommy—a keen footballer—in particular. He walked around in the gymnasium and looked around him. 'Do you wanna play?' Tommy asked rhetorically. But his presence was such that no one dared to say that they wanted to play. 'Come on! Look, no one wants to play!' When Tommy finally left (after several minutes), things cooled down. Seeing that no one was playing, Chloe and Stacey, two of the younger members, each took a bat, ran up on the court and started playing. About an hour later, in the middle of a game of badminton, Tommy walked in again and loudly proclaimed: 'Let's play football! No one wants to play!' Again, none of the other youths said anything. Tommy and a few others started taking away the equipment. Then Gary walked in and reprimanded Tommy.

Thus, we can see how Tommy's display of status was enacted through aggressive, masculine forms of display. This was shown in his confrontational, forceful manner in attempting to get his way, particularly apparent when he decided to remove the equipment, although such decisions could only be made by the staff.

Status differences created a pecking order among the boys. And one's position in this pecking order was closely bound up with one's ability to put up a 'tough' masculine front. I will illustrate this through discussing two situations. The first occurred during a game of table tennis between Chad and Liam at Greenwood. Chad, aged 14, was known to display 'tough' manners. Described by a youth worker as 'that chubby boy in a hat', he wore a black hat, black T-shirt with 'fcuk' (the French Connection logotype) written on the chest and tracksuit bottoms. Liam was two years younger than Chad. He was a sociable and talkative person, and unlike many others, particularly older boys, had not developed the self-consciousness and awareness, nor learnt and embodied the skills, of putting up an assertive, aggressive front. Like Chad, Liam was also slightly larger than the norm. He was fair-skinned, had a freckled face and short-cropped blond hair. On this particular evening, he wore a T-shirt, grey cotton tracksuit bottoms with a large Umbro logotype in white letters across one leg and black Nike Air Max trainers.

It is clear from the beginning that Chad is the superior table tennis player, and throughout the game, Chad repeatedly puts Liam down for his playing skills. With slightly downturned lips, his face appears to display contempt, while he comments in a low voice on Liam's game. He scolds Liam for missing balls and once mutters 'fucking cunt' under his breath. A few times, he also—provocatively—and aggressively slams the table tennis rack on the tennis table. In contrast to Chad's display of assertive, aggressive masculinity, Liam doesn't answer back and is mostly quiet, often looking down and avoiding eye-contact. It looks like he is trying to concentrate on the game. When I rebuke Chad for his behaviour, his manner changes completely. He suddenly becomes very polite, standing with a straight back listening to me with full attention, saying that he will do as I say. Similarly, in another situation, this time at Northside, Chad is playing table-tennis with Tommy. And this time, Chad is dominated and bullied. Here, Tommy is the superior player and puts Chad down during the game, saying things like, 'You're pretty fast for a fat boy'. Chad looks down, saying nothing. The tables have been turned. From having been the older and the bully in the situation with Liam, he has now become the younger and the bullied. My argument here is that one's social status relative to other boys decides one's position in the pecking order. Status, in turn, is heavily dependent upon one's ability to put up a 'tough' masculine front. This was no means the only way of getting status; proficiency in sports, particularly football, as well as success with girls, were other obvious sources of recognition. And boys like Mike, who had good verbal skills, could also use these as a resource to master social relations and receive respect from others (though of course, verbal skills were highly useful in displays of 'tough' manners, as will be explored later on in the incident with Nicky).

Although it usually entailed performing 'tough', of course, masculine performances of status could also be displayed in ways not involving aggressive, hostile or reserved forms of impression management. Status could also be displayed in more good humoured ways through, for instance, bragging and other ways of showing off. In the following situation, Bobby, aged 17, brags to Tom, who is three years younger, about shoplifting. 'I've robbed JD [Sports] many times of, like, jackets. But I robbed Poundland once and got caught', Bobby goes. 'What [did] you steal?' Tom asks. 'A pack of biscuits or something. [I] think it was them Marylands'. Then Tom says: 'Can you rob me a phone?' 'I got one here', Bobby jokes and picks up his mobile phone from his back pocket.

Bobby here points to the irony of repeatedly stealing expensive clothes and accessories from JD Sports without problems, and then getting caught the first time he steals something from a store where everything costs one pound. But most importantly, by telling this story, Bobby also shows off in front of Tom. By bragging about his exploits as a shoplifter, he presents himself as someone with a daring, 'tough' demeanour.

Masculine identity performances, status and working-class space

Having explored the masculine performances of identity among boys in Satellite Town, I have argued that such performances often involve putting up a 'tough' front. Here, issues of face, which are bound up with upholding self-respect and being treated with respect by others, play a central part. On the one hand, this involves maintaining one's self-respect by trying to uphold a 'tough' demeanour, and not show any signs of weakness. On the other hand, this involves that one is treated with respect by others through being shown proper deference. In situations where this is not the case, where one is disrespected and thus one's face is threatened, to protect one's self-respect, a tough demeanour craves a swift response, often involving confrontational, aggressive face-work. Putting up a 'tough' masculine front also involves appropriating visual markers embodied in dress and appearance as well as body techniques.

Moreover, I have shown how masculine identity performances in Satellite Town are intimately tied to social status. The ability to put up a 'tough' front depends on one's status relative to the status of the other interactants. If the other person has higher status he may feel free to put you down and thus disrespect you. In such situations, as we saw when Tommy bullied the usually 'tough' Chad, it is difficult to uphold a 'tough' demeanour and be able to protect one's self-respect, especially if the other person is bigger, stronger and older than you. Rather, one is forced to perform in a submissive fashion.

In the pecking order among boys, then, the ability to put on an aggressive display and successfully show that one is a person not to be denigrated, is the difference between being dominant or dominated.

In this way, I would argue that putting up a masculine front through aggressive display is a cultural resource, a form of embodied knowledge of cultural codes. The ability to put up a 'tough' front is dialectically related to social status, in the sense of both being a means and a consequence of status attainment. My argument is that these performances are bound up with the boys' positioning as working-class, and thus part of the working-class culture in Satellite Town. An essential aspect of this is that the cultural codes performed and embodied through putting up a 'tough' front function as performance criteria by which social encounters in the spaces of Satellite Town are interpreted and negotiated. In this way, these masculine performances are not only tied to people but also to the particular context of Satellite Town as a place. My argument here is that the performances of masculinity are bound up with the relative lack of economic and cultural resources, and the dense social relationships of familiarity and proximity in this marginalized working-class space. In this context, we can understand the rationale for bullying someone. In a marginalized socio-economic context where few sources for value and recognition may seem available, to bully or otherwise 'put down' someone can be understood as bound up with the quest for status and respect as it may give one a sense of recognition and show that the person has 'tough' demeanour (cf. Phillips, 2003).

These observations can be related to Elijah Anderson's (1999) seminal analysis of public behaviour in a Philadelphia ghetto. In these extremely violent and deprived spaces, he argues that people have to orient their behaviour to what he calls 'the code of the street', that is, 'a set of informal rules governing interpersonal public behaviour, particularly violence' (p. 33). This code is tied to issues of respect, deference and aggressive display. Anderson argues that the code has arisen in a situation where law and order have broken down and a street law has taken its place. And his point is that a failure to perform according to this code can be a matter of life and death. Thus Anderson portrays a much grimmer situation than the one in Satellite Town, but the similarities lie, firstly, in the fact that a 'tough' front functions as performance criteria in interpersonal encounters in a particular place. Secondly, putting up a front can be interpreted as a protection in a milieu, which as we saw in Chapter 4, other people are perceived to be violent (see also Trondman, 1999, pp. 163-195; Willis, 1978)

The importance of 'tough' masculine identity performances in Satellite Town showed that it was the dominant form of masculinity in this space. The prevalence of these codes of interaction created an environment where the younger boys had to learn to put up a front as they got older. They had to manage their performances correctly—to act 'tough', aggressive and 'cool', to hold their nerve so as to not appear weak. Liam, still only 12, had yet to learn this. Diane, a youth worker at Greenwood, once told me that some of the younger boys could be really 'sweet', but as they got older, could in a short time turn into real 'mean' boys that were a 'nightmare' to handle in the youth club. During a debrief at Greenwood, the staff talked about one of the younger members, a small blond boy with braces. He was well-liked among the staff; one woman said: 'That boy is so sweet'. Then someone said: 'He'll probably turn out like his brother'. His older brother was apparently like him when younger but had recently become 'rude'.

Challenging Authority

Some of the ways in which the young people put up a tough front entailed various ways of challenging the authority of the youth workers. In this section, I will explore the meaning of acting 'tough' through challenging authority, and I will particularly explore how this is connected to performances of masculine identity. Lee, a boy of 14 years who went to Greenwood, often displayed a 'cool' front. He did not talk much and rarely smiled. During one evening at Greenwood he was alone in the gymnasium playing basket ball. He hit one of the strip lights in the gymnasium with the basket ball. Anthony from the staff went in with a broom and shovel to clean up the splinters from the broken strip light. Then shortly after it happened again, with Lee once more claiming it was an accident. During the debrief, people in the staff agreed that he obviously did it on purpose. 'Okay if it happens once. But twice? Come on!' Diane said. 'What are you gonna do?', Anthony said. 'We were short staffed the whole evening and both times Lee was by himself in the gymnasium with no one to watch him'. According to the staff once he had also broken a pool cue. He said that it was an accident but people in the staff thought otherwise. 'We gotta watch him', said one youth worker. Apparently Sarah had spoken with him and said that if he continued to break things, his parents would have to pay for the damage.

Not only boys, but also some girls challenged authority. Two such 'tough' girls were Mel and Lianne. They were both in their early teens. Lianne had long dark blonde hair, eyes made up with eyeliner and white eyeshadow, and wore jeans, brown ugg boots and a grey, very loose-fitting sweatshirt with a Nike logo on the chest. Mel had blonde shoulder-length hair, eyeliner accentuating her eyelashes, tracksuit and black ugg boots. The first time I saw them was one evening at Northside. From the moment they entered, they were playing and joking. Among other things, they reset the time of the clock on the wall, removed the 'No change given' sign on one of the vending machines, played around with the balls for the pool game, and poked me and David, a member of the staff, on our legs and behinds with pool cues. They were eventually thrown out by Gary, and I didn't see them at Northside again, although I met them at Greenwood, as we will see in the next section.

Behaving like a 14 year-old

I will now explore how challenges to authority are tied to performances of masculine identity. I will do this through exploring a series of interactions which led to an incident at Greenwood between me and a 14 year-old boy called Nicky. As will become apparent, during the incident, I came to perform masculinity very much like a 14 year-old in Satellite Town. In general, I usually tried to be and act 'like myself' or 'like a youth worker', but in some contexts, I sometimes started to perform—often routinely and largely unconsciously—in some ways like the young men, that is, according to the masculinely coded behaviour prevalent in Satellite Town. Following the argument in Chapter 2, I will include my own thoughts, emotions, affects and performances in the description and analysis of the incident. Doing this, I argue, brings further understanding of the meanings of masculine performances of identity in Satellite Town and how they are related to challenging authority.

The first I remember of Nicky was during one session at Greenwood when I saw a boy with short-cropped dark blonde hair in a fringe, wearing a bright red hooded jumper, tracksuit bottoms, trainers and a small shoulder bag (which was something of a fad among many boys at the time). He was all smiles while riding a mini bike from the entrance through to the emergency exit at the other end of the youth club. After the session, during the debrief, someone in the staff said that his name was Nicky and that he was known to be 'difficult'. I wrote this down in my fieldnotes and didn't think much more about it. It was some time later that I started to notice him more. He used to come in with a few other boys in his own age group, particularly Dazza, Leon and Dave.

I have my first prolonged face-to-face interaction with Nicky before one session at Greenwood. I arrive early, and in a good mood, feeling relaxed and self-confident, looking forward to the session. No one is at the staff entrance, so I go to the main entrance to ring the door bell. Outside the entrance I see a group of five young people in their early teens. It's Nicky and two other boys, one of them the tall and slender boy called Dazza, and two girls, Mel and Lianne.

The youths immediately approach me, with Nicky taking the lead. But theirs are not friendly expressions of deference. Rather, they spread out around me and comment on my appearance, ask me things and joke with me in a way that surprises me by its intensity and nature. 'Are you gay?' one of the girls asks me. 'You asking me if I'm gay? Why are you so interested? Are *you* gay?' I answer to challenge them, hoping to embarrass them. But they are completely unfazed and in a completely matter-of-fact tone, they provocatively say: 'Yeah, we are lesbians', then turn their faces towards each other and make a movement as if to kiss, though they never actually do so. Then Lianne, recalling the evening at Northside described above, says to me: 'Didn't I poke you with a stick?' 'Yeah, you did', I answer in what I feel is an easy-going way. She and the others laugh.

I ring the door bell, but nothing happens. I'm surprised; the door bell should work. Dazza, who has been quiet so far, points towards a section at the wall with a neutral expression and calmly tells me: 'The door bell's there'. Easily fooled, I look to where he is pointing, searching for a door, obviously without finding one.

Meanwhile, the verbal attacks continue. Lianne asks me if I'm sore in the bum after having been poked with the pool cue. This is the moment when the jokes turn sour. This is beyond joking. I'm surprised, completely taken aback by what to me is the malevolence of the verbal attack, and its unprovoked nature. From my original easy-going manner, I now try to maintain an adult stance, taking the role of the morally righteous youth worker. I say: 'If you don't treat others with respect, you can't expect to be treated with respect'. Hearing this, Nicky laughs and turns his face away with a mocking smile and says: 'Oh come on! Don't give me that!' as if to emphasize how hollow and pathetic my words are.

As I realize that I won't get into the youth club, I turn around to go back to the fire entrance to see if anyone with a key has arrived. 'What? You going home?' someone says to my back as I'm about to walk out. I ignore her. 'Yeah, fuck off', Nicky says in a low voice, barely audible. I stop and turn around to face him. 'Look, maybe you shouldn't come tonight [to the youth club]', I say seriously. To my surprise, his 'mask' falls—his 'cool' and aggressive manners fail him and he mumbles, something hardly audible, like 'Yeah...', and looks down. For a few seconds it is as though a more vulnerable person underneath appears. As I would learn later, this generally reflected his behaviour.

I walk back to the staff entrance and this time Sarah has arrived. She tells me that she usually turns off the door bell before sessions to prevent kids from abusing it. During the session, it becomes clear to me that I am Nicky's—and to some extent Lianne and Mel's—target for jokes and ridicule. This they do through sidelong glances, denigratory words said under the breath so to be just barely audible, and open insults. For instance, Nicky makes a very fast movement pointing his middle-finger making a 'fuck you' sign at me. This is a skilfully accomplished performance. Made in a subtle manner, it creates a more provocative and effective way of showing disrespect and undermining my authority than if made explicitly. 'Why did you make that gesture?' I ask. 'Gesture', he mimics in a mock 'posh', high pitched voice, all the while an ironic smile plays on his lips. Again, this is skilfully executed. Making fun of my speech, this time he puts me down in a more explicit manner, showing how pathetic I appear. He makes it clear that

I speak and behave in a snobbish, effeminate manner, which of course is the very opposite of putting up a 'tough' front.

My way of getting back at him is to be a nuisance. In a low-key, non-aggressive way, I disturb him by my very presence. For instance, when he is playing PlayStation I stand close by, looking at him play. It works. 'Just go!' he says after awhile. Towards the end of the evening he offers a sort of pact of mutual avoidance: 'Okay, I'll leave you alone from now on. I won't do anything to you'.

However, although initially, I pay little attention to the verbal and non-verbal assaults, I gradually get more and more provoked and finally I switch from trying (albeit unsuccessfully) to maintain the stance of an adult and youth worker, to someone who wants respect, who no-one is going to put down. In other words, I alter, rather unconsciously, my behaviour and start to orient my performances to the codes of interaction prevailing among many of the boys in Satellite Town. While Nicky is offering to leave me alone, I am determined not to let him get away that easily: I refuse to let him dictate the interactions that will follow. They will not be on his terms, due to his goodwill, but I will be the one to set the conditions. Moreover, I have a score to settle with Nicky. He is not going to get away with behaving like he have without consequences. He has to be put in place.

Two weeks later I'm back at Greenwood—jetlagged, having just returned from the United States. Among the first to enter are Nicky and his friends, including Leon, Dave and Dazza. When I see Nicky, anger boils up inside me, and it is like I am back to where we left off two weeks before. Nicky and Leon, a black boy of Nicky's age, go into the pool room, where I am standing, and they start to play. When Leon sees me, his face lights up in a grin and he greets me with an 'You alright'. He was not at Greenwood two weeks ago and probably doesn't know what happened. Leon's friendly greeting may confuse Nicky as he meets my gaze and mumbles 'Alright', too. He displays more vulnerable, insecure impressions, which he only showed in glimpses during our previous encounter.

I, on the other hand, want to show him that I am not going to show deference for him. Because of how he acted last time, he should not think I've got respect for him. But naively, I also thought that I had 'won', that he would not try to get back at me. That's why I was surprised at what came to happen. It begins while Nicky is playing pool, now with Dazza, and I am standing nearby (I am the staff member currently responsible for the room). Suddenly he goes and gets a table tennis bat. He uses the handle of the bat to hit the ball lying on the table. He hits the ball but the handle also smashes against the table. He does this a few times. Shortly after, he does the same thing but uses a pool cue, hitting the ball with force. All the while, a smile is playing on his lips. Of course, he does this to provoke me. And I know that he knows that I know.

'For fuck's sake', I mutter twice under my breath, and then tell him to stop. One basic rule as a youth worker is to challenge young people's use of swearwords, and here I am swearing at one of the boys known for his 'bad language'. 'For fuck's sake', he mimics me, triumphantly. He knows that he is getting me where he wants, that is, provoked and angry. Then he leans closely to Dazza's ear and in a low voice says something that I can't hear. Dazza answers with a sneer. It's obviously all part of a performance to provoke me further.

Leon stands several meters away from the rest of us, saying nothing, looking down with a serious look in his face. In fact, he looks grieved at what is happening, and it seems that he wants to stay out of the situation, and for the moment, not take any sides. Meanwhile, I respond to Nicky' provocations by teasing him back. I stand near the pool table and fix him with my gaze. He seems to become self conscious as he shoots a weak shot. 'Good shot', I say ironically, to mock him. 'Yeah...' he mumbles. Again, he displays a vulnerable, insecure side. But he is not the type to fold. A few seconds later, he has composed himself. It is as if he switches personality, and back is the seemingly self-assured boy. And he continues to wind me up in the same manner as earlier through a mix of very fine, subtle ways—small winks, gestures, glances, scornful smiles—and outright verbal taunts. And as before, he succeeds in 'winding me up'. He is winning. I try to beat him at his own game, but it is a game at which he is a master.

After a while, I decide to walk to the entrance where Diane and Simone from the staff are sitting. I tell them that I'm too angry at Nicky to remain in the pool room, so I switch place with Simone. 'Try to let it go', Diane tells me. I make an attempt and we try some small talk but I find it hard to focus on what we are talking about. Some minutes later, Nicky, Dave and Dazza pass us as they walk towards the exit. For some reason, they are left standing there. Nicky turns around and looks at me. He fixes me for several seconds with his eyes wide open and a playful smile, just to make me angrier and more upset. And this is where I 'lose the plot'. My blood boils and I look at him, furious. 'What? You angry?', he says smiling. 'Yeah', I answer, and then it all comes out: 'If you continue, I will go to jail because I will break your neck'. Nicky laughs at this, obviously not the reaction I'm after, so I say: 'No, I'm serious'. Of course, in reality, I would never do such a thing. His expression changes. He becomes very serious, even shocked. Diane tells him to leave and he goes out. Simone reappears. Outside, there is a loud commotion. Nicky is standing there with his friends and sounds upset as he says in a loud voice: 'He said he'll break my neck!' My words have sparked a scene.

Shell-shocked by my own words and by all that is happening, I rise, as if on autopilot, from the chair and walk up the stairs to the entrance, and stand in front of Nicky. We square up. Dave, looking upset, warns me that I'm standing too close to Nicky. As he says this, I suddenly realize what I have caused, namely a war-like situation. In this moment, all my adrenaline and anger disappears and is replaced by sadness at what is happening. They are just boys, and I've been behaving like one of them. I turn and walk back into the youth club.

Some minutes later, I speak with Diane and Simone. I tell them I should probably not work with young people any longer and that I better go home. They tell me that it would not be a good idea to go out by myself since Nicky and his friends ran off to collect sticks to attack me. Diane adds that she and Simone took the sticks from them. Nicky also called his dad. 'So they're out there, it's not safe to go out'. I decide to remain until the end of the session, and then take the bus home.

A few weeks after the incident, I was sacked and never worked at either of the two youth clubs again.[25] This was, formally speaking, the end of my relation with Nicky and his friends. But a month after the incident, I encounter Nicky again. It is a Sunday noon and the sun is blazing. Sleeping in and slightly hung over, I leave my flat to get the newspaper at the corner shop, next to the park, a few minutes' walk. Reaching the corner shop I'm disappointed to see that it is closed. The door to the neighbouring corner shop is open, but I know from experience that they mostly sell tabloids and do not stock the broadsheet I want. Still, I decide to walk in to have a look. I notice that Dave is standing at the counter and he glances in my direction. I realize that his friends—among them Nicky—are probably there, too. In a fraction of a second, I have to decide whether to turn around and walk back or continue walking in, but walking back was never really an option as that would be a display of weakness, of not daring to walk in and confront Nicky and his friends, so I continue entering, all the while trying to maintain expressive control (Goffman, 1959).

To the left of the counter where Dave is standing, I see Nicky in a knitted hat with his back towards me. Nearby, and also standing with their backs against me, are two of their friends. Since I know that the newspaper stand is just at the right of the entrance, I directly turn right when I walk in, take a quick look only to find that they haven't got my choice of newspaper, then walk straight out again. It cannot have taken longer than ten or fifteen seconds. It is a tense moment.

---

[25] The main reason for sacking me was bureaucratic. At the time of the incident I was not registered with the Criminal Registration Bureau (CRB), which is compulsory for all youth workers. But since I was a volunteer, I was allowed to start working even while still not registered. By the time of the incident, I thought the registration had gone through as several months had passed since my application was submitted, and no one had told me anything about encountering any obstacles. But after the incident I was informed that the CRB had been declined as one of the three documents I had submitted to prove my identity was deemed invalid. Consequently, it was a great embarrassment to Sarah, the caretaker at Greenwood, to have a misbehaving youth worker without a CRB. And obviously, without a CRB I could no longer work at any of the youth clubs.

As I walk out I can hear one of the boys say something, but I cannot hear what. I walk back rather slowly, not only because I now feel rather relaxed, but also to show the boys this, in case they've gone out of the shop and see me. I also make sure not to turn around, as I don't want to show them that I 'care' about them, which also would be a sign of weakness. Only after I've walked some distance do I turn around, but I cannot see them. Maybe they've gone to the bus stop, I ponder. Shortly after, I see the bus approaching and as I reach the crossing, the bus stops next to me, waiting for cars driving by. Now, this is another tense moment, as I realize that they're probably in the bus. I mobilize my strengths to make the right impressions. Self-consciously, I ignore the bus until it stops next to me and then I turn my head to look at it. I see several youths inside the bus, among them Nicky and his three friends. They turn and see me, too. I brace myself for what I think is to come: hostile, mocking gestures. But while they shout and wink, and someone thumps his palms on the window, they do so while smiling and laughing. Surprised and amused, I return the greeting in a 'cool' manner by raising my eyebrows and offer a little smile.

Afterwards, I start to think that it would be nice to become reconciled with these boys—indeed, I very much interpreted their greeting as their way of showing that we are no longer 'at war' with each other. But as it happened, I never saw Nicky again.

How can we make sense of this incident? As in other situations described throughout this chapter, Nicky, his friends and this time, also myself, all performed in a 'tough' manner according to the codes of interaction in Satellite Town. But the ways in which Nicky and his friends ridiculed and 'put me down' were particular in their intensity and persistence. And we should also note how volatile and fragile Nicky's performances of masculinity were. Beneath his assured, arrogant face-work, an insecure, vulnerable child sometimes appeared. And in Nicky's reputation as a serial trouble-maker, there was a sense that he was going down a dangerous, self-destructive path. Sarah told me that a week after the incident Nicky was banned from Greenwood after threatening another member of the staff. A youth officer I spoke with told me that if Nicky continued on this trajectory, when he became older, he would eventually encounter other institutions such as the police.

Thus, while Satellite Town in general is a relatively marginal space, Nicky's situation seemed particularly insecure. Nicky performed what Raewyn Connell (2005 [1995]) has called 'protest masculinity'. It is formed in volatile situations such as Nicky's, which was characterized by poor prospects, economic marginality and a lack of cultural resources with wider legitimacy outside of the boundaries of Satellite Town. To develop the argument made earlier, in such a volatile life situation, performances of self in social interaction become a source of value. That is why notions of respect, keeping up a front and facework become so important. In this sense, Connell notes that protest masculinity often entails spectacular display, whether it is through clothes, body techniques, gestures, words or the use of physical violence.

As I argued earlier, displaying a 'tough' front and bullying other boys increased one's standing and was a source for respect, which gave the person a form of value or recognition. In this context, to denigrate and ridicule a youth worker functioned in the same way. Thus, we can understand why Nicky and his friends put me down for being snobbish and effeminate or 'gay'. And this was far from an isolated event. The staff at Greenwood told me that Nicky had bullied a former youth worker for an extended period, amongst other things repeatedly calling him 'gay'. Here Nicky defined his own masculine identity through drawing boundaries against mine and others' effeminate, 'posh' performances. By devaluing and femininizing the performances of others, he enhanced his own worth and sense of manliness. Similar dynamics can be identified in Mairtin Mac an Ghaill's (1994) interviews with the 'rasta boys', a group of Afro-Caribbean working-class boys who taunted academic black boys in their school, referring, among other things, to the latter using the homophobic term 'batty men'.

Moreover, in arguing that Nicky and others' challenges to authority were connected to a quest for status and value, my analysis is similar to the one made by Anette Hemmings (2002) in her study of violence, respect and aggressive display in two inner city high schools in the United States. This also means that I don't interpret these challenges of authority as forms of counter-cultural resistance against a Bourgeouis institution as Willis does in his analysis of 'the lads' in *Learning to Labour* (Willis, 1977).

Nicky's concern with face could also be observed by his impression management in front of his friends. Nicky knew that I was not literally going to break his neck, but since he was playing to an audience of his friends, he had to respond as if this public threat should be taken literally. I had challenged him, and he had to protect his honour. Similarly, his friends reacted to the threat posed to one of the members in their group. By threatening Nicky, I threatened the entire group. Thus, the boys reacted as if a war had broken out and they went out and fetched sticks.

Lastly, as regards my own performances, we could see how I left the stance of the 'adult' or 'youth worker' and instead started to perform according to similar codes of behaviour as those adopted by Nicky and his friends. Thus, I played according to their rules. My ways of performing masculinity during the incident can be seen as a reaction to their disrespect and ways of feminizing me.

Conclusion

In this chapter, I have explored how the young respondents construct their identities through face-to-face performances. I here distinguished between 'friendly' and 'tough' performances, which on a general level, were characterized by showing and withholding deference, respectively. Moreover, 'tough' performances were often characterized by displays of 'cool' manners, such as distance, reserve, arrogance and boredom. I then primarily focused on the performances particular among the boys and how they served to express masculine identity. I argued that the dominant form of masculine identity performances in Satellite Town entails putting up a 'tough' front distinguished, not only by a 'cool' display, but frequently, by aggression as well. Central to putting up a 'tough' masculine front is upholding face. This means maintaining self-respect through performing with a 'tough' demeanour, on the one hand, and securing respect by being shown deference by others, on the other hand. To uphold a 'tough' masculine demeanour means that one protects one's self-respect in situations where others disrespect you through performing aggressive face-work. It is crucial to maintain one's nerve and not become subservient to others and appear 'soft'. It also entails adopting certain body techniques as well as visual markers of taste embodied in dress and appearance.

In Satellite Town, 'tough' masculine identity performances are intimately tied to social status. The ability to put on an aggressive display and successfully show that one is a person whom no one 'puts down', is both a source and consequence of status attainment, and thus a way of acquiring recognition from others. It is the difference between being dominant or dominated. In this way, I have argued that keeping up a 'tough' front is a cultural resource taking the form of embodied, often tacit, knowledge of cultural codes.

My argument here is that these performances of are bound up with Satellite Town as a relatively marginalized working-class space with a lack of economic and cultural resources, and dense social relationships of familiarity and proximity. In this context, where few sources for value and recognition may seem available, putting up a 'tough' front functions as such a source. While certainly an element in the construction of most types of heterosexual masculinity (Connell, 1995 [2005]), such performances become more emphasized and important in this space. This is especially the case for boys like Nicky who are in a particularly volatile, marginalized situation. To bully another boy or undermine the authority of a youth worker can be understood as bound to the quest for status and respect, as it may give one a sense of recognition and show that one has 'tough' demeanour. Unlike Willis' (1977) analysis of 'the lads', the young people in Satellite Town do not form a counter-culture engaging in resistance against dominant Bourgeois culture.

Moreover, mastering the cultural codes of putting up a 'tough' front is not only tied to status but also functions as performance criteria for how encounters in Satellite Town are interpreted and negotiated. In this way, these masculine performances are not only tied to people but also to the places in which these performances occur. In this sense, I have drawn out the importance of place in constraining and enabling certain forms of identity performances to be articulated. This may partly explain why an outsider like myself sometimes came to behave in a 'tough' manner during my stay in Satellite Town.

Connell (2005 [1995]) would probably classify the working-class masculinity performed by many boys in Satellite Town as 'marginalized masculinity', or in the case of Nicky, 'protest masculinity'. In her framework, these would be subordinated to 'hegemonic' middle-class masculinity. My argument here, however, is that in the context of Satellite Town, it is the 'marginal' masculinity which is the dominant type. But of course, this doesn't mean that tough performances reap approval from everyone. For instance, Katie complained that 'everybody seems to have an attitude problem' in Satellite Town. Moreover, people like Mark could deviate from the norm and still be well-liked and respected—though it should be added that he could do so by virtue of being integrated into the local community and by embodying a certain assertive demeanour.

Furthermore, in the wider British context, such 'tough' manners, particularly among volatile white working-class boys like Nicky, are frequently pathologized. Linda McDowell (2003, 2007) argues that in policy discourse, young working-class boys are conceived as yobbish, unruly and dangerous, and in need of control. Not the least is this apparent with the issuing of Anti-Social Behaviour Orders (ASBOs), discussed in Chapter 3. But the most powerful way in which this pathologization of white working-class boys appears has been through the figure of the chav. As we saw in Chapter 3, chav males are frequently portrayed as loutish, violent, yobbish and associated with vandalism, assault and muggings. They are also strongly associated with ASBOs, not the least shown in the expression 'chav ASBO'. Lastly, the boys' masculine identity performances also position them in the negative place images constructed around Satellite Town and its residents, as discussed in Chapter 4. These place images include Satellite Town's history as a council estate and its portrayal as a 'chav town'—a deprived space full of single mothers, 'dole scroungers', violence and criminality.

7. Conclusions

The central aim of this study is to examine processes of identity formation among the white, working-class youths of Satellite Town—particularly through the interpretative frames of class and place. In so doing, I have explored the dialectical interplay between identity constructed from the 'outside' through processes of social categorization, and from the 'inside' through processes of identification and boundary work. This echoes C. Wright Mills' (1959) contention that the aim of sociological research is to relate public issues to individuals' concerns and biographies. Thus, while primarily an ethnographic investigation, a crucial aspect has also been to study public discourse.

Exploring identity formation, I have proceeded from the 'outside and in'. The motivation behind the study was the recent moral panic over chavs in the British public realm and how it was related to the lives and identities of my respondents. Consequently, my first step was to study the public discourse on chavs, as reflected on web sites, in newspapers and in popular culture. I then turned to Satellite Town and its residents and explored the dialectics of peoples' identification with the area, conceived as a place and space. Subsequently, I examined the young respondents' construction of identity in relation to visual markers of taste. Lastly, I focused on the boys and how they constructed their identities through face-to-face performances.

In the following sections, I will discuss the main findings of the book and identify their wider implications and contributions, particularly in relation to our knowledge of the chav phenomenon and research on youth (sub)cultures and social class. I begin, however, by discussing the findings of this study in relation to the chav phenomenon.

'Chavs', Subcultural Theory and Working-Class Culture

On the level of public discourse, I contribute to our understanding of this social identity by framing it as a moral panic. I show that the figure of the chav has been constructed as a pathologized, non-respectable fraction of the white British working-class against which middle-class and respectable working-class people distinguish themselves and construct their identities. I also show that the chav phenomenon incorporates two historically familiar folk devils, distinguished along gender lines: young, violent working-class males and young, single, welfare dependent working-class mothers.

Moreover, I demonstrate that the figure of the chav has been a contested public issue explicitly discussed in terms of class, and to some extent whiteness. This is important in the light of recent arguments about the silence around issues of class in public discourse (e.g. Savage, 2000; Skeggs, 2004), including the debate about chavs (Lawler, 2005a, p. 800; Moran, 2006, pp. 19-20). I also argue that it is precisely because 'chav' is a label of class contempt directed towards white people that explains why this strongly derogatory discourse has gained such wide legitimacy. Indeed, my point is that this vocabulary would have been unthinkable if directed against, for example, gays or people of non-white ethnicity.

In the context of Satellite Town, I show how this stigmatizing discourse influenced the young respondents' identities in often powerful ways. Firstly, Satellite Town and its residents were positioned in the public representations of chavs and the places and spaces that they were said to inhabit. In local news papers and on the internet, Satellite Town was portrayed as a 'chav town' full of dole scroungers, teenage mothers, loutish kids, violence and anti-social behaviour. Moreover, aspects of the local style in Satellite Town, particularly appropriated by young people, also featured as elements in the public discourse on chavs. As a consequence, many respondents' ways of styling their clothing and appearance were associated with chavs.

Secondly, their positioning in these discourses was also apparent in how they constructed their self-identities. When interpreting the term, the respondents drew on similar codes and narratives as those circulating in public discourse. 'Chav' was therefore a stigmatizing label against which they drew strong moral-aesthetic boundaries. Thus, they actively disidentified with the term and used it to categorize others. Some respondents also identified Satellite Town as a place with many chavs, though they added that those so labelled were also likely to disidentify with the term. A few respondents claimed that 'some' or 'few' people might use the label, though I never met anyone who did. However, as some visual markers appropriated by the respondents positioned them in the stigmatizing 'chav' discourse, it was sometimes difficult not to be associated with the term, which led some to draw very minute distinctions between 'chavy' and 'normal'. In this way, their markers of taste had become symbolically tainted by the chav discourse.

What are the implications of this study for subcultural theory? I found that there was little evidence to suggest that in Satellite Town, the notion of chav constituted a subculture. This runs counter to Anoop Nayak's (2003, 2006) analysis of 'charver kids' living in a deprived and isolated area in Newcastle characterized by high crime rates and unemployment. Nayak identified the charvers as a subculture based on visual markers of style, 'illicit activities', music and the social stigmatization by others. He explained the emergence of this subculture as a 'survivalist' response to the effects of deindustrialization among 'socially and spatially excluded' youths (Nayak, 2003, p. 75). Similarly, Greg Martin (2009), through a reading of secondary sources (including Nayak's study), interpreted 'chav style' explicitly in classic CCCS fashion (see Chapter 1) as a subcultural response, that is, as an attempt to symbolically or 'magically' resolve structural contradictions among members of the 'post-industrial "youth underclass"' (p. 141). For both Nayak and Martin, then, chav subculture seems to have formed primarily among youths living under much marginalized conditions. In other studies conducted in the North of England, white working-class kids who are labelled as chavs can also be interpreted as displaying some subcultural tendencies, characterized by collective identification with, for instance, place of residence or to groups in this locality (McCulloch et al., 2006) and with music such as 'new monkey' (Rimmer, 2010) or 'donk' (VBS.TV, 2009).

However, an essential element of 'subcultural substance' (Hodkinson, 2002) lacking in these studies, is any evidence of collective identification with the term chav. This is also acknowledged by Martin (2009), although presumably he thought it unimportant. The only evidence of identification with the term chav that I have been able to find in these studies was in an interview conducted by Nayak (2003) with a 12 year old girl. Moreover, I also showed that in the public realm, self-identified chavs were largely absent, with well-known journalist Julie Burchill being a conspicuous exception. Rather, the overwhelming evidence is in line with this study in that 'chav' is first and foremost a stigmatizing signifier. Like the respondents in Satellite Town, the youths labelled chavs in Rimmer's (2010) and McCulloch et al.'s (2006) studies, used the term as a derogatory classification for others.

Previous studies of chavs, then, give some, but rather limited evidence of subcultural substance. In Satellite Town, however, the adoption of visual markers associated with chavs did not constitute a 'subcultural style' adopted among certain groups of young people who were, for instance, interested in a certain type of music, members of certain gangs or positioned as 'socially excluded'. Rather, these markers of taste were much more widely adopted as part of the local style or fashion, and thus were expressions of popular taste. Although they were particularly embraced by young people, to some extent they were also popular among people of all ages. The local style or fashion was rooted in the wider working-class culture of the area. Moreover, the respondents' appropriation of these markers of taste was first and foremost expressions of personal identity rather than forms of collective identification.

Thus, a general contention of this study is, first, that to understand the social category of chav, we cannot limit our analysis to particular groups or categories of youths or subcultures. We must also examine more widely the aspects of white British working-class culture that have been demonized by being positioned in the codes and narratives constructed around chavs.

A second argument is that the appropriation of local taste reflects an individualized rather than collective form of consumption. This points to a more general pattern of class formation in the contemporary moment, namely that individualization is a fundamentally classed process (Savage, 2000; Skeggs, 2004). Theorists such as Beck (1992) and Giddens (1991) argue that individualization processes are breaking down traditional class structures. This leads to increased reflexivity among people to choose and to construct their identities. Similar arguments are advocated by post-subculturalists (e.g. Bennett, 1999; Polhemus, 1996; Redhead, 1990) in relation to youth cultural forms. Moreover, Diana Crane (1999) argues that there has been a general shift in the consumption of fashionable clothing, from reflecting people's identifications with social classes to expressing their personal tastes.

Yet, while the respondents' appropriation of taste very much took an individualized form, theirs were not freely chosen lifestyles unconstrained by class. Instead, these markers of taste, *qua* elements in the local style or fashion, were part of the wider working-class culture in Satellite Town. Although the styles of the respondents very much reflected personal taste, and thus choices in the market, these choices were structured by their positioning as working-class in terms of their access to economic, cultural and social resources. This structuring of taste was also shown by the aesthetic and moral distinctions respondents made against markers of middle-class taste.

But the local style did not reflect what Bourdieu (1984 [1979]) calls a 'taste of necessity'. His argument is that the working-class adapt their preferences to material constraints and form a practical and informal taste oriented to satisfying basic needs. In contrast, many respondents adopted highly stylized, and often conspicuous, forms of dress and appearance, suggesting creativity and careful attention to detail. Branded goods were also important; this might be explained by the availability of inexpensive counterfeit items, but also suggests that the access to economic resources was not as limited as Bourdieu's analysis of working-class taste implies.

In addition to the aesthetic dimension, this study also bears testament to the power of moral boundaries in the formation of classed identities. While Bourdieu (1984 [1979]) emphasized how the middle-classes constructed their identities by othering the working-class through aesthetic distinctions, recent studies have shown an increasing interest in the moral dimensions of classed identities and boundary work (e.g. Lawler, 2005a; Reay, 2004; Sayer, 2005; Skeggs, 1997, 2004; Watt, 2006, 2009). Here, aesthetics is often conceived as interlinked with morality.

This moral-aesthetic denigration of working-class culture, and its consequences for identity formation, has been most powerfully formulated by Beverley Skeggs (1997) in her study of white working-class women in the North West of England. The pathologization of working-class femininity, Skeggs has argued, prevented it from serving as a positive form of identification for these women, who therefore resisted being categorized as working-class. These processes of pathologization and disidentification have been even more apparent in relation to the notion of chav. As a figure of non-respectable working-class people, it has become a word of abuse used to categorize others rather than oneself. Like Skeggs' work, this study shows the power of certain working-class markers in positioning and shaping people's identities. My point is that the symbolic power of these markers is not the same for everyone. While those who are positioned as chavs are pathologized, and constituted as lacking cultural and economic resources, for the middle-class person who dresses up in tracksuits and jewellery during a 'chav night', this lack is ransformed into a useful resource and source of enjoyment and identity formation, since by playing they can show what they are not.

Spatiality and the Formation of Classed Identities

In this final section, I will discuss the role of spatiality in the formation of classed identities in Satellite Town and more generally. Classed identifications and distinctions to a great extent informed both public representations and respondents' conceptions of Satellite Town. In Britain, council house estates are generally the spaces where the marginalized white working-class is most densely concentrated, and to an important extent, these spaces form segregated enclaves (Webster, 2008). They are also frequently stigmatized (Hanley, 2007; Hastings, 2004; Reay & Lucey, 2000). This was also the case in Satellite Town. As we have seen, the area and its residents were positioned in the place images constructed around 'chav towns' and some respondents identified Satellite Town as a place with many chavs. Moreover, most respondents acknowledged, at least partly, the spoiled identity of Satellite Town by drawing on similarly negative place images as those circulating in public discourse. The respondents' particularly expressed accounts of violence and muggings. But their social relations in, and images of, Satellite Town were also characterized by a 'strong sense of community', including strong social ties, familiarity, interpersonal trust as well as sense of safety. I therefore argue that social relationships in the area functioned as useful resources or social capital. Respondents also displayed a tension when negotiating place images of danger on the one hand, and place images of safety and familiarity on the other hand. Moreover, accounts of 'community' were coupled with suspicion and hostility against 'strangers', reflecting the long-standing distinction in British community studies between established and outsiders (e.g. Elias & Scotson, 1965; Frankenberg, 1957; Stacey, 1960; Strathern, 1981). Respondents also constructed negative place images of other areas they considered more dangerous.

The respondents' 'sense of place' was also strongly shaped by living in the physical and social milieu of Satellite Town. While very few displayed any sense of permanent attachment to the area, most respondents' sense of elective belonging (Savage et al., 2004) reflected a desire to live in a provincial area like Satellite Town with greenery, slow pace and sense of familiarity, but without the danger and violence they associated with the latter. Similarly, the urban, central parts of London appeared at both a cultural and spatial distance for most respondents who rarely went there. The city was conceived as an anonymous, busy and crowded space lacking 'community'.

The presence of 'community' in Satellite Town serves to counter the narrative in recent studies that the working-class communities of the industrial age have disintegrated due to deindustrialization and have become spaces characterized by loss, despair, suffering and displacement (Charlesworth, 2000; Turner, 2000; Wacquant, 2008). The area's history of being a council estate and its long-standing social and spatial isolation may partly explain the cohesion and familiarity as well as the boundaries reasidents drew against outsiders. Similar patterns of familiarity and close social networks have been observed in deprived, isolated neighbourhoods in the North East of England (MacDonald & Marsh, 2001; MacDonald et al., 2005; Nayak, 2003).

Moreover, I show that the performances of masculine identity among the boys in Satellite Town were not only related to class, but also to the characteristics of the place. A relatively marginalized working-class space with a lack of economic and cultural resources, few sources for value and recognition seemed to be available to the boys. As a consequence, performances of masculine identity through displaying a 'tough' front became such a source of value. It also generated social status. As the dominant form of masculinity in Satellite Town, the ability to perform such 'tough' displays was a cultural resource taking the form of embodied, often tacit, knowledge of cultural codes. Mastering these cultural codes, not only generated status and recognition, but more generally functioned as performance criteria for how encounters in Satellite Town were interpreted and negotiated. In this way, displays of masculinity were not only tied to people but also to the places in which these performances were situated. However, in the British public realm, including the place images of Satellite Town, these masculine identity performances were associated with chavs, ASBOS, 'yobbish' behaviour, violence, vandalism, assaults and muggings. Thus, what has the status of dominant masculinity in Satellite Town, is positioned as pathologized in the wider British context, and can in Connell's (2005 [1995]) terms more aptly be characterized as 'marginalized' masculinity.

Lastly, the study demonstrates the importance of place for understanding the formation of classed tastes. While the local style embodied the dominant taste in Satellite Town, we saw that in British public discourse it was associated with chavs and thus highly denigrated. Conversely, while some visual markers of middle-class taste may embody 'good' or legitimate taste in the wider British or 'Western' context, in the local context of Satellite Town, they most often signified bad taste. In this sense, there was a social and spatial distance between working-class markers of taste appropriated in Satellite Town and those embodying middle-class taste.

In relation to taste formation and performance of masculinity, then, notions of 'dominant culture' need to be spatially situated. What is dominant taste or masculinity in the working-class space of Satellite Town has a largely marginalized and denigrated status in a wider British context, and vice versa. In this sense, the formation of class identities and the valuing of resources are spatially dependent—symbolic class hierarchies and notions of 'dominant culture' may play out in very different ways from one locality to another.

The findings also show the importance of face-to-face interaction in locales for the constitution of classed identities, including notions of 'community', taste formation and performances of masculinity. This is particularly important in relation to recent arguments that identity and belonging have largely transcended locales in the wake of globalization (e.g. Scholte, 2000). This has led to an increasing focus on 'the symbolic construction of community' (A. P. Cohen, 1985). Consequently, the role of social relations in constructing and sustaining notions of community, has been underplayed or overlooked (Amit, 2002; Neal & Walters, 2008). In this study, I have not only studied the ways in which notions of community are 'imagined' (B. Anderson, 1991 [1983]), but also how they are tied to, and to an important extent rooted in, the social relationships and interaction situated in locales.

Appendix: Non-Ethnographic Sources

Newspapers

Qualitative content analysis was made of all articles published in six major National British newspapers featuring the term 'chav' (see Table A.1). In addition, I analyzed 36 articles from *Daily Star*, 11 articles from *Daily Express* and 21 articles from *Metro* in which term featured. Lastly, I analyzed in total 103 articles from two local newspapers, mentioning Satellite Town.

Table A.1. *National British newspapers*

Newspaper	2004	2005	2006	2007	2008	2009
The Daily Telegraph	7	19	7	9	14	15
The Daily Mail	8	20	33	30	63	41
The Guardian	41	123	78	88	66	41
The Independent	34	52	46	62	39	26
The Sun	44	87	65	27	47	40
The Times	60	183	111	98	43	39

Web sites

http://www.bbc.co.uk/news
http://www.chavfreebies.co.uk
http://www.chavscum.co.uk
http://www.chavtowns.co.uk
http://www.chavworld.com
http://www.communities.gov.uk/
http://www.dooyoo.co.uk
http://www.eastlondonlines.co.uk/
http://encyclopediadramatica.com/
http://en.wikipedia.org/
http://fiveprime.org/
http://www.freewebs.com
http://www.geofftech.co.uk/
http://glasgowsurvival.co.uk
http://www.hannahmorezider.co.uk/
http://www.homedefenceuk.com/
http://www.met.police.uk/
http://www.metafilter.com

http://www.nedculture.com
http://www.ons.gov.uk
http://www.openmagazine.co.uk/
http://rds.homeoffice.gov.uk/
http://www.retrotogo.com
http://uk.answers.yahoo.com/
http://www.utterpants.co.uk
http://www.viceland.com

Weblogs

http://www.aroundtheplanet.org
http://bigfatme.blog.co.uk
http://blog.peta.org
http://blogs.warwick.ac.uk/jodiefranklin
http://blogs.warwick.ac.uk/zoebrigley
http://chavblog.ohlog.com
http://chavspeak.info
http://cornerstonegroup.wordpress.com
http://davidthompson.typepad.com
http://dba-oracle.blogspot.com
http://dreamingarm.wordpress.com
http://emoskaterchick.spaces.live.com/blog
http://www.fetch-the-nets.blogspot.com
http://fitchavlads.blogspot.com
http://london.metblogs.com
http://www.muzzerino.com
http://peterreynolds.wordpress.com
http://secretperson.wordpress.com
http://www.septicisle.info/
http://stina-dontyoujusthate.blogspot.com
http://thecitydream.blogspot.com
http://www.tworepressedegotists.co.uk
http://vic-tim-project.blogspot.com

Internet discussion forums

http://boxrec.com/forum
http://britishexpats.com/forum
http://www.chavscum-resurrection.co.uk
http://www.chavworld.com/forum
http://www.cpfc.org/forums
http://www.eurogamer.net
http://www.facebook.com
http://www.israelmilitary.net
http://mydeathspace.com

Video clips

On the website *YouTube*, I searched for the word 'chav', then selected and analyzed the first 100 video clips that came up in the search results.

Broadcasted material

CHAV! 2005 (television program).
Eden Lake, 2008 (film).
Harry Brown, 2009 (film).
Lee Nelson's Well-Good Show, 2010 (television series).
Little Britain, 2003-2006 (television series).
Prescott: The Class System and Me, 2008 (television program).
Shameless, 2008-2009 (television series).

References

Adams, Matthew & Jayne Raisborough. (2008). 'What Can Sociology Say About Fairtrade? Class, Reflexivity and Ethical Consumption', *Sociology, 42*(6), 1165-1182.

Adams, Stephen. (2008). '"Chav" Nativity Casts Mary as A "Kappa-Slapper"', *The Daily Telegraph*, 9 December.

Agnew, John. (2005). 'Space : Place' in Paul J. Cloke & Ron Johnston (eds.), *Space of Geographical Thought: Deconstructing Human Geography's Binaries*. London: Sage.

Ajzenstadt, Mimi. (2009). 'Moral Panic and Neo-Liberalism: The Case of Single Mothers on Welfare in Israel', *British Journal of Criminology, 49*(1), 68-87.

Albion. (2009). *Jarvis Cocker Announces Melbourne Show*. Available at: http://albionblog.wordpress.com/2009/08/25/jarvis-cocker-announces-melbourne-show/ [Accessed 1 June 2010].

Amit, Vered. (2002). 'Reconceptualizing Community' in Vered Amit (ed.), *Realizing Community: Concepts, Social Relationships and Sentiments*. London: Routledge.

Anderson, Benedict. (1991 [1983]). *Imagined Communities: Reflections on the Origin and Spread of Nationalism* (2nd ed.). London: Verso.

Anderson, Elijah. (1999). *Code of the Street: Decency, Violence, and the Moral Life of the Inner City*. New York; London: Norton.

Anderson, Nels. (1923). *The Hobo: The Sociology of the Homeless Man*. Chicago: University of Chicago Press.

Anti Chav. (2008). *Congratulations Son, First Asbo*. Available at: http://www.anti chav.com/gallery.html%3Bsa=view%3Bid=18 [Accessed 3 November 2009].

Appadurai, Arjun. (1996). *Modernity at Large: Cultural Dimensions of Globalization*. Minneapolis; London: University of Minnesota Press.

Ask Lo Pan. (n.d.). *Lo Pan's Guide to Being an Emo*. Available at: http://www.ask lopan.com/archive3.html [Accessed 29 July 2010].

Aspers, Patrik. (2006). *Markets in Fashion: A Phenomenological Approach*. London: Routledge.

Aspers, Patrik. (2007). *Etnografiska Metoder*. Lund: Liber.

Asthana, Anushka. (2007). 'Names Really Do Make a Difference', *The Observer*, Sunday 29 April

Back, Les. (1996). *New Ethnicities and Urban Culture: Racisms and Multiculture in Young Lives*. London: UCL Press.

Back, Les. (2007). *The Art of Listening*. Oxford: Berg.

Bäckman, Maria. (2009). *Miljonsvennar: omstridda platser och identiteter.* Göteborg; Stockholm: Makadam.

Bailey, Brian. (2005). 'Emo Music and Youth Culture' in Pirya Parmar & Birgit Shirley Steinberg & Richard (eds.), *Encyclopedia of Contemporary Youthculture.* Westport, CT: Greenwood Press.

Barth, Fredrik. (1969). 'Introduction' in Fredrik Barth (ed.), *Ethnic Groups and Boundaries: The Social Organization of Culture Difference.* Bergen: Universitetsforlaget.

Bauman, Zygmunt. (1982). *Memories of Class: The Pre-History and after-Life of Class.* London: Routledge & Kegan Paul.

BBC News. (2008). *"Chav-Free Holidays" Defended.* Available at: http://news.bbc.co.uk/2/hi/uk_news/7853360.stm [Accessed 14 December 2009].

Beck, Ulrich. (1992). *Risk Society: Towards a New Modernity.* London: Sage.

Beck, Ulrich & Elisabeth Beck-Gernsheim. (2001). *Individualization: Institutionalized Individualism and Its Social and Political Consequences.* London: Sage.

Becker, Howard S. (1997 [1963]). *Outsiders: Studies in Sociology of Deviance.* New York: Free Press.

Bennett, Andy. (1999). 'Subcultures or Neo-Tribes? Rethinking the Relationship between Youth, Style and Musical Taste', *Sociology, 33*(3), 599-617.

Bennett, Andy. (2000). *Popular Music and Youth Culture: Music, Identity, and Place.* Basingstoke: Macmillan.

Bennett, Andy & Keith Kahn-Harris. (2004a). *After Subculture: Critical Studies in Contemporary Youth Culture.* Basingstoke: Palgrave Macmillan.

Bennett, Andy & Keith Kahn-Harris. (2004b). 'Introduction' in Andy Bennett & Keith Kahn-Harris (eds.), *After Subculture: Critical Studies in Contemporary Youth Culture.* Basingstoke: Palgrave Macmillan.

Bird, Sharon R. (1996). 'Welcome to the Men's Club', *Gender & Society, 10*(2), 120-132.

Blackman, Shane. (2005). 'Youth Subcultural Theory: A Critical Engagement with the Concept, Its Origins and Politics, from the Chicago School to Postmodernism', *Journal of Youth Studies, 8*(1), 1-20.

Boëthius, Ulf. (1995). 'Youth, the Media and Moral Panics' in Johan Fornäs & Göran Bolin (eds.), *Youth Culture in Late Modernity.* London: Sage.

Böse, Martina. (2003). '"Race" and Class in the "Post-Subcultural" Economy' in David Muggleton & Rupert Weinzierl (eds.), *The Post-Subculture Reader.* Oxford: Berg.

Bothwell, Claire. (2005). *Burberry Versus the Chavs.* Available at: http://news.bbc.co.uk/2/hi/business/4381140.stm [Accessed 30 July 2010].

Bottero, Wendy. (2004). 'Class Identities and the Identity of Class', *Sociology, 38*(5), 985-1003.

Bottero, Wendy. (2005). 'Interaction Distance and the Social Meaning of Occupations' in Lynne Pettinger, Jane Parry, Rebecca Taylor & Miriam Glucksmann (eds.), *A New Sociology of Work?* Oxford: Blackwell.

Bourdieu, Pierre. (1984 [1979]). *Distinction: A Social Critique of the Judgement of Taste.* Cambridge, Mass.: Harvard University Press.

Bourdieu, Pierre. (1985). 'The Social Space and the Genesis of Groups', *Theory and Society, 14*(6), 723-744.

Bourdieu, Pierre. (1986a). 'The Forms of Capital' in John G. Richardson (ed.), *Handbook of Theory and Research for the Sociology of Education*. Westport, CT: Greenwood Press.

Bourdieu, Pierre. (1986b). 'What Makes a Social Class? On the Theoretical and Practical Existence of Groups', *Berkley Journal of Sociology 32*(1), 1-17.

Bourdieu, Pierre. (1989). 'Social Space and Symbolic Power', *Sociological Theory, 7*(1), 14-25.

Bourdieu, Pierre. (1999 [1993]). *The Weight of the World: Social Suffering in Contemporary Society*. Oxford: Polity.

Bourdieu, Pierre. (2003). 'Participant Objectivation', *Journal of the Royal Anthropological Institute, 9*(2), 281-294.

Bradshaw, Ted K. (2008). 'The Post-Place Community: Contributions to the Debate About the Definition of Community', *Community Development, 39*(1), 5-16.

Brewis, Joanna & Gavin Jack. (2010). 'Consuming Chavs: The Ambiguous Politics of Gay Chavinism', *Sociology, 44*(2), 251-268.

Brubaker, Rogers. (1985). 'Rethinking Classical Theory', *Theory and Society, 14*(6), 745-775.

Brubaker, Rogers & Frederic Cooper. (2000). 'Beyond "Identity"', *Theory and Society, 29*(1), 1-47.

Brush, Lisa D. (1997). 'Worthy Widows, Welfare Cheats: Proper Womanhood in Expert Needs Talk About Single Mothers in the US 1900-1988', *Gender and Society, 11*(6), 720-746.

Burchill, Julie. (2005). 'Yeah but, No but, Why I'm Proud to Be Chav', *The Times*, 18 February.

CaptiveInnocencePhotography. (2008). *Chardonay Has Never Worked in Her Life*. Available at: http://www.flickr.com/photos/captiveinnocence/2339909691/in/photostream/ [Accessed 31 May 2010].

Castells, Manuel. (1997). *The Power of Identity*. Oxford: Blackwell.

Charlesworth, Simon J. (2000). *A Phenomenology of Working-Class Experience*. Cambridge: Cambridge University Press.

Chavs Test. (n.d.). *Chavs Test: Is U a Chav?* Available at: http://chavstest.com/quiz/index.php [Accessed 4 December 2009].

Clarke, Gary. (1982). 'Defending Ski-Jumpers: A Critique of Theories of Youth Subcultures', *Stencilled Occasional Paper No. 71*. Centre for Contemporary Culture Studies, University of Birmingham.

Clarke, John, Stuart Hall, Tony Jefferson & Brian Roberts. (2006 [1976]). 'Subcultures, Cultures and Class' in Stuart Hall & Tony Jefferson (eds.), *Resistance through Rituals: Youth Subcultures in Post-War Britain*. London: Routledge.

Clifford, James & George E. Marcus (eds.) (1986). *Writing Culture: The Poetics and Politics of Ethnography*. Berkeley: University of California Press.

Coffey, Amanda. (1999). *The Ethnographic Self: Fieldwork and the Representation of Identity*. London: Sage.

Cohen, Albert K. (1955). *Delinquent Boys: The Culture of the Gang.* New York: Free Press.

Cohen, Anthony P. (1985). *The Symbolic Construction of Community.* Chichester: Ellis Horwood.

Cohen, Phil. (1972). 'Subcultural Conflict and Working Class Community', *Working Papers in Cultural Studies, 2,* 5-52.

Cohen, Stanley. (2002 [1972]). *Folk Devils and Moral Panics: The Creation of the Mods and Rockers* (3rd ed.). London: Routledge.

Coleman, James S. (1990). *Foundations of Social Theory.* Cambridge, Mass.: Harvard University Press.

Collins, Michael. (2004). 'White Trash, the Only People Left to Insult', *The Sunday Times,* 17 July.

Company. (n.d.). *Chav Namer.* Available at: http://www.company.co.uk/other/chav namer/game [Accessed 4 November 2009].

Connell, R. W. (2005 [1995]). *Masculinities* (2nd ed.). Berkeley: University of California Press.

Crane, Diana. (1999). 'Diffusion Models and Fashion: A Reassessment', *The ANNALS of the American Academy of Political and Social Science, 566*(1), 13-24.

Cressey, Paul Goalby. (1932). *The Taxi-Dance Hall: A Sociological Study in Commercialized Recreation and City Life.* Chicago: University of Chicago Press.

Crow, Graham. (2002). 'Community Studies: Fifty Years of Theorization', *Sociological Research Online, 7*(3).

de Certeau, Michel. (1984). *The Practice of Everyday Life.* Berkeley: University of California Press.

Dennis, Norman, Louis Fernando M. Henriques & Clifford Slaughter. (1969 [1956]). *Coal Is Our Life: An Analysis of a Yorkshire Mining Community* (2nd ed.). London: Tavistock Publications.

Dent, Susie. (2004). *Larpers and Shroomers: The Language Report.* Oxford: Oxford University Press.

Denzin, Norman K. (1997). *Interpretive Ethnography: Ethnographic Practices for the 21st Century.* London: Sage.

Denzin, Norman K. (2002). 'Confronting Ethnography's Crisis of Representation', *Journal of Contemporary Ethnography, 31*(4), 482-490.

DETR. (2000). *Indices of Deprivation 2000.* London: Department of the Environment, Transport and the Regions.

Devine, Fiona. (1992). *Affluent Workers Revisited: Privatism and the Working Class.* Edinburgh: Edinburgh University Press.

Devine, Fiona & Mike Savage. (2005). 'The Cultural Turn: Sociology and Class Analysis' in Fiona Devine, Mike Savage, John Scott & Rosemary Crompton (eds.), *Rethinking Class: Cultures, Identities and Lifestyles.* Basingstoke: Palgrave Macmillan.

Digitaltoast. (2008). *Activities Abroad Offers Chav-Free Holidays.* Available at: http://www.digitaltoast.co.uk/activities-abroad-chav-free-holidays [Accessed 3 November 2009].

Class, Place and Identity in a Satellite Town

Elias le Grand

Academic dissertation for the Degree of Doctor of Philosophy in Sociology at Stockholm University to be publicly defended on Friday 29 October 2010 at 10:00 in hörsal 7, hus D, Universitetsvägen 10 D.

Abstract

The central aim of this study is to examine processes of identity formation among white, working-class youths in a marginalized area located on the outskirts of South London. It is primarily based on long-term ethnographic fieldwork but also on analyses of web sites, newspapers and popular culture. The study contributes to research on 'chavs', and on youth (sub)cultures and social class.

Identity is conceived as constructed through the dialectical interplay between 'external' processes of social categorization and 'internal' processes of identification and boundary work. The context of the study is the recent moral panic in Britain over 'chavs'. In public discourse, the term chav emerged as a way of pathologizing white working-class youths adopting specific visual markers of taste. The study shows that most respondents, and the area in general, were positioned in the stigmatizing discourse on chavs, and the spaces and places that they are associated with. When interpreting the meaning of chav, the respondents drew strong boundaries against the term, and used it to categorize others. In contrast to earlier research, the notion of chav is not related to a subcultural style adopted by socially excluded groups of youths, but primarily a form of categorization serving to pathologize important aspects of the working-class culture in the area.

The findings support the contention that spatiality plays an essential role in the formation of classed identities. In light of the stigmatizing perceptions of the area, the study explores the often ambiguous ways in which the respondents negotiated their sense of belonging, community and safety. Moreover, in relation to taste and masculinity, the study demonstrates how the construction and performance of classed identifications and distinctions, and thus symbolic class hierarchies, are related to the spatial context.

Keywords: *class, identity, place, chav, stigma, symbolic boundaries, youths, moral panics.*

Stockholm 2010
http://urn.kb.se/resolve?urn=urn:nbn:se:su:diva-43045

ISBN 978-91-86071-50-9
ISSN 0491-0885

Department of Sociology

Stockholm University

Stockholm University, 106 91 Stockholm

Durkheim, Emile. (1984 [1893]). *The Division of Labour in Society*. New York: Free Press.

Dyer, Richard. (1997). *White*. London: Routledge.

Edensor, Tim. (2009). 'Illuminations, Class Identities and the Contested Landscapes of Christmas', *Sociology, 43*(1), 103-121.

Elias, Norbert & John L. Scotson. (1994 [1965]). *The Established and the Outsiders: A Sociological Enquiry into Community Problems* (2nd ed.). London: Sage.

Ellis, Carolyn. (2004). *The Ethnographic I: A Methodological Novel About Autoethnography*. Walnut Creek, CA: AltaMira Press.

Evans, Gillian. (2006). *Educational Failure and Working Class White Children in Britain*. Basingstoke: Palgrave Macmillan.

Evans, M. D. R., Jonathan Kelley & Tamas Kolosi. (1992). 'Images of Class – Public Perceptions in Hungary and Australia', *American Sociological Review, 57*(4), 461-482.

Fay, Brian. (1996). *Contemporary Philosophy of Social Science: A Multicultural Approach*. Oxford: Blackwell.

Frankenberg, Ronald. (1957). *Village on the Border: A Social Study of Religion, Politics and Football in a North Wales Community*. London: Cohen & West.

Frankenberg, Ruth. (1993). *White Women, Race Matters: The Social Construction of Whiteness*. Minneapolis: University of Minnesota Press.

Fraser, Nancy. (2000). 'Rethinking Recognition', *New Left Review, 3*, 107-120.

Garland, David. (2008). 'On the Concept of Moral Panic', *Crime, Media, Culture, 4*(1), 9-30.

Geertz, Clifford. (1973). *The Interpretation of Cultures: Selected Essays*. London: Fontana, 1993.

Geertz, Clifford. (1983). *Local Knowledge: Further Essays in Interpretive Anthropology*. London: Fontana, 1993.

Geertz, Clifford. (1988). *Works and Lives: The Anthropologist as Author*. Cambridge: Polity.

Giddens, Anthony. (1979). *Central Problems in Social Theory: Action, Structure and Contradiction in Social Analysis*. London: Macmillan.

Giddens, Anthony. (1984). *The Constitution of Society: Outline of the Theory of Structuration*. Cambridge: Polity.

Giddens, Anthony. (1990). *The Consequences of Modernity*. Cambridge: Polity Press.

Giddens, Anthony. (1991). *Modernity and Self-Identity: Self and Society in the Late Modern Age*. Cambridge: Polity Press.

Gilroy, Paul. (1993). *The Black Atlantic: Modernity and Double Consciousness*. London: Verso.

Goffman, Ervin. (1956). 'The Nature of Deference and Demeanor', *American Anthropologist, 58*, 473-502.

Goffman, Erving. (1951). 'Symbols of Class Status', *The British Journal of Sociology, 2*(4), 294-304.

Goffman, Erving. (1959). *The Presentation of Self in Everyday Life*. New York: Doubleday.

Goffman, Erving. (1963). *Stigma: Notes on the Management of Spoiled Identity.* Englewood Cliffs, N.J.: Prentice-Hall.

Goffman, Erving. (1967). *Interaction Ritual: Essays on Face-to-Face Behaviour.* New York: Doubleday.

Goldthorpe, John H. (1996). 'Class Analysis and the Reorientation of Class Theory: The Case of Persisting Differentials in Educational Attainment', *The British Journal of Sociology, 47*(3), 481-505.

Goldthorpe, John H. (2007). *On Sociology* (2nd ed.). Stanford, Calif.: Stanford University Press.

Goode, Erich & Nachman Ben-Yehuda. (1994). *Moral Panics: The Social Construction of Deviance.* Cambridge, Mass.: Blackwell.

Grusky, David B. & Kim A. Weeden. (2001). 'Decomposition without Death: A Research Agenda for a New Class Analysis', *Acta Sociologica, 44*(3), 203-218.

Habermas, Jürgen. (1989). *The Structural Transformation of the Public Sphere: An Inquiry into a Category of Bourgeois Society.* Cambridge, Mass.: MIT Press.

Hall, Stuart. (1990). 'Cultural Identity and Diaspora' in Jonathan Rutherford (ed.), *Identity: Community, Culture, Difference.* London: Lawrence and Wishart.

Hall, Stuart. (1996). 'Introduction: Who Needs Identity?' in Paul Du Gay & Stuart Hall (eds.), *Questions of Cultural Identity.* London: Sage.

Hall, Stuart, Charles Critcher, Tony Jefferson, John Clarke & Brian Robert. (1978). *Policing the Crisis: Mugging, the State, and Law and Order.* London: Macmillan.

Hall, Stuart & Tony Jefferson. (2006 [1976]). *Resistance through Rituals: Youth Subcultures in Post-War Britain* (2nd ed.). London: Routledge.

Hampson, Tom & Jemima Olchawski. (2008). 'Ban the Word "Chav"', *The Guardian*, 15 July.

Hanley, Lynsey. (2007). *Estates: An Intimate History.* London: Granta.

Hannah More Zider. (2004). *Chav Christmas Decorations 2004.* Available at: http://www.hannahmorezider.co.uk/chavychristmas.htm [Accessed 2 May 2009].

Hannerz, Ulf. (1996). *Transnational Connections: Culture, People, Places.* London: Routledge.

Haraway, Donna. (1988). 'Situated Knowledges: The Science Question in Feminism and the Privilege of Partial Perspective', *Feminist Studies, 14*(3), 575-599.

Hardt, Michael & Antonio Negri. (2000). *Empire.* Cambridge, Mass.: Harvard University Press.

Harries, Rhiannon. (2009). 'Checks and Balances: Why You Can Now Bring That Burberry Scarf out of the Closet', *The Independent*, 18 October.

Harvey, David. (1989). *The Condition of Postmodernity: An Enquiry into the Origins of Cultural Change.* Oxford: Basil Blackwell.

Hastings, Annette. (2004). 'Stigma and Social Housing Estates: Beyond Pathological Explanations', *Journal of Housing and the Built Environment, 19*(3), 233-254.

Hay, Colin. (1995). 'Mobilization through Interpellation: James Bulger, Juvenile Crime and the Construction of Moral Panic', *Social and Legal Studies, 4*(2), 197-224.

Hayes, John. (2007). *Thought for the Day – May 24th – by John Hayes MP.* Available at: http://cornerstonegroup.wordpress.com/2007/05/24/thought-for-the-day-may-24th-by-john-hayes-mp/ [Accessed 31 May 2010].

Hayward, Keith & Majid Yar. (2006). 'The "Chav" Phenomenon: Consumption, Media and the Construction of a New Underclass', *Crime, Media, Culture, 2*(1), 9-28.

Hebdige, Dick. (1979). *Subculture: The Meaning of Style.* London: Methuen.

Hemmings, Annette. (2002). 'Youth Culture of Hostility: Discourses of Money, Respect, and Difference', *International Journal of Qualitative Studies in Education, 15*(3), 291-307.

Hide, Will. (2009). 'News in Brief: BA Finds Horse Sperm on Plane', *The Times*, January 31.

Hodkinson, Paul. (2002). *Goth: Identity, Style, and Subculture.* Oxford: Berg.

Hollingworth, Sumi & Katya Williams. (2009). 'Constructions of the Working-Class "Other" Among Urban, White, Middle-Class Youth: "Chavs", Subculture and the Valuing of Education', *Journal of Youth Studies, 12*(5), 467-482.

Hollyzone. (2006). *Chavs and the Working Class.* Available at: http://blogs.warwick ac.uk/hollycruise/entry/chavs_and_the/ [Accessed 22 November 2009].

Holstein, James A. & Jaber F. Gubrium. (1995). *The Active Interview.* Thousand Oaks; London: Sage.

Home Office. (2009). *Anti-Social Behaviour.* Available at: http://www.asb. homeoffice.gov.uk/article.aspx?id=9066 [Accessed 3 November 2009].

Honneth, Axel. (1986). 'The Fragmented World of Symbolic Forms: Reflections on Pierre Bourdieu's Sociology of Culture', *Theory, Culture & Society, 3*(3), 55-66.

Huq, Rupa. (2006). *Beyond Subculture: Pop, Youth and Identity in a Postcolonial World.* London: Routledge.

Jacobs, Ronald N. (1996). 'Civil Society and Crisis: Culture, Discourse, and the Rodney King Beating', *The American Journal of Sociology, 101*(5), 1238-1272.

Jameson, Fredric. (1991). *Postmodernism, or, the Cultural Logic of Late Capitalism.* London: Verso.

Jenkins, Richard. (2008 [1996]). *Social Identity* (3rd ed.). London: Routledge.

Jensen, Sune Qvotrup. (2006). 'Rethinking Subcultural Capital', *Young, 14*(3), 257-276.

Johnson, Paul. (2008). '"Rude Boys": The Homosexual Eroticization of Class', *Sociology, 42*(1), 65-82.

Johnston, Les, Robert Macdonald, Paul Mason, Louise Ridley & Colin Scott Webster. (2000). *Snakes & Ladders: Young People, Transitions and Social Exclusion.* Bristol: Policy Press.

Jokes Forum. (2009). *Chavette Jokes.* Available at: http://www.jokesforum.com/ adult-jokes/11047-chavette-jokes.html [Accessed 2 November 2009].

Kelle, Udo. (1995). 'Introduction: An Overview of Computer-Aided Methods in Qualitative Research' in Udo Kelle (ed.), *Computer-Aided Qualitative Data Analysis: Theory, Methods, and Practice*. London: Sage.

Kelley, Jonathan & M. D. R. Evans. (1995). 'Class and Class Conflict in 6 Western Nations', *American Sociological Review, 60*(2), 157-178.

Kirk, John. (2007). *Class, Culture and Social Change: On the Trail of the Working Class*. Basingstoke: Palgrave Macmillan.

Kobayashi-Hillary, Nobumi. (2008). 'Brands and Class', paper presented at *SCUD Workshop: Cultural Capital and Class*, 27-28 October, University of Aalborg.

Lamont, Michèle. (2000). *The Dignity of Working Men: Morality and the Boundaries of Race, Class, and Immigration*. Cambridge, Mass.: Russell Sage Foundation; Harvard University Press.

Lamont, Michèle & Virág Molnár. (2002). 'The Study of Boundaries in the Social Sciences', *Annual Review of Sociology, 28*, 167-195.

Larcombe, Duncan. (2006). 'Future Bling of England', *The Sun*, 10 April.

Lawler, Steph. (2005a). 'Disgusted Subjects: The Making of Middle-Class Identities', *Sociological Review, 53*(3), 429-446.

Lawler, Steph. (2005b). 'Introduction: Class, Culture and Identity', *Sociology, 39*(5), 797-806.

Lawler, Steph. (2008). *Identity: Sociological Perspectives*. Cambridge: Polity.

Lefebvre, Henri. (1991). *The Production of Space*. Oxford: Blackwell.

Lewis, Jemima. (2004). 'In Defence of Snobbery', *The Daily Telegraph*, 31 January

Liddle, Rod. (2004). 'Everyone Hates the White Working-Class Male', *The Sunday Times*, 14 November.

Liebow, Elliot. (1967). *Tally's Corner: A Study of Negro Streetcorner Men*. London: Routledge & Kegan Paul.

Likilla, Al. (2004). *Chav TV Becomes a Reality*. Available at: http://www.homedefenceuk.com/lifestyle_chavTV.html [Accessed 24 September 2010].

Link, Bruce G. & Jo C. Phelan. (2001). 'Conceptualizing Stigma', *Annual Review of Sociology, 27*, 363-385.

Mac an Ghaill, Máirtín. (1994). 'The Making of Black English Masculinities' in Harry Brod & Michael Kaufman (eds.), *Theorizing Masculinities*. London: Sage.

MacDonald, Robert. (1996). 'Welfare Dependency, the Enterprise Culture and Self-Employed Survival', *Work Employment Society, 10*(3), 431-447.

MacDonald, Robert & Jane Marsh. (2001). 'Disconnected Youth?', *Journal of Youth Studies, 4*(4), 373-391.

MacDonald, Robert & Jane Marsh. (2005). *Disconnected Youth? Growing up in Britain's Poor Neighbourhoods*. Houndmills: Palgrave Macmillan.

MacDonald, Robert & Tracy Shildrick. (2007). 'Street Corner Society: Leisure Careers, Youth (Sub)Culture and Social Exclusion', *Leisure Studies, 26*(3), 339-355.

MacDonald, Robert, Tracy Shildrick, Colin Webster & Donald Simpson. (2005). 'Growing up in Poor Neighbourhoods', *Sociology, 39*(5), 873-893.

Maffesoli, Michel. (1996). *The Time of the Tribes: The Decline of Individualism in Mass Society*. London: Sage.

Mahoney, Elisabeth. (2007). 'Celebrating 50 Years of Today', *The Guardian*, 28 October.

Marshall, Gordon. (1988). *Social Class in Modern Britain*. London: Hutchinson.

Massey, Doreen. (1994). *Space, Place and Gender*. Minneapolis, MN: University of Minnesota Press.

Mauss, Marcel. (1973). 'Techniques of the Body', *Economy and Society, 2*(1), 70-88.

Mauss, Marcel. (1979). *Sociology and Psychology: Essays*. London: Routledge.

McCulloch, Ken, Alexis Stewart & Nick Lovegreen. (2006). '"We Just Hang out Together": Youth Cultures and Social Class', *Journal of Youth Studies, 9*(5), 539-556.

McDowell, Linda. (2003). *Redundant Masculinities? Employment Change and White Working Class Youth*. Oxford: Blackwell.

McDowell, Linda. (2007). 'Respect, Deference, Respectability and Place: What Is the Problem with/for Working Class Boys?', *Geoforum, 38*(2), 276-286.

McGuffey, C. Shawn & B. Lindsay Rich. (2008). 'Playing the Gender Transgression Zone: Race, Class, and Hegemonic Masculinity in Middle Childhood' in Joan Z. Spade & Catherine G. Valentine (eds.), *The Kaleidoscope of Gender: Prisms, Patterns, and Possibilities*. Thousand Oaks: Pine Forge Press.

McRobbie, Angela. (1978). 'Working-Class Girls and the Culture of Femininity' in Women's Studies Group Centre for Contemporary Cultural Studies (ed.), *Women Take Issue: Aspects of Women's Subordination*. London: Hutchinson.

McRobbie, Angela. (2002). 'A Mixed Bag of Misfortunes?', *Theory, Culture & Society*, 129-138.

McRobbie, Angela & Jenny Garber. (1976). 'Girls and Subcultures' in Stuart Hall & Tony Jefferson (eds.), *Resistance through Rituals*. London: Hutchinson.

McRobbie, Angela & Sarah Thornton. (1995). 'Rethinking "Moral Panic" For Multi-Mediated Social Worlds', *British Journal of Sociology, 46*(4), 559-574.

Merrifield, Andrew. (1993). 'Place and Space: A Lefebvrian Reconciliation', *Transactions of the Institute of British Geographers, 18*, 516-531.

Metro. (2005). 'Chav Teen Gets Asbo', *Metro*, 3 May.

Metro. (2007). 'Chav Yourself a Merry Christmas', *Metro*, 12 December.

Miles, Steven. (2000). *Youth Lifestyles in a Changing World*. Buckingham: Open University Press.

Millie, Andrew. (2008). 'Anti-Social Behaviour, Behavioural Expectations and Urban Aesthetic', *British Journal of Criminology, 48*(1), 379-394.

Mills, C. Wright. (1959). *The Sociological Imagination*. Oxford: Oxford University Press.

Mitch's Blog. (2004). *Chavs – Is There Really Any Need?* Available at: http://blogs.warwick.ac.uk/mwilson/entry/chavs_is_there/ [Accessed 7 May 2009].

Mitchell, Kevin. (2005). 'Simply Rooney', *The Observer*, 7 August.

Moore, Christopher M. & G. Birtwistle. (2004). 'The Burberry Business Model: Creating an International Luxury Fashion Brand', *International Journal of Retail & Distribution Management, 32*(8), 412-422.

Moran, Joe. (2006). 'Milk Bars, Starbucks, and the Uses of Literacy', *Cultural Studies, 20*(6), 552-573.

Muggleton, David. (2000). *Inside Subculture: The Postmodern Meaning of Style*. Oxford: Berg.

Muggleton, David. (2005). 'From Classlessness to Clubculture: A Genealogy of British Youth Cultural Analysis', *Young, 13*(2), 205-219.

Muggleton, David & Rupert Weinzierl. (2003). *The Post-Subcultures Reader*. Oxford: Berg.

Nayak, Anoop. (2003). *Race, Place and Globalization: Youth Cultures in a Changing World*. Oxford: Berg.

Nayak, Anoop. (2006). 'Displaced Masculinities: Chavs, Youth and Class in the Post-Industrial City', *Sociology, 40*(5), 813-831.

Naylor, Bronwyn. (2001). 'The "Bad Mother" In Media and Legal Texts', *Social Semiotics, 11*(2), 155-176.

Neal, Sarah & Sue Walters. (2008). 'Rural Be/Longing and Rural Social Organizations: Conviviality and Community-Making in the English Countryside', *Sociology, 42*(2), 279-297.

Newmahr, Staci. (2008). 'Becoming a Sadomasochist: Integrating Self and Other in Ethnographic Analysis', *Journal of Contemporary Ethnography, 37*(5), 619-643.

Okely, Judith. (2001). 'Visualism and Landscape: Looking and Seeing in Normandy', *Ethnos, 66*(1), 99-120.

Okely, Judith. (2007). 'Fieldwork Embodied', *Sociological Review, 55*(S1), 65-79.

Okely, Judith. (2008). 'Knowing without Notes' in Narmala Halstead, Eric Hirsh & Judith Okely (eds.), *Knowing How to Know*. Oxford: Berghahn.

Oliver, Smith. (2009). 'Travel Company Offers Discounts to 'Chavs", *The Daily Telegraph*, 20 March 2009.

Ottenberg, Simon. (1990). 'Thirty Years of Fieldnotes: Changing Relationships to the Text', in Roger Sanjek (ed.), *Fieldnotes: The Making of Ethnography*. Ithaca: Cornell University Press.

Oxford University Press. (n.d.). *Word of the Month: Bogan*. Available at: http://www.oup.com.au/dictionaries/wotm/bogan [Accessed 4 September 2010].

Pahl, R. E. (1989). 'Is the Emperor Naked? Some Questions on the Adequacy of Sociological Theory in Urban and Regional Research', *International Journal of Urban and Regional Research, 13*(4), 709-720.

Patrick, Guy. (2009a). 'Video Hero Is a Gulf War Black Belt', *The Sun*, 8 October.

Patrick, Guy. (2009b). 'Yob-Smacked', *The Sun*, 7 October.

Patrick, Guy. (2009c). 'Yob Got a Beating... Now He's Bleating', *The Sun*, 9 October.

Phillipov, Michelle. (2009). '"Just Emotional People"? Emo Culture and the Anxieties of Disclosure', *M/C Journal, 12*(5), Available at: http://journal media-culture.org.au/index.php/mcjournal/article/view/181 [Accessed 1 June 2010].

Phillips, Coretta. (2003). 'Who's Who in the Pecking Order?', *British Journal of Criminology, 43*(4), 710-728.

Phoenix, Anne. (1996). 'Social Constructions of Lone Motherhood' in Elizabeth Bortoloaia Silva (ed.), *Good Enough Mothering? Feminist Perspectives on Lone Mothering*. London: Routledge.

Polhemus, Ted. (1996). *Style Surfing: What to Wear in the 3rd Millennium*. London: Thames and Hudson.

Price, Katie. (2008). 'Katie Price: Why Was I Snubbed by the Polo Snobs?', *The Times*, 1 August.

Putnam, Robert D. (2000). *Bowling Alone: The Collapse and Revival of American Community*. New York: Simon & Schuster.

Raisborough, Jayne & Matt Adams. (2008). 'Mockery and Morality in Popular Cultural Representations of the White, Working Class', *Sociological Research Online, 13*(6).

Reay, Diane. (1998). 'Rethinking Social Class: Qualitative Perspectives on Class and Gender', *Sociology, 32*(2), 259-275.

Reay, Diane. (2004). '"Mostly Roughs and Toughs": Social Class, Race and Representation in Inner City Schooling', *Sociology, 38*(5), 1005-1023.

Reay, Diane. (2005). 'Beyond Consciousness? The Psychic Landscape of Social Class', *Sociology, 39*(5), 911-928.

Reay, Diane & Helen Lucey. (2000). '"I Don't Really Like It Here but I Don't Want to Be Anywhere Else": Children and Inner City Council Estates', *Antipode, 32*(4), 410-428.

Redhead, Steve. (1990). *The End-of-the-Century Party: Youth and Pop Towards 2000*. Manchester: Manchester University Press.

Redhead, Steve. (1997). *Subculture to Clubcultures: An Introduction to Popular Cultural Studies*. Oxford: Blackwell.

Rimmer, Mark. (2010). 'Listening to the Monkey: Class, Youth and the Formation of a Musical Habitus', *Ethnography, 11*(2), 255-283.

Robertson, Roland. (1995). 'Glocalisation: Time-Space and Homogeneity-Heterogeneity' in Mike Featherstone, Scott Lash & Roland Robertson (eds.), *Global Modernities*. London: Sage.

Rose, David & Karen O'Reilly. (1998). *The ESRC Review of Government Social Classifications*. London and Swindon: ONS and ESRC.

Rose, David & David J. Pevalin. (2003). *A Researcher's Guide to the National Statistics Socio-Economic Classification*. London: Sage.

Savage, Mike. (2000). *Class Analysis and Social Transformation*. Buckingham: Open University Press.

Savage, Mike, Gaynor Bagnall & Brian Longhurst. (2001). 'Ordinary, Ambivalent and Defensive: Class Identities in the North West of England', *Sociology, 35*(4), 875-892.

Savage, Mike, Gaynor Bagnall & Brian Longhurst. (2004). *Globalization and Belonging*. London: Sage.

Sayer, Andrew. (2005). *The Moral Significance of Class*. Cambridge: Cambridge University Press.

Scholte, Jan Aart. (2000). *Globalization: A Critical Introduction*. Basingstoke: Palgrave.

Scott, John. (2002). 'Social Class and Stratification in Late Modernity', *Acta Sociologica, 45*(1), 23-35.

seriouslymcmillan. (2008). *A Crash Course in UK "Trash": The Chav*. Available at: http://www.zimbio.com/Chavs/articles/6/Crash+Course+UK+Trash+Chav [Accessed 3 November 2009].

Shank, Barry. (1994). *Dissonant Identities: The Rock'n'roll Scene in Austin, Texas*. Hanover, NH: University Press of New England.

Shields, Rob. (1991). *Places on the Margin*. London: Routledge.

Shildrick, Tracy. (2006). 'Youth Culture, Subculture and the Importance of Neighbourhood', *Young, 14*(1), 61-74.

Shildrick, Tracy, Shane Blackman & Robert MacDonald (eds.). (2009). *Journal of Youth Studies, special issue: Young People, Class and Place, 12*(5).

Skeggs, Beverley. (1997). *Formations of Class and Gender: Becoming Respectable*. London: Sage.

Skeggs, Beverley. (2004). *Class, Self, Culture*. London: Routledge.

Sørensen, Aage B. (2005). 'Foundations of a Rent-Based Class Analysis' in Erik Olin Wright (ed.), *Approaches to Class Analysis*. Cambridge: Cambridge University Press.

Stacey, Margaret. (1960). *Tradition and Change: A Study of Banbury*. Oxford: Oxford University Press.

Straight from the heart. (2009). *The Devil Wears Prada*. Available at: http://ze2red. blogspot.com/2009/12/devil-wears-prada.html [Accessed 1 June 2010].

Strathern, Marilyn. (1981). *Kinship at the Core: An Anthropology of Elmdon, a Village in North-West Essex in the Nineteen Sixties*. Cambridge: Cambridge University Press.

Straw, Will. (1991). 'Systems of Articulation, Logics of Change: Scenes and Communities in Popular Music', *Cultural Studies, 5*(3), 368-388.

Straw, Will. (2002). 'Scenes and Sensibilities', *Public, 22/23*, 245-257.

Superfuture. (2009). *Supernews*. Available at: http://www.superfuture.com/super news/wp-content/uploads/2009/11/jarvis-cocker.jpg [Accessed 1 June 2010].

Sweetman, Paul. (2004). 'Tourists and Travellers? "Subcultures", Reflexive Identities and Neo-Tribal Sociality' in Andy Bennett & Keith Kahn-Harris (eds.), *After Subculture*. Basingstoke: Palgrave Macmillan.

The Daily Mail. (2006). 'Woman Mugged by Vicky Pollard Look-a-Like', *The Daily Mail*, 24 August.

The Daily Mail. (2009). 'As Emma Watson Wows at Burberry's London Catwalk Comeback, We Look at the History of the Luxury Brand', *The Daily Mail*, 24 September.

The Guardian. (2005). 'No but Yeah but No', *The Guardian*, 12 May.

The Independent. (2004a). 'Black Watch, America and Others', *The Independent*, 8 November.

The Independent. (2004b). 'Sneering Britain ', *The Independent*, 28 January.

The Student Room. (2008). *The Official Chav Jokes Thread*. Available at: http://www.thestudentroom.co.uk/showthread.php?t=756371 [Accessed 2 November 2009].

The Times. (2004). 'Questions Answered', *The Times*, 4 August.

The Times. (2005). 'Should Baseball Caps and Hoods Be Banned from Our Shopping Centres?', *The Times*, 12 May.

Thomas, David. (2004). 'I'm a Chav Get Me out of Here', *The Daily Mail*, 12 February.

Thornton, Sarah. (1995). *Club Cultures: Music, Media and Subcultural Capital*. Cambridge: Polity.

Thrasher, Frederic Milton. (1927). *The Gang. A Study of 1,313 Gangs in Chicago*. Chicago: Chicago University Press.

Tolonen, Tarja. (2005). 'Locality and Gendered Capital of Working-Class Youth', *Young, 13*(4), 343-361.

Tönnies, Ferdinand. (2001 [1887]). *Community and Civil Society*. Cambridge, UK: Cambridge University Press.

Trondman, Mats. (1999). *Kultursociologi i praktiken*. Lund: Studentlitteratur.

Tuan, Yi-Fu. (1974). 'Space and Place: Humanistic Perspective' in Stephen Gale & Gunnar Olsson (eds.), *Philosophy in Geography*. Dordrecht: Reidel.

Tuan, Yi-Fu. (1977). *Space and Place: The Perspectives of Experience*. Minneapolis: Minnesota University Press.

Tungate, Mark. (2005). *Fashion Brands: Branding Style from Armani to Zara*. London: Kogan Page.

Turner, Royce Logan. (2000). *Coal Was Our Life: An Essay on Life in a Yorkshire Former Pit Town*. Sheffield: Sheffield Hallam University Press.

Tweedie, Neil. (2004). 'Cheltenham Ladies and the Chavs', *Daily Telegraph*, December 14.

Tyler, Imogen. (2008). '"Chav Mum Chav Scum"', *Feminist Media Studies, 8*(1), 17-34.

Tyler, Imogen & Bruce Bennett. (2010). 'Celebrity Chav: Fame, Femininity and Social Class', *European Journal of Cultural Studies, 13*(3), 375-393.

Ueno, Toshiya. (2003). 'Unlearning to Raver: Techno-Party as the Contact Zone in Trans-Local Formations' in David Muggleton & Rupert Weinzierl (eds.), *The Post-Subcultural Reader*. Oxford: Berg.

Urry, John. (2000). *Sociology Beyond Societies: Mobilities for the Twenty-First Century*. London: Routledge.

Van Maanen, John. (1988). *Tales of the Field: On Writing Ethnography*. Chicago; London: University of Chicago Press.

VBS.TV. (2009). *Donk*. Available at: http://www.vbs.tv/watch/music-world/donk# [Accessed 14 August 2010].

Venkatesh, Sudhir. (2002). '"Doin' the Hustle": Constructing the Ethnographer in the American Ghetto', *Ethnography, 3*(1), 91-111.

Wacquant, Loïc J. D. (2006). 'Pierre Bourdieu' in Rob Stones (ed.), *Key Contemporary Thinkers*. Basingstoke: Palgrave Macmillan.

Wacquant, Loïc J. D. (2008). *Urban Outcasts: A Comparative Sociology of Advanced Marginality*. Cambridge: Polity.

Watt, Paul. (1998). 'Going out of Town: Youth, "Race", and Place in the South East of England', *Environment and Planning D: Society and Space, 16*, 687-703.

Watt, Paul. (2006). 'Respectability, Roughness and "Race": Neighbourhood Place Images and the Making of Working-Class Social Distinctions in London', *International Journal of Urban and Regional Research, 30*(4), 776-797.

Watt, Paul. (2009). 'Living in an Oasis: Middle-Class Disaffiliation and Selective Belonging in an English Suburb', *Environment and Planning A, 41*(12), 2874-2892.

Weber, Max. (1979). *Economy and Society: An Outline of Interpretive Sociology.* Berkeley; London: University of California Press.

Webster, Colin. (2008). 'Marginalized White Ethnicity, Race and Crime', *Theoretical Criminology, 12*(3), 293-312.

Webster, Colin, Donald Simpson, Robert MacDonald, Andrea Abbas, Mark Cieslik, Tracy Shildrick & Mark Simpson. (2004). *Poor Transitions: Social Exclusion and Young Adults.* Bristol, UK: Policy Press.

Whyte, William Foote. (1993 [1943]). *Street Corner Society: The Social Structure of an Italian Slum* (4th ed.). Chicago: University of Chicago Press.

Williams, J. Patrick. (2007). 'Youth-Subcultural Studies: Sociological Traditions and Core Concepts', *Sociology Compass, 1*(2), 572-593.

Willis, Paul E. (1977). *Learning to Labour: How Working Class Kids Get Working Class Jobs.* Aldershot: Ashgate.

Willis, Paul E. (1978). *Profane Culture.* London: Routledge and Kegan Paul.

Willis, Paul E. (1990). *Common Culture: Symbolic Work at Play in the Everyday Culture of the Young.* Milton Keynes: Open University Press.

Wood, Helen & Beverley Skeggs. (2004). 'Notes on Ethical Scenarios of Self on British Reality TV', *Feminist Media Studies, 4*(1), 205-208.

Wray, Matt. (2006). *Not Quite White: White Trash and the Boundaries of Whiteness.* Durham; London: Duke University.

Wulff, Helena. (1988). *Twenty Girls: Growing up, Ethnicity and Excitement in a South London Microculture.* Stockholm: Almqvist & Wiksell.

Young, Gavin. (2004). 'Good News for Chavs: They May Be Cool People Soon', *The Times*, 19 October.

Zatz, Marjorie. (1987). 'Chicano Youth Gangs and Crime: The Creation of a Moral Panic', *Crime, Law and Social Change, 11*(2), 129-158.

Stockholm Studies in Sociology. N.S.
Published by Stockholm University
Editor: Jens Rydgren

1. KARIN HELMERSSON BERGMARK Anonyma Alkoholister i Sverige (Alcoholics Anonymous in Sweden). Stockholm 1995, 195 pages.

2. APOSTOLIS PAPAKOSTAS Arbetarklassen i organisationernas värld: en jämförande studie av fackföreningarnas sociala och historiska förutsättningar i Sverige och Grekland (The Working Class in the World of Organizations). Stockholm 1995, 239 pages.

3. HÅKAN LEIFMAN Perspectives on Alcohol Prevention. Stockholm 1996, 174 pages.

4. HASSAN HOSSEINI-KALADJAHI Iranians in Sweden: Economic, Cultural and Social Integration. Stockholm 1997, 201 pages.

5. ILKKA HENRIK MÄKINEN On Suicide in European Countries. Some Theoretical, Legal and Historical Views on Suicide Mortality and Its Concomitants. Stockholm 1997, 218 pages.

6. ANDERS KASSMAN Polisen och narkotika problemet: från nationella aktioner mot narkotikaprofitörer till lokala insatser för att störa missbruket (The Police and the Drug Problem). Stockholm 1998, 212 pages.

7. ÖRJAN HEMSTRÖM Male Susceptibility and Female Emancipation: Studies on the Gender Difference in Mortality. Stockholm 1998, 177 pages.

8. LARS-ERIK OLSSON Från idé till handling. En sociologisk studie av frivilliga organisationers uppkomst och fallstudier av: Noaks Ark, 5i12-rörelsen, Farsor och Morsor på Stan (From Idea to Action. A Sociological Study of the Emergence of Voluntary Organizations). Stockholm 1999, 185 pages.

9. KRISTINA ABIALA Säljande samspel. En sociologisk studie av privat servicearbete (Selling Interaction. A Sociological Study of Private Servicework). Stockholm 2000, 197 pages.

10. PER CARLSON An Unhealthy Decade. A Sociological Study of the State of Public Health in Russia 1990–1999. Stockholm 2000, 162 pages.

11. LOTTA CONVIAVITIS GELLERSTEDT Till studiet av relationer mellan familj, ekonomi och stat. Grekland och Sverige (A Study of Relations Between Family, Economy, and State. Greece and Sweden). Stockholm 2000, 166 pages.

12. EVA CHRISTENSON Herraväldets processer. En studie av förslitningsskadesituation och könade processer i tre olika slags

arbetsorganisationer (Patriarchal Processes. A Study of Women's Muscloskeletal Pain Situation and Gendered Processes in Three Different Types of Work Organizations). Stockholm 2000, 174 pages.

13. JENNY-ANN BRODIN Religion till salu? En sociologisk studie av New Age i Sverige (Religion for Sale? A Sociological Study of the Swedish New Age Movement). Stockholm 2001, 142 pages.

14. ADRIENNE SÖRBOM Vart tar politiken vägen? Individualisering, reflexivitet och görbarhet i det politiska engagemanget (Where is Politics going? On individualization, Reflexivity and Makeability in Political Commitments). Stockholm 2002, 255 pages.

15. MIEKO TAKAHASHI Gender Dimensions in Family Life. A Comparative Study of Structural Constraints and Power in Sweden and Japan. Stockholm 2003, 175 pages.

16. ABBAS EMAMI Att organisera oenighet. En sociologisk studie av Iranska Riksförbundet och dess medlemsorganisationer (To organize Disunity. A Sociological Study of the Confederation of Iranian Associations and its Member Organizations). Stockholm 2003, 210 pages.

17. MEHRDAD DARVISHPOUR Invandrarkvinnor som bryter mönstret. Hur makt-förskjutningen inom iranska familjer i Sverige påverkar relationen (Immigrant Women who Break Established Patterns. How changing Power Relations within Iranian Families in Sweden influence Relationships). Stockholm 2003, 216 pages.

18. CARL LE GRAND AND TOSHIKO TSUKAGUCHI-LE GRAND (eds.) Women in Japan and Sweden: Work and Family in Two Welfare Regimes. Stockholm 2003, 239 pages.

19. ROBERT SVENSSON Social Control and Socialisation: The Role of Morality as a Social Mechanism in Adolescent Deviant Behaviour. Stockholm 2004, 124 pages.

20. SANJA MAGDALENIĆ Gendering the Sociology Profession: Sweden, Britain and the US. Stockholm 2004, 200 pages.

21. SÉBASTIEN CHARTRAND Work In Voluntary Welfare Organizations: A Sociological Study of Voluntary Welfare Organizations in Sweden. Stockholm 2004, 204 pages.

22. MARCUS CARSON From Common Market to Social Europe? Paradigm Shift and Institutional Change in EU Policy on Food, Asbestos and Chemicals, and Gender Equality. Stockholm 2004, 278 pages.

23. NAOMI MAURO, ANDERS BJÖRKLUND AND CARL LE GRAND (eds.) Welfare Policy and Labour Markets: Transformation of the Japanese and Swedish Models for the 21st Century. Stockholm 2004, 275 pages.

24. ELISABET LINDBERG Vad kan medborgarna göra? Fyra fallstudier av samarbetsformer för frivilliga insatser i äldreomsorg och väghållning (What Can the Citizens Do? Four Case Studies of Voluntary Contribution in Public Elderly Care and Road Maintenance). Stockholm 2005, 374 pages.

25. MIKAELA SUNDBERG Making Meteorology: Social Relations and Scientific Practice. Stockholm 2005, 259 pages.

26. ALEXANDRA BOGREN Female Licentiousness versus Male Escape? Essays on intoxicating substance use, sexuality and gender. Stockholm 2006, 169 pages.

27. OSMAN AYTAR Mångfaldens organisering: Om integration, organisationer och interetniska relationer i Sverige (Organizing Diversity: On Integration, Organizations and Inter-ethnic Relations in Sweden). Stockholm 2007, 253 pages.

28. ERIK LJUNGAR Levebröd eller entreprenörskap? Om utlandsfödda personers företagande i Sverige (Survival or Entrepreneurship? Self-employment among Immigrants in Sweden). Stockholm 2007, 181 pages.

29. AKVILĖ MOTIEJŪNAITĖ Female Employment, Gender Roles, and Attitudes: the Baltic Countries in a Broader Context. Stockholm 2008, 141 pages.

30. ZHANNA KRAVCHENKO Family (versus) Policy. Combining Work and Care in Russia and Sweden. Stockholm 2008, 184 pages.

31. LISA WALLANDER Measuring Professional Judgements: An Application of the Factorial Survey Approach to the Field of Social Work. Stockholm 2008, 253 pages.

32. MIKAEL KLINGVALL Adaptablity or Efficiency: Towards a Theory of Institutional Development in Organizations. Stockholm 2008, 144 pages.

33. MONICA K. NORDVIK Contagious Interactions. Essays on social and epidemiological networks. Stockholm 2008, 190 pages.

34. ÅSA TORKELSSON Trading out? A study of farming women's and men's access to resources in rural Ethiopia. Stockholm 2008, 303 pages.

35. DANA SOFI Interetnisk konflikt eller samförstånd. En studie om etnopolitik i Kurdistan/Irak. Stockholm 2009, 286 pages.

36. TINA FORSBERG KANKKUNEN Två kommunala rum: Ledningsarbete i genusmärkta tekniska respektive omsorgs- och utbildningsverksamheter. (Two municipal spaces: Managerial work in genderized municipal technical services versus social care and education services). Stockholm 2009, 161 pages.

37. REBECCA LAWRENCE Shifting Responsibilities and Shifting Terrains: State Responsibility, Corporate Social Responsibility, and Indigenous Claims. Stockholm 2009, 229 pages.

38. MAGNUS HAGLUNDS Enemies of the People. Whistle-Blowing and the Sociology of Tragedy. Stockholm 2009, 248 pages.

39. DANIEL CASTILLO Statens förändrade gränser. En studie om sponsring, korruption och relationen till marknaden. (State Boundaries in Transition. A Study of Sponsoring, Corruption and Market Relations). Stockholm 2009, 244 pages.

40. DANIEL LINDVALL The Limits of the European Vision in Bosnia and Herzegovina: An Analysis of the Police Reform Negotiations. Stockholm 2009, 278 pages.

41. LOVE BOHMAN Director Interlocking and Firm Ownership: Longitudinal Studies of 1- and 3-Mode Network Dynamics. Stockholm 2010, 155 pages

42. NINA-KATRI GUSTAFSSON Bridging the World: Alcohol Policy in Transition and Diverging Alcohol Patterns in Sweden. Stockholm 2010, 175 pages.

43. PAUL FUEHRER Om tidens värde: En sociologisk studie av senmodernitetens temporala livsvärldar. (Über den Wert der Zeit. Eine soziologische Studie der zeitlichen Lebenswelten in der Spätmoderne). Stockholm 2010, 311 pages.

44. LAMBROS ROUMBANIS Kierkegaard och sociologins blinda fläck (Kierkegaard and the blind spot of sociology). Stockholm 2010, 247 pages.

45. STINA BERGMAN BLIX Rehearsing Emotions: The Process of Creating a Role for the Stage. Stockholm 2010, 237 pages.

46. THOMAS FLORÉN Talangfabriken: Om organisering av kunskap och kreativitet i skivindustrin (The Talent Factory: The Organization of Knowledge and Creativity in the Record Industry). Stockholm 2010, 256 pages.

47. ELIAS LE GRAND Class, Place and Identity in a Satellite Town. Stockholm 2010, 182 pages.

Subscriptions to the series and orders for single volumes should be addressed to any international bookseller or directly to the publishers:

eddy.se ab
P.O Box 1310, SE-621 24 Visby, Sweden
Phone: +46 498 253900
Fax: +46 498 249789
E-mail: order@bokorder.se
http://acta.bokorder.se

ACTA UNIVERSITATIS STOCKHOLMIENSIS

Corpus Troporum
Romanica Stockholmiensia
Stockholm Cinema Studies
Stockholm Economic Studies. Pamphlet Series
Stockholm Oriental Studies
Stockholm Slavic Studies
Stockholm Studies in Baltic Languages
Stockholm Studies in Classical Archaeology
Stockholm Studies in Comparative Religion
Stockholm Studies in Economic History
Stockholm Studies in Educational Psychology
Stockholm Studies in English
Stockholm Studies in Ethnology
Stockholm Studies in Film History
Stockholm Studies in History
Stockholm Studies in History of Art
Stockholm Studies in History of Ideas
Stockholm Studies in History of Literature
Stockholm Studies in Human Geography
Stockholm Studies in Linguistics
Stockholm Studies in Modern Philology. N.S.
Stockholm Studies in Musicology
Stockholm Studies in Philosophy
Stockholm Studies in Psychology
Stockholm Studies in Russian Literature
Stockholm Studies in Scandinavian Philology. N.S.
Stockholm Studies in Sociology. N.S.
Stockholm Studies in Social Anthropology. N.S.
Stockholm Studies in Statistics
Stockholm Theatre Studies
Stockholmer Germanistische Forschungen
Studia Baltica Stockholmiensia
Studia Fennica Stockholmiensia
Studia Graeca Stockholmiensia. Series Graeca
Studia Graeca Stockholmiensia. Series Neohellenica
Studia Juridica Stockholmiensia
Studia Latina Stockholmiensia
Studies in North-European Archaeology

Printed in Sweden 2010, www.us-ab.com